Just Money

Just Money

A Critique of
Contemporary American Philanthropy

MICHELE COURTON BROWN · DENNIS COLLINS
JOEL L. FLEISHMAN · DAVID FORD · PETER GOLDMARK
ANNA FAITH JONES · H. PETER KAROFF · SCOTT McVAY
STEVEN A. SCHROEDER, M. D. · BRUCE SIEVERS
ADELE SIMMONS

Edited by H. PETER KAROFF

TPI EDITIONS

For information, address:
TPI Editions
77 Franklin Street
Boston, MA 02110

Designed and composed by
Scott-Martin Kosofsky at The Philidor Company, Cambridge.
Typeset in Philidor Bell.

ISBN 0-9753311-0-8 hardcover
0-9753311-1-6 paperback

Educational, community, foundation and non-profit boards or groups
wishing to order this book at attractive quantity discounts may contact TPI.

*TPI wishes to express its gratitude to all the clients and friends who helped
make this book possible. In particular we thank Allen and Joan Bildner
and the Bildner Family Foundation, and the Mallon Family Foundation
for their kind support, which has been so important to the work
of Peter Karoff and the Karoff Center at TPI.*

Distributed by Publishers Shipping and Storage Corp.

10 9 8 7 6 5 4 3 2 1
PRINTED IN CANADA BY FRIESENS

CONTENTS

Acknowledgments   ix

Introduction: *Serious Travelers*   xi

Saturday Morning   H. PETER KAROFF   3

> H. Peter Karoff's essay, which provided the impetus for this book, begins and ends with a walk in the garden. In between, he makes the case for respecting the multiple forms of human knowing— analysis, fact gathering, intuition, imagination, and faith. These epistemological puzzles run like the currents through the stream of the book. Karoff believes they are at the heart of the meaning of generosity and the meaning of philanthropy.

Before the Storm   PETER GOLDMARK   23

> Peter Goldmark throws down a gauntlet, challenging the reader to stand up and be counted and to look deep within heart and soul. Goldmark presents a bold and even radical social commentary on the state of the times and advocates for his belief that philanthropy has a critical role to play in a dangerous and troubled world. Identifying the two ultimatums facing humanity, this chapter is both a compelling analysis and a stirring call to action.

Doors and Mirrors   ANNA FAITH JONES   51

> Anna Faith Jones shares her deep conviction that the source for meaningful philanthropy is in listening to the intelligence, wisdom, and experience of the community. For Jones, this realization

is not abstract but influenced by her vivid personal experience as a young woman in Washington, D.C., and at Howard University during the early days of the civil rights movement. Those days shaped her awareness of the potential for philanthropy to be a powerful mechanism for enabling all of us to transcend the constraints of history and circumstance.

The Art of Philanthropy   DENNIS COLLINS   63

Denis Collins reflects on the role of process and how it relates to attitude as he defines it. He looks at the powerful effect that attitude has on outcomes in the field of philanthropy—an important consideration for every gift-giver. In addition, Collins argues for less reliance on "metrics" in a field where exact measurement of results is elusive. His call to treat philanthropy as an art that relies on instinct and wisdom sets up a challenge to current trends in the field.

The Philanthropic Tipping Point   SCOTT McVAY   73

Scott McVay names curiosity, imagination and courage as the most essential characteristics for philanthropists. He also offers ideas about supporting excellence and splendid leadership in the field, and about how to master the art of being both prudent and bold at the same time. Arguing for realism, McVay notes that philanthropy is only one actor on a big stage, and almost never the star, but he also points out that philanthropic gifts can leverage tipping points to effect social change in communities both large and small.

Simply Doing Good or Doing Good Well   JOEL L. FLEISHMAN   101

Joel L. Fleishman offers a candid portrayal of the philanthropic world, including its foibles—considering the issues of accountability, transparency, and thoughtful governance, especially within large foundations. He cautions donors against the potential for hubris and examines the risks in strategic and venture philanthropy. He also argues that too much donor direction can derail the true mission and capability of nonprofit organizations, tempting grant seekers to rise to the bait of resources and undermining the innovation that fuels change.

Philanthropy's Blindspots   BRUCE SIEVERS   129

Bruce Sievers contributes to the dialectic of what constitutes good philanthropic process by suggesting that this work requires the attitude of students and champions bent on improving the human condition, not cost accountants or social engineers. He argues for limits on the use of the business model in a field where the mission-driven dimension is the primary one. Sievers also names and makes a strong case for a number of neglected social agendas and examines the concept of the bottom line as it relates to philanthropy.

Making the Case for
Corporate Philanthropy   MICHELE COURTON BROWN   151

Michelle Courton Brown tells the story of how a major financial organization successfully integrated social concerns and business goals through applied strategic philanthropy. This is a story of leverage, more about the overall resources of the institution than its limited charitable giving budget. Brown provides examples of what can be gained when funders collaborate and argues that even in a corporate setting it is possible to take social risks and still meet business objectives. From the perspective of an African-American woman who has also been the president of a corporate foundation, she makes the case for including a diversity of voices around the philanthropic table.

Ruminations upon Ruminations   DAVID FORD   165

David Ford is wary of attempts to transform large social systems and warns of wide swings in the availability of corporate philanthropic resources, swings that reflect the vicissitudes of the economy. He writes from the perspective of one who has run charitable giving at two major corporations and cautions against over-reliance on collaboration, based on the difficulty of sustaining it. Ford also advocates for more common sense in philanthropy while at the same time illustrating the effectiveness and impact of well-designed programs.

When Execution Trumps Strategy
STEVEN A. SCHROEDER, M.D.   179

Under Steven A. Schroeder, the Robert Wood Johnson Foundation took on two tough transformational issues: an ambitious effort to reduce the use of tobacco by teenagers, and an initiative—unsuccessful but potentially path breaking—to help secure national health care coverage for all Americans. Believing that "execution trumps strategy," Schroeder cautions against spending too much time on developing carefully honed strategic plans and too little time on execution. In his essay Schroeder candidly shares insights, victories, and a few regrets.

Global Giving   ADELE SIMMONS   203

To Adele Simmons, context matters, especially in her experience in "cross-border giving" at the John D. and Catherine T. MacArthur Foundation. Simmons traces the development of the foundation's global social investment portfolio and the rise of international coalitions around the world. As one of the few major foundations to venture outside the United States, MacArthur's work has included the creation of major international institutions as well as indigenous NGOs. Her essay is an ambitious and enlightening story of global social investing.

Epilogue   235

Stillness—A poem   240

Glossary of Terms   241

Acknowledgments

❦

T HIS BOOK owes its existence to a covey of talented people, foremost among them the authors who generously contributed their time and their knowledge. Through the "slings and arrows" of the editing process, these writers were surely but gently guided by Emily Hiestand, a wonderful writer in her own right, whose developmental editing and guidance was immensely helpful. My partner from beginning to end at TPI has been Jane Maddox. Jane's excellent editorial eye and judgment have been invaluable, and she has led us along a steep and interesting learning curve. We are also indebted to John Schneider of Tufts University and the University Press of New England for his good and productive comments.

The decision to publish *Just Money* as a "TPI book," as opposed to a trade or university press publication, was influenced by several factors, including our desire to bring the book to the market in a time frame consistent with the content. The major reason for this decision, however, was the renewed commitment at TPI, led by its president, Joe Breiteneicher, to dedicate significant time and resources to the development and dissemination of new ideas and materials relevant to the field of philanthropy. The establishment of the Karoff Center at TPI and the publication of this book are among the first products of this endeavor. We hope *Just Money* will be the beginning of a series of publications that will add value and substance to our collective understanding of the ways that philanthropy can uniquely and most effectively address the critical issues and needs of our society.

Finally, I want to thank those extraordinary clients and friends who have provided the financial support that has made this book possible.

—H. PETER KAROFF

Introduction: Serious Travelers

༜

A BOOK about philanthropy should begin with a good definition. Here is one from my friend Sam Miller:

> *philanthropy understood as flow, process truly possible,*
> *how to mean, how to learn it's all evidence,*
> *it's an accounting, it's traveling to the journey,*
> *it's an exchange of visible and invisible goods.*[i]

I like the notion of philanthropy as a literal transaction on one level and on another level something figurative, something just beyond reach. This blend of facts and figures, intellect and intuition, emotion and spirit is magnetic, it draws us in—if we allow it.

This book is an odyssey, a voyage of discovery, a Grand Tour more intriguing than a ride on the Orient Express, a journey into the little known and powerful world of American philanthropy. It is a book about *serious travelers* in the tradition of Marco Polo, who brought the mysteries of the East and the West together and bridged two worlds that were remarkable and strange to each other; of Alexis de Tocqueville, who observed and chronicled the uniquely American phenomenon of everyday citizens taking responsibility for and acting in the public interest; and of Johnny Appleseed, who in the early 1800s planted thousands of apple orchards throughout the Midwest.

We travel with those who, among other things, are bridge builders, shrewd observers of society, and creators of orchards.[ii]

Our *serious travelers*, our guides, our conductors, are men and women who have had the rare experience of leading major philanthropies—large national, community, and corporate foundations. They write on meaning and purpose, imagination and courage, and the conditions that lead to meaningful generosity and action. By turns practical and visionary, their essays capture the wisdom and the lessons learned, sometimes the hard way, by a generation of philanthropic leaders, and their collective aim is to inspire readers to reconsider their own generosity and action in the world.

After you have read this book you will know more about how large charitable organizations go about their business, but you will also know more about the nature of generous action in the complex world in which we live—the risks and the rewards, the opportunities, the imperatives, and the challenges of such action.

In the classic novel *Invisible Cities,* by Italo Calvino, Marco Polo reports to the Great Kublai Khan his vivid impressions of the many different cities he visits, all of which have unique and defining characteristics. By the end of the novel, however, it is revealed that all these remarkable tales were actually about one city—a huge, complex, interconnected metropolis as varied as the Khan's vast empire, a metaphor for the world itself. The same is true for this book. Told by people who have led major philanthropies, the stories and experiences represent different contexts and perspectives, but the lessons they hold are relevant for every individual gift giver, from the smallest family foundation or donor-advised fund to the very largest funder. Many of the questions the authors grapple with are things we struggle with in our own lives. How should we act on our generous impulses? How can we best use finite resources? How can we act with hope and creativity in the face of large and stubborn problems? Thus the phrase *serious travelers* includes all of those who rise to the challenge, to the imperative, of doing good works.

The catalyst for this collection of essays was a piece I wrote in 2002, titled "Saturday Morning," in which a walk in my garden evolved into a softly critical look at the "golden age" of philanthropy that didn't quite happen. Presented originally as a talk and reprinted here, "Saturday Morning," with its focus on ideas and conditions that lead to heroic philanthropy, seemed to strike a chord and sparked discussion about the condition of philanthropy in American life.[iii] The opportunity to build on the interest in these ideas came when a number of respected figures in the field graciously agreed to contribute their own reflections.

All of the authors, including this writer, share one common characteristic—a recent transition from running a philanthropic organization to other professional pursuits. The hope was that this small distancing would allow us all, as representatives of a generation of philanthropic leadership, more freedom to speak our minds. The goal was to provide a kind of collective knowledge transfer that would provide insight to anyone and everyone who cares about the promotion and practice of philanthropy.

An Overview of This Book

From diverse perspectives, then, the authors who have contributed to *Just Money* consider the very nature of generosity and offer seasoned insights about the art and practice of philanthropy. Their essays offer a wide spectrum of ideas—from calls for a more international worldview among philanthropists and all citizens, to pointing out the critical importance of listening to grant recipients, to communities of interest, and to the voices that come out of each neighborhood with an attitude of respect and openness.

Reflecting on their craft, the authors nominate qualities that mark great philanthropy and define through their stories the nature of what constitutes philanthropic leadership. They also speak candidly about the limitations and foibles of this field, recognizing that hubris and ambition, as well as generosity and genius, figure in the complex motivations that fuel philanthropy and affect its impact. These essays reveal concerns about governance, accountability, and transparency in large private foundations; about the ways foundations treat people; and about the fine line between too much and too little donor influence. Challenging some of the prevailing views in the field, the contributors to this book caution and question the excessive application of strategy, measurement, and the focus on results and make a case for a more holistic approach to philanthropic practice. Because of the nature of their work, these men and women have become keenly aware of the realities that put our species and planet at risk. They face these struggles squarely, and offer sobering but hopeful outlooks that encourage readers to consider the positive roles they can play. And while the authors of these essays understand well the ambiguities and uncertainties latent in any attempt to do good works, their writings reaffirm the profound promise in every generous deed.

Just Money looks in two directions. Its contributors reflect on the historic decades between 1980 and 2000, a period when philanthropic leaders had reason to hope that an influx of new wealth and new ideas would translate into a golden age of social progress. In the aftermath of that era, with all its hype and rhetoric, they look to the future, proposing effective ways for American philanthropists to engage with emerging and sometimes daunting realities and addressing contemporary issues—among them, justice, poverty, hunger, health, equity, education, peace, and security—as well as perennial questions about humanity and generosity.

This book comes at a critical time in America and around the world, a time of great individual, social, and political change and instability.

Presented in these pages are worldviews and personal perspectives that help inform us about what the important issues are, and which ones have been neglected.

Here is one characterization of the times in which we live:

> The waves of change sweeping the world—digitalization, globalization, demographic shifts, migration, and individualization, as well as the rapid degradation of social and natural capital—are giving rise to arenas of clashing forces. These clashing forces play out as tensions between multiple polarities: speed and sustainability, exploration and exploitation, global and local ways of organizing, top-down and bottom-up approaches to leadership.[iv]

Against that backdrop, we mere mortals have to deal with a continuous flow of new information and the impact it has on us. Some suggest that while the world is becoming more interconnected through technology, people are becoming more disconnected and isolated. What's more, as Andy Grove of Intel has put it, this business about speed has its limits. Brains don't speed up. The exchange of ideas doesn't really speed up; it's just that the overhead that slows down that exchange has been reduced.[v]

How to cope with these changes and process an overwhelming amount of information, never mind turning it into knowledge, challenges every thinking person today. And yet this is the complicated world through which we travel; this is the raw material that makes up our lives.

The Role of Philanthropy Today

American philanthropy represents the largest pool of private capital available in the world that is free from the constraints of governments or the marketplace. More than 200 billion dollars a year flows from charitable foundations and individual donors into a vast range of programs and initiatives.[vi] Even though philanthropy's resources are

finite, and it is only one source of program funding and social investment among many, this intersection of freedom and enormous wealth
has a profound effect on American culture and, increasingly, on life
beyond our borders. Each writer in *Just Money* offers a certain slant on
the purpose of philanthropy and much of this book deals with the question of what is the highest and best use of these resources.

Professional philanthropy, what is referred to as organized philanthropy, especially the domain of the large private and corporate foundations that play a key leadership role, remains a veiled and little
understood world. These charitable organizations, within which the
authors have lived and worked, sit at the very top of the pyramid of
America's remarkable largesse, a pinnacle that often seems shrouded in
heavy fog. One of the goals of this book is to help disperse that mist.

In many respects, philanthropy doesn't fit into any box very well. It
lies outside of the normal conventions that neatly define the role of
government and the role of the market economy. There is no perfect
definition for philanthropy, one that succinctly describes what it is and
what it does. Some would say philanthropy is about a love for
humanity, because of its roots in the Greek words *philos* and *anthropos*,
which mean "love" and "human being," respectively. Some would say
philanthropy is a highbrow word for charity. Some would say that philanthropy in the United States is defined by the entire Independent
Sector, which includes the one million plus nonprofit organizations of
all shapes and sizes that in the aggregate represent a resounding 8 percent of the U.S. GNP, and has links to thousands of non-governmental
organizations (NGOs) around the world.

In the United States, this remarkable energy grew out of elements of
the American experience that can be traced back to the early days of
the nation. Our society has a two-hundred-year history of citizen
action and involvement in effecting positive change in the quality of life
in our communities. That tradition remains robust and, as all of the

authors of this book agree, philanthropic resources may be more important today than at any time in the past.

Most recently, private philanthropy has moved further into the realm of policy issues that relate to the functions of government. There are different views of what its role should be. Some would say that philanthropy should do what the government and the market cannot do or should not do; others see philanthropy as taking up the slack when government resources are reduced. Some would argue that philanthropy has no business being involved in social engineering or attempting to influence public policy, that the role of philanthropy should be simply to cure the sick and feed the poor; others, including most major foundations, argue that this is far too limiting a role, one that in fact allows government to shirk its own fundamental responsibilities.

Since President Reagan's administration, the private sector in the United States has been asked, encouraged, and given incentives to do more on behalf of society. The managers of private philanthropic resources are caught in the middle of larger political and ideological debates about the role and size of government and the devolution of control and resources from federal to state and local authority. This is an uncomfortably hot spot to be in, and wrestling with the implications is a test of the beliefs and courage of donors.[vii]

A similar axis of complications and confrontation exists at the intersection between philanthropy and the market economy, where there are both opportunities and the potential for conflict. Conflict arises when environmental degradation, depletion of natural resources and unfair labor practices, for instance, are created or exacerbated by actions of corporations. On the other hand, when capital markets and corporate know-how are harnessed for social good, the leverage gained can be enormous.[viii]

Philanthropy's Sea Change

The field of philanthropy is undergoing immense change, which is one of the major subjects of the essays in *Just Money*. Some of that change is internal to the field. The craft of philanthropy, discernment and careful management of the way in which grants and social investments are made, has become more challenging with an increase in the depth and the quality of engagement in the process. This is true across the donor spectrum, for private and corporate foundations and individual and family donors alike. Another part of this change involves scale. There is a great deal more money in the system than ever before. There has been a huge increase in the number of new donors, many of whom have challenged the standard operating procedures and assumptions of the past. Put simply, philanthropy plays on a bigger stage today than ever before and the actors are more serious in wanting to make a difference. That fact has not gone unnoticed, and powerful external forces are at work as well.

It was an event when *Time* magazine did a cover story on philanthropy in 2002. But *Time* was not alone as the media's fascination with wealth and the wealthy caused reporters to quickly beat a hot trail to the doorstep of philanthropy. Much of this attention has been critical, with a steady stream of news articles on actual or presumed violations of the public trust within the philanthropic/nonprofit sector. To many, there were troubling analogies with the abuses of fiduciary trust that seemed to be running rampant in corporate America.

In tandem with the media attention, and certainly influenced by it, federal and state legislation has been proposed to monitor the not-for-profit sector and in some cases "reform" the operations of large foundations. In fact, one can read the Sarbanes-Oxley Act of 2002, the legislation passed in response to corporate scandals, as a precursor to the kind of legislation that could easily be on the horizon for foundations and not-for-profit organizations.[ix] The proposed Charitable

Giving Act of 2003, which was not passed by Congress in 2003, originally contained a provision that struck at the heart of a long-held assumption about how foundations could allocate and expense administrative costs as part of the 5 percent pay-out requirement. These changes were viewed as a serious attack, and the philanthropic trade associations, urged on by many large foundations, rallied a lobbying effort that challenged that particular provision. The defensiveness of that reaction demonstrated how unfamiliar and uncomfortable leaders in the field are with the rough and tumble of media and politics. More importantly, it showed how vulnerable are those things that we assume to be sacrosanct. The reality is that there are many such assumptions (with far bigger implications than an adjustment in the payout rules for private foundations) that could easily be challenged. We live in a culture of debate and spotlights. Everything is on the table for questioning, including the historical tensions, always simmering just below the surface, around the role, purpose, and rationale for allowing tax-exempt organizations within a democratic society.

Being reactive and defensive, however, is not productive. The focus of the authors of *Just Money* on accountability, transparency, attitude, and meaning pinpoints some of the fundamental issues that leave the field of philanthropy vulnerable to criticism. These issues need to be taken seriously and addressed proactively. All indications are that the field of philanthropy is at the beginning of an extended period of increased media and public scrutiny. The best answer to the critics, by far, and the best defense for philanthropy, will be in demonstrating how well we manage the public trust, how well we utilize the resources for which we are responsible, and how well we assess and communicate the results.

Major Foundations

Most of the authors of this book have worked for very large philanthropies, some with several billion dollars in assets. What earns these actors the designation *serious traveler?* Why are they so influential in the scheme of things?

It is certainly not the total amount of giving by major foundations. Out of the $240 billion given to charity in the United States in 2002, all foundations—and there are more than 60,000—gave just under $30 billion. The one hundred largest foundations provided a relatively modest $11 billion. But large philanthropies are influential because they have the unique potential and capacity to focus and direct substantial resources in a targeted way over a sustained period of time on issues and institutions that are important to society. Large foundations can function as learning organizations, acquire knowledge and practical experience, and in the best of worlds, share that knowledge with others who care about similar issues. Foundations also have the advantage of full-time professional staffs and exceptional leadership.

Organized philanthropy represented by large foundations has long been the center of power in philanthropy, and that center is now in flux. Many wealthy individuals are making very large gifts and grants on a sustained basis without establishing an endowed foundation. They argue that these direct gifts produce as much or more creativity, thoughtfulness, and impact as do large foundations, plus, in avoiding bureaucratic structures, they gain the advantage of a certain nimbleness. In addition, new networks of more modest donors are collaborating and pooling knowledge and funds through a wide range of vehicles and mechanisms, including community foundations. These new resources are having a flattening and democratizing influence on the field.

The authors in the book speculate about what these trends portend for the future, but today it is still the major foundations—corporate and private—that are on the "A" list of every individual or organization seeking grant money. For the myriad nonprofit organizations looking for financial support in the United States, how to access and unlock foundation resources remains a subject of immense interest.

The Life of Philanthropy

If no one is certain where this train is going, why does it continue to attract so many talented passengers? Why is philanthropy so robust?

I believe its very independence attracts people. Not having to wait or ask permission, the option to invent and reinvent, to make up the rules as you go along, makes for pure entrepreneurial individualism at work. If you are looking for an arena where original and creative thinking coexists with almost unfettered action, philanthropy is that place. This independence is one of the reasons why philanthropy can be so exciting, why the process continues to engage so many people.

So how would one characterize our guides, our *serious travelers?*

The contributors to this book are by turn optimistic, romantic, spiritual, realistic, moderate, conservative, and revolutionary. They make several primary and sometimes seemingly opposing arguments, yet for all of their differences they are remarkably congruent in their assessments. Among their arguments are:

- While philanthropy is a small actor on the world stage, its disciplined and catalytic role is critically important. Of philanthropy's two great roles, conservation and constructive change, the latter is most important.
- Philanthropy is part of the "American polyarchy," with an almost infinite number of players and approaches. While chaotic, this diversity is a major strength. To restrict philanthropy's pluralism in order to fix its problems would be a net loss to society.
- Philanthropy as art is not well understood, but it is the art that speaks to the soul, to the substance of the work, and to meaning.

' Philanthropy is at best a *messy science*, and thus all attempts to organize, strategize, and measure are bound to be incomplete.

' Philanthropy is primarily about building upon the values and institutions of civil society to engage critical social needs and promote human growth.

' Meaningful philanthropy is possible only when one listens to the voices, input, and guidance of the community—"No amount of giving can do for the community what the community can do for itself."

' Corporate philanthropy can have an impact on challenging social issues, even risky ones, by marshalling the total resources of a corporation. There is, or there can be, a "triple bottom line."

' Cross-border giving and global social investing, a minor factor to date in American philanthropy, is on the rise and its time has come.

' The focus on quantifying and measuring results makes funders more risk adverse and less willing to take on the tough issues where success is hard to measure.

' Organized philanthropy has attitude and control problems. Foundation staff members do not always treat people with respect and courtesy, and major donors too often exert excessive and counter-productive control.

Finally, taken together, these essays create a new lexicon for philanthropy, one that contains words and phrases like *curiosity, courage, splendid leadership, ambition, discipline, excellence,* and *the elevation of the human spirit.*

What *Just Money* represents is a philanthropic inquiry in which knowledge is presented from an ethnographic perspective, one that is based on practice, learning, listening, watching, and *walking around.*[x] For the *serious traveler* the journey begins with close observations from the wide windows of the train as it winds up and down and around the valleys and mountaintops of the vast, chaotic, troubling, fascinating, magnificent world in which we are privileged to live.

—H. PETER KAROFF

---

i.   Sam Miller is the executive director of the New England Foundation for the Arts. NEFA, *Annual Report* 2002.

ii. Johnny Appleseed's real name was John Chapman. He did not scatter seeds but was a skilled nurseryman who started an amazing number of nurseries and orchards throughout the newly settled Midwest in the early 1800s.

iii. The talk was first presented at the Delaware Valley Grantmakers annual meeting in October of 2002.

iv. From *Illuminating the Blind Spot: Leadership in the Context of Emerging Worlds*, by C. Otto Scharmer, W. Brian Arthur, Jonathan Day, Joseph Jaworski, Michael Jung, Ikujiro Nonaka, Peter M. Senge-McKinsey (Society for Organizational Learning [SOL] Leadership Project, 1999-2000).

v.   Ibid.

vi. A look at the numbers is instructive. In 2002 Americans gave more than $240 billion to charity. The overall breakdown is as follows:

2002 Donors	Amount	% of Total
Individuals	$183.73 billion	76.3
Foundations	26.9 billion	11.2
Bequests	18.1 billion	7.5
Corporations	12.19 billion	5.1
Total:	$240.92 billion	

Looking at funding given out by foundations, the breakdown is

Independent Foundations	$23.3 billion
Corporate Foundations	3.4 billion
Community Foundations	2.46 billion
Total:	$29.16 billion

Source: American Association of Fundraising Counsel, *Giving USA 2003*.

vii. For example, who has what job? Should a foundation focused on the issue of homelessness provide food and shelter to homeless people, or is that government's responsibility? The Connecticut-based Melville Charitable Trust, which focuses exclusively on the issue of homelessness, has determined that their role is to work on systemic problems, and that it is government's role to provide basic food and shelter to homeless citizens.

viii. Two interesting examples are the Henry J. Kaiser Foundation's work with Viacom on the AIDS pandemic and the Bill & Melinda Gates Foundation's investment with drug companies to develop new medications for diseases that have not received much public attention in this country, medications that would otherwise not have been developed.

ix. The Sarbanes-Oxley Act of 2002: Reforms in Corporate Governance, Accounting, and Disclosure.

x. Gerald D. (Jerry) Yoshitomi, 2003 presentation to the board of the New England Foundation for the Arts.

THE ESSAYS

H. PETER KAROFF

Saturday Morning:
A Reflection on the Golden Age of Philanthropy

SATURDAY MORNING in the garden. The once-a-season changeover from spring flowers to the heat and heart of summer. A bit of a grunt, the weeds are tough and have had a field day; at least it's cool and the mosquitoes are on holiday. The art is in the pruning of pansies now leggy and faded, snapdragons gone by, dianthus a shadow of its brilliant self, all with the idea that properly cut back these lovelies will bloom again in the fall. I go about this piecework of renewal with satisfaction, and carefully cultivate around the tall Oriental lilies, still in exotic bloom. How self-restorative it is to do work that leads to certain restoration. All the time knowing that I will ignore my wife's protestations to stop obsessing, knowing that I will later go to the nursery, buy more plants—perhaps salvia, amaranthus, and sage?—to back and fill smartly in between the lilies.

H. Peter Karoff founded The Philanthropic Initiative to help donors increase the impact of their philanthropy and at the same time make "giving" more meaningful in their own lives. President of TPI from 1989 to 2002, he is a senior fellow at the Tufts University College of Citizenship and Public Service. Peter has written extensively, taught, lectured and motivated hundreds of audiences in the U.S. and around the globe on the successful practice and art of philanthropy—reflecting his experience through his philosophy, passion and poems. He is a graduate of Brandeis University and Columbia University, and holds an honorary degree from Lesley University.

Meanwhile the Dow dropped another four hundred points on Friday and the era of affluence, as we have known it for more than a decade, has been plowed under. There is no certain restoration on that horizon. They say there are really only two kinds of stockbrokers: those who have lived through a depression and a major decline in the market, and those who have not. Not that such experience builds character or even wisdom, but it may grant us the perspective to see that what goes down eventually goes back up. Nonetheless, there's no question that anxiety is in the air. Intertwined with the fear of violence that has followed September 11th and its aftermath, the market free fall only exacerbates the general mood of unease. So many comforting aspects of the world we have known are gone, our comfortable sense of invincibility, on more than one level, is eroding away. It's disturbing.

Some years ago, on the island of Molokai, I had a similarly disturbing experience, one than has haunted me ever since. I was part of a mission of goodwill, an effort to make a better world. One evening, under the spell of a magical place, we sat in a circle, good people from every continent, and each person was asked to say in turn why they were there, what they most wanted from our work together. From one came this response: "What I am looking for is a shred of hope."[i]

If it was not hard to feel that hope was elusive ten years ago, it is even harder to sustain optimism today. The threat of terrorism, the reality of environmental degradation, and the increasing gap between the rich and the poor portend an era of reckoning for our species and the planet itself. The end of the "afluenza" period has kicked away another prop, the illusion that a ton of money could be brought into the philanthropic "garden of goodness" to increase the odds for hope.

In the late 1980s and the 1990s, the community of philanthropy, like so many other sectors of American life, adopted the "bull market" mentality and was swept up in a set of delusions of its own. Now, however, the terms of philanthropic engagement have clearly changed. As with stockbrokers, perhaps there are two kinds of donors: those who still exist, and those who don't. Whether it's the Guggenheim Museum trying to raise several hundred million for a new pad in lower Manhattan, or a rural co-op in West Virginia scrounging for the next $75,000 to keep the doors open for another six months, the world of philanthropy seems, in July of 2002, very different than it did even a few short months ago.

So perhaps this is a good time to take a step back, to see what has happened in the garden of goodness, what is left, what we have learned, and what we might prune in order to renew the bloom again.

To BEGIN WITH, it seems clear enough that we romanticized the surge of presumptive wealth. The expectation was that if every nonprofit in the land, every social entrepreneur, could just get their act together, they could surf a perfect wave of infinite resources. It was hard not to get caught up in a kind of feeding frenzy. fundraising even took on elements of the lascivious as the buzz around the "new wealth" turned into a cacophony, complete with its own pop sociology and psychobabble. An industry of instant experts swarmed around the bewildered crowd of suddenly wealthy people and came knocking on the doors of those whose existing wealth had dramatically increased. In most instances, the people they importuned were not ready—not ready to know their own minds, not ready to accept the awkward mantle of "donor"—and the world of organized philanthropy wasn't ready either.

Despite all the noise and commotion, from the point of view of most investors and most people, this "wave of wealth" was more offshore than on. In fact, the concentration of monetary resources in the United States had never been greater; the top 1 percent of the population held 41 percent of the wealth. In many instances, however, this was paper money, both literally and figuratively. In some cases, the inherent instability of assets with potential for huge gyrations in value (which of course turned downward in due time) prevented people from becoming significant donors. Others held back for reasons that are not unique to this era: concern that the money would not be used wisely, or a lack of passion, or knowledge, or time. Not wanting the publicity, the exposure. Not knowing where to go or how to go about the process of giving. Concern that "no good deed goes unpunished." Worry about the first rule of philanthropy—and of life—which is to "do no harm."

All in all, our expectations of a "golden age" of philanthropy grew too high and too fast. It takes a while for people to get used to the idea of wealth; sometimes they never do. It takes time to sort out how to be a thoughtful donor. It takes a lot of time—it sometimes takes a lifetime—to learn what to do that will make a difference, and even then you haven't finished. The truth is we expected too much.

At the same time, there were real signs of progress during this period. Charitable giving in the United States increased by 28 percent from 1997 to 2001 (a substantial improvement from the 7 percent increase from 1992 to 1996, which saw a drop from an average 12 percent increase over the previous two five-year periods). Also on the plus side, there were a few stunning examples of big philanthropic bets being placed, many new foundations—large and small—were being formed, and we saw robust growth in some community foundations and charitable gift funds.[ii] Yet in other ways all these increases did was to keep pace in relation to other economic indicators. During this period, total charitable giving in the United States remained constant at 2 percent of GNP, where it has hovered for the past fifteen years. The huge potential for dramatic growth in giving simply never materialized, and in fact, for most nonprofit organizations, the outlook has been business as usual.

Some did benefit from the boom of the 1990s. No surprise, the rich got richer and universities, colleges, and other large cultural institutions, with their sophisticated development operations, got the lion's share. Giving to higher education increased sharply; college endowments almost doubled from 1995 to 2000, and a substantial amount of that increase came from new contributions. But the vast, chaotic universe of small, community-based organizations continued to operate on a catch-as-catch-can basis.

Why wasn't the world of philanthropy as a whole ready to take advantage of new opportunites in the 1990s? During this same period, philanthropy moved from the back page onto the cover of *Fortune* and *Forbes*. Media fascination with the "wealth syndrome" spilled over into philanthropy, and reporters, cultural commentators, and analysts scrutinized the whole field. In the process, all the warts, paradoxes, and failings of the sector surfaced. Many new donors, and would-be donors, who came to take a look and kick the tires found the scene wanting. To many observers, both from within the field and from outside, organized philanthropy seemed provincial, a kind of cottage industry not equal to the task of fulfilling its stated mission.

What were their critiques and accusations? They make up quite a litany.

To begin with, critics would say, organized philanthropy is not necessarily a welcoming place. The large foundations have almost no transparency and only limited accessibility; they are run by an old boy/girl network of people who carry out their work in insulated silos or bunkers and resist anything "not invented here." Furthermore, they are lousy listeners, bureaucratic, unimaginative, slow, accountable only to themselves, and risk-adverse (mired in a 5 percent payout mode as though immortality is more important than the critical needs of today). When observers looked closely at foundations, they saw a lack of collaboration, very little investment in the infrastructure of the field (through techniques like knowledge management), and ambivalence even around the efficacy of promoting philanthropy. As a result, the phrase "the Achilles heel of philanthropy"—referring to the difficulty in knowing if you have made a difference or had an impact—has become a kind of mantra for those in search of the Holy Grail of the perfect metric.

These critiques have struck a chord in a field that has historically been awash in a paradoxical mix of arrogance and insecurity. Apparently there are lots of tough weeds in the garden of philanthropy, and, unlike in my garden, the strategies for renewal are not always so clear.

We have, on the one hand, a universe of new potential resources that is truly mind-boggling, and on the other hand, all of these off-putting aspects that either anger people, frustrate them, or confuse them. What screams out, of course, is opportunity. What has happened over the last ten-plus years is a combination of the creative and intriguing mixed with the counter-productive and foolish and a strong dose of overt opportunism. What happened is also what *didn't* happen.

HERE, THEN, is an analysis, complete with an admittedly silly-putty rating of six major trends or bents that give us an inkling of how far we have come, and of how much farther we need to go toward restoring the promise of a golden age of philanthropy. In what follows, I use the terms "low point" to mean there's a long way to go, "mid-point" to mean there's been fair progress toward the promise, and "high point" to mean that the wave has crested and the potential for growth, and in some cases sustainability, has been exhausted.

1. Philanthropy with a Capital "P": If organized philanthropy started the decade of the 1990s as a kind of obtuse, impenetrable fortress, it soared into the new millennium with new language, ideas, mechanisms, and intermediaries, all presuming to make the way into the field easier, more user friendly, and more effective. We see regional associations of grantmakers breaking out of their trade-association mode and becoming promoters of philanthropy, affinity groups of those interested in specific issues morphing into sources of knowledge and networks for collaboration, and many new associations catering to donors of all stripes.

The "advice business" is booming on all levels with a profusion of new and old answers to the challenges facing the field. Where there was one choice for a donor in 1990, there are now a dozen. The number of private foundations and donor-advised funds has increased dramatically. The field is in great flux, with much sorting out to be done. The role and relationship of "organized" philanthropy (of national organizations and of large foundations) to the many emerging donors, new associations, and networks (as well as to for-profit interventions) is a work in progress. There has been a shift in the market, an ongoing amalgamation of these various actors fraught with unanswered questions about who can deliver value. (Overall, I think philanthropy is a more interesting garden today than in it was 1990, one with lots of potential and energy; it is approaching, but has not reached, its mid-point of development.)

2. *Community Foundations:* As a group, community foundations, other federated giving programs, and a few United Ways came into their own in this period and were helped, rather than hurt, by the Fidelity factor and its clones. Many community foundations have become or are becoming more holistic in ways that will continue to attract new donors. Many are themselves fledgling organizations and out of necessity are focused on building financial capital; far fewer are as intent on developing intellectual capital around the critical issues facing their communities—the very asset that is their unique advantage. Big operational challenges include how to educate donors about community needs, how to integrate the development side of the organization with the program side, and how to find the talent and the operating funds to do all these things at once. Too often community foundations are still a well-kept secret. There is, however, increased self-awareness, and a healthy dialogue about the issues facing the field.

(In my view, community foundations have enormous unrealized potential to serve increasing numbers of donors and to promote philanthropy, and they are in between the low and the mid-point on the scale.)

3. *Innovating Forms:* New forms of user-friendly intermediary organizations—variations on the old notion of community combined with the new notion of networks—are growing profusely. Some of these organizations are collectives, where the donor invests in an intermediary that has the responsibility to manage and re-grant the funds.[iii] Many are Web-based or have a Web component. Giving circles, learning circles, and collective and collaborative approaches to funding are coming of age both domestically and globally.

Here are some examples: Social Venture Partners, now in over twenty cities, has moved beyond "Philanthropy 101" and is developing advanced educational programs for participants. Right in the midst of the current stock market free fall, a new Boston-based "circle" has formed, with fourteen families committing $10 million plus—evidence that the trend for new forms of collective giving is continuing. People have found intriguing, even radical, uses of these mechanisms in response to specific crises; one example is The Voice of the Faithful, an organization established in the wake of the child-abuse scandals that have racked the Catholic Church, which is using both the Web and a donor-advised fund to organize its work. All of these efforts emphasize collaboration, learning, and higher levels of engagement. They also represent a shift in the nature of the donor/donee relationship from a top-down process to one more like a partnership in which two-way learning is possible.

In some ways this movement flies in the face of the tradition of the individualistic donor who wants to do her or his own thing. Perhaps we want and need both models. How effective over the long term, and how sustainable these efforts will be, are open questions, but their impact on our field is energizing. (I think this innovation will continue, that there will also be a shakeout—some new initiatives will run out of gas, and some will be merged as more traditional organizations learn how to provide similar experiences for donors. My sense is that in this realm of philanthropy we have passed the mid-point.)

4. *Mixed Motive Players:* More for-profit organizations and professionals are taking up the cause and becoming indirect and direct marketers of philanthropy.[iv] There are two aspects to this trend. One is product driven, and the other is occurring within the broader realm of advisors to the wealthy. Products such as charitable gift funds, originated by Fidelity, are now offered by many financial institutions and have clearly created a new market that is here to stay. At the same time, private banks, investment firms, law firms, financial planners, and life insurance agents have discovered philanthropy for all the right business reasons. There was a time when every neighborhood had a Fuller Brush man, and every home had a Sears catalogue. Nearly as ubiquitous now are the basic messages of philanthropy, along with toolkits for donors and "foundations in a box" that come delivered ready to use. While good, much of this activity is product driven, complete with a sales pitch that directs clients toward specific mechanisms or vehicles. In some situations, of course, donor education is more objective. Its focus, however, is almost always around process, and seldom includes the thoughtful examination of programmatic substance concerning social issues. Instead, individuals get only snippets of information, which leaves them without enough knowledge to make truly informed decisions. (Of the two pieces here, I think the commercial gift-fund business is between its mid-point and its high point, as community foundations will become more competitive. With regard to the other, advisors of all stripes have only begun to integrate philanthropy into the mainstream of their work and are between the low and mid-point of their potential.)

5. Public and Private—and Somewhere in Between: The line that once separated the market economy and not-for-profit activities has now become blurred. For-profit companies now operate schools, prisons, and social service programs that were once the domain of nonprofit organizations (NPOs) exclusively, and nonprofits themselves have established for-profit subsidiaries in search of new and more stable forms of revenue. Sometimes these efforts create a conflict of both culture and mission within the same organization. Meanwhile, the terms "social venture" and "social entrepreneur" are gaining definition and credibility. Many for-profit businesses view their mission, legitimately, as a blend of profit and social enterprise, and many more, despite the current crisis in corporate governance, have a strong ethic of corporate social responsibility. As a result, there are several areas of possible "mix-up" in this blended reality. One may occur when the balancing act between social mission and market imperatives becomes corrupted. There is also real concern that the market will take the more profitable pieces of the social services domain, leaving NPOs weakened and unable to serve the most needy. Overall, this puts more pressure on philanthropic leaders to navigate between these worlds and ensure that the social mission is protected.

Another, even bigger potential for "mix-up" stems from the immense influence of corporations, multinationals in particular, on cultural, social, and environmental systems. In many instances, the impact of corporate behavior on the very issues that philanthropy aims to address dwarfs even governmental influence. While the term "public/private partnership" is gaining increasing currency, the idea of partnerships between the for-profit and nonprofit sectors has almost none. (This "mix-up" is going to escalate over the next few years—I think we are at the low point of these developments but approaching a high point of concern.)

6. *Strategic Philanthropy—the Standard:* Strategic philanthropy, once the province of only a few large foundations, is fast becoming the norm for thoughtful donors. Language makes all things new, and the themes initiated by strategic philanthropy—among them the notion of the investor/donor, high-impact philanthropy, and venture philanthropy—have attracted many new donors. Strategic philanthropy, in all of its iterations, has raised the level of discourse in our field and led almost every established foundation to examine and reassess how they function. The trends are toward making fewer and bigger bets, staying the course longer, building organizational capacity, and, in a few instances, developing programs in which collaboration is at the heart of the endeavor.

Strategic thinking calls for more research, more due diligence, and increased measurement of program results, all of which will presumably increase the odds for positive impact. Whether "strategic philanthropy" represents new thinking or simply new terminology is beside the point; the question is whether it makes a difference. At this stage, I think the answer must be both "yes" and "we don't know." Certainly the rhetoric of "venture" and "high-impact" giving is out in front of actual experience and results. Without diminishing the value or utility of having a well-thought-out strategy, the process of strategic philanthropy, which can be prescriptive and formulaic, may be too dry in a field and arena where the human and emotional component is so large, where, say, a donor may be drawn by deep compassion to help people, provide relief, and reduce suffering. One thing is certain: linking good process with the passion and art that are central to the philanthropic experience is all-important. Perhaps these are some of the reasons that the vast majority of private foundations and donor-advised funds are not strategically driven but act primarily as checkbooks.[v] (Strategy writ large has great potential, and in my view is still at a low point in its development.)

Has the pendulum swung too far in one of these directions, and will it retrace its path, as pendulums do? I have some thoughts.

It's good to see an increased focus on building organizational capacity, on effectiveness, metrics, and impact—all logical extensions of the trend to be more strategic. And yet, I believe, there are risks inherent in this approach.

One example is the false application of the for-profit concept of competitiveness. If building the capacity of a single organization works to the detriment of other important players in the system, any social gain will be muted, or even lost. It is worse than foolish to follow the "market share" notion to an extreme. For example, if the children's health services program on one side of town focuses exclusively on building its own market share to the detriment of the other providers in other neighborhoods, the community is not being well served. Currently there's a great deal of focus on helping organizations improve performance. Well and good. But I believe we need an equal amount of focus on encouraging collaboration, coordination of services and advocacy, and thinking systemically. As one foundation trustee observed after being frustrated by the lack of interest on the part of nonprofits in the same field in working together, "There's a constant danger and seduction of parochialism in a world where collaboration is the key to moving beyond the status quo."[vi] His comment points to the importance of "building an industry" as opposed to a single company or organization.

Organizations need to look beyond their own bunkers and think more broadly about systemic impact. The fierce competition for scarce resources forces nonprofits to focus on their own organizational purposes, but the philosophy of "each tub on its own bottom" doesn't get the job done. Collaboration between organizations and multiple stakeholders is complex, difficult work, but it's hard to see how major, long-lasting change can occur without it. Caution is the watchword I would offer to donors drawn to the idea of building capacity and to nonprofit organizations rising to the same bait. The power of collaboration is one reason that efforts among increasing numbers of funders to create "place-based" giving, where the strategy is to address issues from a whole-community perspective, are so interesting.[vii]

Another risk is that "impact-driven" philanthropy pushes unintentionally in the direction of funding those projects and programs whose results, by their nature and/or their design, can be most easily measured; at the same time, the quest for measurement pushes donors away from engagement with the tougher, more ambiguous, and more complicated issues and problems that defy, or seem to defy, linear evaluation. An emphasis on metrics can make donors risk-adverse, leading them to choose small risks instead of big ones or to back away from promising but really tough projects because they require a leap of imagination and faith. Information, data, and formulaic evaluations do not in themselves constitute knowledge, although they are often confused with it.[viii]

A related risk lies in the over-emphasis on "business plans" without equally well thought out "programmatic plans." A worst-case scenario would be "growing to scale" a youth organization, getting all of its organizational and financial plans in order, only to discover that it promotes a treatment program or an approach that may actually cause harm to the young people involved. My fear is that this scenario will happen, or has happened. As Warren Buffet has said, "Anything not worth doing is not worth doing well." We need to review more diligently the essential quality of an idea before we begin to even imagine its implementation.

What can we do besides wring our hands?

Donor insecurity within the field of philanthropy arises chiefly from the fear that at the end of the day our efforts may not matter, and this concern exists on several levels. We are drawn to improve process. We are not, however, always confident about what actually constitutes "good" philanthropic practice, and this uncertainty allows us to be influenced easily, even mesmerized, by other disciplines and their rhetoric, in particular the business-speak of management science. After all, philanthropy sometimes seems like a weakling compared to the powerhouse of business.

Efforts to marry the best of business practice with philanthropy are fine, but I remain skeptical of over-reliance on presumptive experts. I am more interested in hearing from those who have had the direct, day-to-day, long-term, on-the-ground experience—the kind of real-world experience that includes its fair share of failure. I think we need to guard against a tendency to look outside of an organization for solutions when the answers are frequently right under our noses, in the hearts and heads of our colleagues.

Another source of insecurity within the philanthropic community stems from a concern about the modesty, in the end, of our resources. This raises the question of how effective our efforts can be when we're dealing with big and difficult social issues, a question made more troubling by the fundamental realization that "social change is incremental at best."[ix] It is these questions and reflections that return me to that moment on Molokai. What if there is no shred of hope? What if, despite our best efforts and good intentions, the die is cast?

Surely it is paradoxical that professionals in a field so often accused of arrogance are also racked by so much doubt. What would give us confidence to be the best that we can be? What kind of philanthropy is needed to deliver hope to our children's children's generation? Try these words.

Here is Steven Spielberg speaking at a Tanglewood tribute celebrating Seiji Osawa's thirty years as music director of the Boston Symphony Orchestra:

What I have come to admire most about you, Seiji, is how you play music from within the music. It's what I want to do, learn to make the film from within the film.[x]

And this is Pierre Omidyar, the founder of eBay, in his speech to the 2002 graduating class at Tufts University:

Prepare for the unexpected. . . . Sometimes ideas have ideas of their own. . . . In the deepest sense, eBay wasn't a business. It was—and is—a community: [an] organic, evolving, self-organized web of individual relationships, formed around shared interests.

I think most people who are serious about wanting to make a difference are also drawn to go deeper, to know more, to understand the core of things. That is why we respond to people, to celebrations, to human suffering and need. It is "the ideas within the ideas," the "philanthropy within the philanthropy," that lights the path of promise.

What does that mean? I think it means being open to learning something we didn't know before, hearing for the first time what people really feel and think, and discovering what's hidden just below the surface. The "music within the music" often comes from surprises, from unexpected and unintended results, from revelation. This kind of discovery is nurtured through close observation, deep listening, and being open to new ideas and to change. Philanthropy does not get to the music if it becomes too dry, too process-fixated, too in love with its own rhetoric and therefore not attuned to the voice within. It is when we can connect that inner voice to our analytical intelligence that we have a shot at discovering the "mystery"—those moments we all recognize when everything comes together and soars.[xi] What counts most in life and what counts most in philanthropy are qualities like judgment, wisdom, and love.

For donors, the first task is to do more listening than talking—perhaps that is the first step in taking hubris out of the equation. If Mr. Spielberg, at the height his profession, still feels humility as a filmmaker, who are we to feel otherwise, either as donors or as nonprofit leaders? Real learning, real technical assistance, takes place when stakeholders are brought together in a safe space and through convening learn from one another. It is in this way that a true "community of interest" is formed. For those who work in philanthropic organizations and programs this translates into never losing sight of why they do this work, what it's really all about. For those with strong beliefs, those "on a mission," it means holding onto those values while at the same time remaining open to alternative ways of thinking. Even more important is experiencing philanthropy through the eyes of the community. Nothing makes sense in philanthropy, in any true way, unless the action meets the needs of the community first, not the needs of the donor or the project or the organization.[xii]

I think of those deep moments when a group of people in a room coalesce around an idea and make a leap of imagination, transforming that idea into action. Or of those moments when we experience the impact of the program a gift has made possible and know it has been "good"—that it has helped, informed, persuaded, cured, rescued, uplifted, inspired, saved, empowered, and, from time to time, even ennobled, a person, a family, a community, a population, an environment. When these things happen I am reminded of the miracle of the second blooming of my annuals, sure to come in the fall.

Where does this kind of thinking lead? I think to substance and meaning.[xiii] Meaning as in passion—elusive, demanding, ambitious, and sometimes all-consuming passion. Meaning as in what we know is right and what we know is wrong. Meaning that transcends the day-to-day and goes beyond self-interest. Meaning is the guide for determining what one should do, and to finding the answers to these central questions: Can we who work in the field of philanthropy become more disciplined? Can we become better at motivating and educating others? Can we become more creative in finding and implementing strategies for social change that work, and more courageous in taking on the tough issues?

Bill McDonough, one of the world's leading "green" architects, once said that everything he has done comes down to this: "What will it take for us to once again become indigenous?" Pondering the meaning of McDonough's question, Peter Senge wrote, "I think it means to be connected—to place, to nature, to life. It also has to do with steward-ship and responsibility."[xiv]

Indigenous, what an interesting slant on substantive philanthropy.

How much of our angst in life, how much of the anxiety that permeates our cultural moment, arises because we do not feel connected and because we are afraid we will loose, literally, figuratively, and spiritually, our place on earth, our place in the sun. Surely this is why working in my garden satisfies so—because it is a direct, simple, grounded way of connecting me to the earth.

As I write about meaning, wisdom, and love, I can feel my fear of wishful thinking, the fear that the notion of giving back, of wanting to be a good person, may be a romantic notion. I wish we had more discussion, reflection, and scholarship on the relationship between soul, heart, spirit, ethics, love, and philanthropic motivation and practice. These issues, so central to our field, are only occasionally addressed directly.[xv] All too often, meaning is treated as though it doesn't matter, when in truth it may be the only thing that does. Questions of meaning are certainly key to understanding why more of the world's private wealth is not in serious philanthropic play, key to making the concept and practice of citizenship more integral to the life and mores of our time, and key to acting on the courage of our convictions.

Perhaps we need a "Journal of Philanthropy," a journal of reflection and practice in this field equivalent in value and influence to the *New England Journal of Medicine* or *Foreign Affairs* in their respective domains.

In order for philanthropy to be great, to be heroic, we have to believe in ourselves and put away the Silly Putty of insecurity. We have to believe that there are untold numbers of unsung heroes in the very communities that we hope to improve. Accept the ambiguity—we know nothing but we know a great deal, we have very little to work with but we have many resources, we have done nothing but we have done a lot.

What is most significant about the last ten years is that we now have a larger philanthropic footprint, a platform with more reach and scale that is better prepared for the unexpected. We also have scores of new recruits, interested parties who are making waves and pushing for change in the system.

I believe we can push harder, and that we can tie the elements together better. Parker Palmer has written about the relationship between intellect, emotion, and spirit. Intellect alone, he says, becomes a cold abstraction, emotion alone becomes narcissistic, and spirituality alone loses its anchor to the world. Wholeness comes when we integrate all three of these ways of knowing.[xvi]

Even though plants do not grow much between morning and afternoon, I'm looking forward to an early evening stroll in my garden—a place where restoration is certain. I will leave you with a tough poem by Adrienne Rich. Her poem does not answer—as this essay does not answer—the existential question of how to find or perhaps create hope in a world of trouble, but it sets the bar higher for all of us, which is where it needs to be in the endless cycle of breaking down and restoring.

In Those Years

In those years, people will say, we lost track
of the meaning of we, of you
we found ourselves
reduced to I
and the whole thing became
silly, ironic, terrible:
we were trying to live a personal life
and, yes, that was the only life
we could bear witness to

But the great dark birds of history screamed and plunged
Into our personal weather
They were headed somewhere else but their beaks
    and pinions drove
along the shore, through the rags of fog
where we stood, saying I

—ADRIENNE RICH, 1991

i.   The speaker was Peter C. Goldmark, Jr., former president of the Rockefeller Foundation. His essay "Before the Storm" appears in this book.

ii. Notably the philanthropy of George Soros, Ted Turner, and Bill and Melinda Gates, and the growth of the Silicon Valley Community Foundation and the Peninsula Community Foundation.

iii. Examples are New Profit Inc.; Youth Venture Partners, a project of the Morino Institute; and Acumen, funded by the Rockefeller Foundation and Cisco Systems.

iv. See Steven Johnson, *Doing Well by Doing Good* (Boston: The Philanthropic Initiative, Inc., 1999).

v.   Ellen Remmer, *What's a Donor To Do?* (Boston: The Philanthropic Initiative, Inc., 2000).

vi.   From a conversation with Kenneth J. Novack, vice chairperson of AOL/Time Warner.

vii. The Annie E. Casey Foundation (Neighborhood Reinvestment Initiative), James Irvine Foundation (the CORAL program), Bill and Melinda Gates Foundation (Small High School Initiative), and the Paul and Phyllis Fireman Foundation (Project Hope Initiative) are examples of place-based giving initiatives.

viii. See John Seely Brown and Paul Duguid, *The Social Life of Information* (Boston: Harvard Business School Press, 2002).

ix.   Memorable words from Mike Sviridoff, former vice president of the Ford Foundation and the founder of LISC.

x.   From the stage at Tanglewood, Lenox, Massachusetts, July 12, 2002.

xi.   From a conversation with Charles Terry, former director of Rockefeller Philanthropic Advisers.

xii. From Alan Broadbent, president of the Toronto-based Maytree Foundation.

xiii. Emmett D. Carson, "Public Expectations and Nonprofit Sector Realities: A Growing Divide with Disastrous Consequences," *Nonprofit and Voluntary Sector Quarterly*, Vol. 31, no. 3, September 2002.

xiv. Peter Senge, "Creating the World Anew," *Systems Thinker*, Vol. 13, no. 3, April 2002.

xv.   See the American Assembly's "Unifying America" initiative, 2002.

xvi. Parker Palmer, *The Courage to Teach* (San Francisco: Jossey-Bass, 1998), 4.

PETER GOLDMARK

Before the Storm

W E REMEMBER storms, but we rarely remember what it was like just before the storm. Today, however, after a period of enormous accumulation of wealth, power, and technology in the North, and during the decline of one international order and the search for a new one, we are, I believe, living in the time before a storm of historic proportions, a period of searing difficulty for the peoples of the world and the planet itself.

Two plays from the beginning of the last century—*The Cherry Orchard,* by Anton Chekhov, and *Heartbreak House,* by George Bernard Shaw—portray a similarly uneasy, hauntingly disturbed era. I am drawn to these plays, set in the period just before World War I and the Bolshevik Revolution, because they capture a mood present again today: a foreboding that deep forces we can barely discern, let alone direct, are reshaping the world we know. Against this unsettling, often reluctant recognition, we are at once appalled and diverted—as we

---

Peter Goldmark has battled on many fronts, as a cub reporter for the *New York Times* covering guerilla uprisings, "British colonial madness," and the Cyprus civil war in 1959; as a teacher of history and as the director of New York's Port Authority; and as publisher of the *International Herald Tribune.* Today he combats global warming and is the director of the Climate and Air Program at Environmental Defense. Goldmark, a graduate of Harvard University, was president of the Rockefeller Foundation from 1988 to 1997.

were at the beginning of the twentieth century—by great wealth, intense artistic exploration, technological breakthroughs, narcissism, and a feeling of helplessness in the public arena.

In common with the generations alive in that pre–World War I period, we see a fading calm marked by glowering storm clouds on the horizon; we feel the psychological impossibility of living every minute with one's consciousness acutely tuned to impending danger, and, at the same time, an attachment to the very last beats and chords of the comfortable, known rhythms of a way of life now substantially undermined.

When will the shifts along the fault lines occur? We cannot know. We sense, fleetingly, that a new world landscape is emerging, but we know only the territories we've navigated before; we know how to dance only to the melodies we have already learned.

Philanthropy: An Erratic Pioneer

There are moments in history when American philanthropy has been farsighted, entrepreneurial, daring, and powerfully attuned to the critical issues of a coming challenge. And there have been moments when American philanthropy has seemed trapped in a curious mix of defensiveness and caution. Perhaps consistent effectiveness and relevance are incompatible with the very nature of philanthropy, which must be speculative and venturesome.

Very few American foundations have agendas that address frontally the newly global dynamics of our present situation. And yet within those dynamics lie the very challenges that will affect the future of both the United States and the world profoundly—perhaps definitively.

To Conserve and to Change

Philanthropy is generally harnessed to one of two great purposes: conservation of something of value, such as a forest or a collection of works of art, or constructive change in some human condition, behavior, or system. The philanthropy of conservation will always have value, but an individual philanthropic enterprise aimed at conservation may turn out to be quixotic or counter-productive if the basic dynamics of social activity have changed and the advocates of conservation have mustered neither the wit nor the means to change with them. For example, it will accomplish nothing to "preserve" a forest if at the same time nothing is done to stabilize the world's population and afford every family and child living near that forest a workable, fair stake in their own economic future. The act of housing and conserving a great work of art will have only temporary meaning unless the society that values and enjoys that art also pursues fairness, opportunity, and sustainability, and makes its commitment to these values compelling enough to disarm those whose indifference or hostility might otherwise undo it.

Therefore I believe it is the second purpose of philanthropy—constructive change in some human condition, behavior, or system as it applies to the new global threats—that is the most important challenge of this generation. And because of the distinctive characteristics of our age, this work—our work—may properly be called the philanthropy of human survival.

The Ultimatums

The human community faces two looming ultimatums. To address them should constitute an important agenda for philanthropy over the next two decades. "Ultimatum" is, of course, a strong and threatening word. But I believe it's an appropriate term to describe the threats we face now, because for the first time in our history these threats are global in scope—capable of changing the outcomes of the whole human adventure on this planet.

The first ultimatum before us is the threat of weapons of mass destruction. This threat presents itself today in two forms: catastrophic terrorism carried out by stateless actors, and the use of weapons of mass destruction (WMD) by one state against another. In these forms, and in others that may later arise, this threat is permanent. As long as there survives on this planet a substantial community of humans who tinker with technology, who explore, exploit, and engineer in the realm of science, then the capacity for inventing and employing instruments of mass destruction will be present as well.

The second ultimatum is the progressive destabilization of the global environment. This danger may seem less acute than the first, but it is relentlessly cumulative in the sense that—like tooth decay—the longer it builds, the more difficult and expensive it becomes to reverse. We have come to understand that environmental degradation is inherent in the particular developmental path that human economic activity on this planet has taken over the last few hundred years, and have come to realize that this model of headlong exploitation of natural resources is no longer workable. The earth is our host and we are its guests, and we are on the verge of destroying the only habitat in which we can live.

For the human community to survive in anything like the condition to which we aspire, these two ultimatums must be addressed successfully. And there is a third dimension of the current global situation that presents a moral and pragmatic imperative for action: the large and growing disparity in wealth and circumstance between the richest and poorest among us.

To understand how these issues connect, and to develop an approach to all three that can command a high degree of allegiance around the globe, is the biggest challenge we have faced during our existence as a species. This challenge should be a central concern of the philanthropic enterprise, with its claims to moral foundation, relevance, freedom from political constraint, and the latitude to tackle mankind's biggest, most controversial problems.

But these issues do not, in fact, constitute the agenda of much of the philanthropic community today. Can we get it, together?

The Challenge for Philanthropy

From what intellectual vantage point can philanthropy engage with these huge issues? A coherent strategic stance might look like this:

1. These are challenges that face all of humanity, and therefore the task of responding is not the preserve, the right, or the burden of any single national, religious, or cultural group. These efforts must be accessible to all, understandable by all, and workable for all. This is a particularly important imperative for American philanthropy, which constitutes the largest and most diverse collection of flexible capital assets in the world. The engagement of American philanthropy and its assets in meeting these challenges must be transparent, it must be generous, and the effort must be eminently "joinable"—or it will be worthless.

2. The time horizon for setting goals and establishing programs that could be part of this effort is probably ten to twenty years. A shorter horizon is not workable; a longer one is not likely to be psychologically sustainable. Furthermore, this engagement must be clearly distinct from any short-term, national political agendas.

3. The enterprise must have a visible and lively dimension of public advocacy. In this era, the process of communication modulates as well as transmits the substance of messages and thought, and influencing public impressions and views,

whether for good or for ill, is a basic part of public life. There
can be no abstention from public engagement in offering new
visions to compete for the hearts and minds of humankind.
And this means that there will be no way to avoid the rough-
and-tumble of public debate. There are more democracies on
this planet today than there have ever been before. No plans
to address the challenges before us can succeed without "a
decent respect" for global public opinion.

Over the past few decades, we in the United States have lived with
the idea that elections are won and lost on domestic issues, and that the
American public is not much engaged by or interested in international
relations. This assumption, plus the "complexity" of international
issues has conditioned many philanthropic foundations to stay out of
international affairs. But there's increasing evidence that now, post-
9/11, American citizens are developing a better grasp of the new global
realities and are reaching the conclusion that they must take an interest in them. This could be a signal that it's time for American foundations to do the same.

American Citizens Are Getting It

From January 10 to12, 2003, a representative group of Americans—
343 of them from all parts of the country—gathered in Philadelphia to
deliberate on the international situation and American foreign policy.
What happened at that gathering was riveting.

Historically, in the United States the formulation and conduct of
foreign affairs is an area of public policy that has been the preserve of
special interests and "insider" experts; only occasionally has the making of our foreign policy been subject to the kind of broad and brawl-
ing interplay of democratic debate and public pressures that surrounds
domestic issues. This condition is a legacy of several attitudes that

course deep within the American tradition: a skeptical aversion to foreign entanglements, a sense that unity in support of the executive branch is important and expected in the field of foreign policy, and a recognition that foreign affairs are unusually complicated and not easily accessible to the average citizen. The American press, with its frequently frugal and occasionally blundering coverage of international issues, has both reflected and contributed to this inaccessibility.

The people who gathered in Philadelphia were participants in a program called By the People, and had been selected to constitute a statistically valid sample of the American electorate. This meant that their views—surveyed both before they arrived and after they had deliberated together—had great potential significance for public officials. The conference afforded an imperfect, but nevertheless dramatic and valuable, insight into patterns of thinking about international affairs, one that was representative of the American people as a whole.

It is not my purpose here to report or assess the substance of those patterns and views.[i] What I find most promising is this: that the delegates clearly grasped that they simply could not ignore foreign issues—that they *had* to be interested in international affairs as citizens, as parents, as human beings. They understood that they weren't experienced in the field and that there was much they didn't know, but they also expressed a strong measure of confidence in their ability to assess the broad outlines of situations and issues, and to question intelligently and listen critically to experts—which they did. Indeed, at one point during the conference, Dr. Zbigniew Brzezinski, formerly national security adviser to President Carter and today professor of American foreign policy at the John Hopkins School of Advanced International Studies—and not a man known for his desire to democratize the formulation of foreign policy—told the assembled group that he was stunned by the quality and common sense of their questions and comments, and that this experience would force him to reassess his views on whether the public could provide useful input in the making of foreign policy.

This sign of hope comes at a moment when the role of the United States in the world has never been more pivotal, and when its preparation for exercising that role wisely and responsibly has rarely seemed more ragged.

Weapons of Mass Destruction and America's War on Terrorism

The first of the two overarching ultimatums cited earlier is that represented by the spread of weapons of mass destruction and the inevitable intersection of the proliferation of increasingly deadly technology with the growth of terrorist movements. In this frightening context, the Bush administration's "war on terrorism" is a disturbing example of what happens when American power is asserted with little understanding of the values and actions needed to build a positive vision around which the world can rally as it faces a global crisis. As we think, as a people, about how to respond more effectively, it will help to consider three broad categories of the use of force.

The first of these is force used by actors who are clearly outside the law or the moral center of society, who use their force for personal gain, or against innocents, or both. This is the *immoral* use of force; it often occurs in an outright criminal mode, as by drug cartels or other organized crime.

The second is the use of force without any apparent or accepted moral rationale other than the ascendancy of one particular group. This is an *amoral* use of collective force, and when it succeeds it does so simply by brute strength. Its use may seem legitimate to some (particularly the users), wrong to others, and simply natural or inevitable to many. This is the "might makes right" mode employed, for example, by the Roman Empire.

The third mode is the use of force on behalf of broadly accepted norms, against actors or ideas widely recognized as illegitimate. The use of Allied force against the Axis powers in World War II is a classic example of the *moral* use of collective force on the international scene.

These categories or modes may be abstract, but they are also understandable on a basic human level, and most people find the distinctions between them important.

Throughout the world, the attack against the World Trade Center was widely understood as an indefensible and repugnant use of force mounted against innocent civilians. Thus the immediate American response against Al Qaeda and the Taliban regime in Afghanistan that had sheltered it carried an inherent measure of logic and a presumptive justification. And the apparent success of the American military effort in limiting civilian casualties, as well as subsequent evidence that much of the Afghan population was delighted to be rid of the Taliban, supported an eventual global verdict that the U.S. action in Afghanistan was on the whole a moral use of force.

But it is not clear that the Bush administration actually sought this result or understands the reasons for it, and today the United States stands embarked upon a planetary "war on terrorism" declared by its executive branch alone. This is a campaign that may continue for decades, a war that even if joined by other nations will generate resistance in unforeseeable ways, and that may seem at best incomprehensible and at worst hostile and immoral to vast numbers of the human beings on this planet. Its second step, the invasion of Iraq, has already weakened the moral stature of the United States in the eyes of the international community. For many, invasion of Iraq belongs to the second of the categories above—that of "might makes right."

A war against rebels, insurgents, or terrorists must be won—as we have been told and history remorselessly teaches us—in the hearts and minds of human beings. No worldwide effort to curtail terrorism and prevent the spread of weapons of mass destruction can possibly succeed without broad support among the community of nations. If this truth does not inform our government's thinking, it must at least instruct its strategy. The evidence of the By the People meeting in Philadelphia suggests that even if the present U.S. administration has not grasped this reality, the American people have.

The Environmental Crisis and Economic Change

The period of deepening environmental deterioration does not lie in the future. It has begun. There are almost no cod left in the great Grand Banks fishery. Every year, massive chunks of tropical and arboreal forests continue to be cut and burned away. There is less fresh water, of lower quality, available in the world for drinking and household use, and water tables beneath the three largest grain-producing plains on the planet are sinking.[ii] The global climate is warming and becoming more volatile.

In scale and impact, the behavior of one species has risen to such a level that we have begun to destabilize the biosphere itself. Swift and discontinuous change has occurred before on the Earth, as the result of geological traumas and external disruptions such as asteroid strikes, and may occur again. But never in the history of this small planet has the activity of a single species metastasized so feverishly that it started to undermine the macro-conditions that allowed it to emerge and flourish in the first place.

To act in response to this environmental challenge will require that we think for the first time within a global framework and out toward time horizons extending several hundred years into the future. There is no other conceptual framework within which we can deal successfully with climate change and ensure the fertility of the oceans, the health of coral reefs, the preservation of potable freshwater, the survival of tropical forests and fauna. We must think more creatively about agricultural productivity, the disposal of toxic waste, the size of the human population upon this earth, energy generation and consumption, the needed shift away from carbon-based transportation systems . . . and more.

It's a long list. Taken as a whole, it involves rethinking our economic models and the largest part of our contemporary industrial system.

The Western economic system has changed before, and it has, in fact, already started to change again, drifting marginally in the direction of patterns more compatible with long-term survival—reduced birthrates, energy efficiency, etc. But government policies regarding these issues are still ambiguous and hesitant, and the pace of change is woefully inadequate. To make the transition to workable and sustainable patterns of life worldwide, that change must be accelerated, it must be guided by a shared framework of global values and objectives, and it must harness the power of the market. This cannot be done overnight, but I believe we can make a good beginning over the next two or three decades. And it is possible, I believe, that we have that much time left. Above all, this transition needs to be embraced and reinforced, rather than resisted, by the leadership of both the public and private sectors.

In the transition to a new and more sustainable development model, the market will not, and should not be expected to, provide the stimuli that cause that model to emerge. The market can only send short-term signals within a larger framework of values and rules. The market, for instance, did not send signals "against" lead-based paint, DDT, or the hydrofluorocarbons that destroy the ozone layer. After experience, research, and advocacy in the public sector, these products were acknowledged to be dangerous, and a framework of values and rules were created by treaty, law, and regulation to ban them. Then, and only then, did the market respond with stimuli that favored safer alternatives and encouraged their use. And in the pre-market phase of new thought and experimentation, I would argue, the catalytic role of philanthropy has been and is vital.

We know today that universal extension of the present Western industrial model is not viable and will not occur; the present model will slowly implode or it will change. As Vaclav Havel reminds us, "The market is a good servant and a bad master." The market is a mechanism, not a direction setter; it is most emphatically not a moral compass, any more than a computer or a stock exchange clearing system can be a moral compass. Only decisions in the public sector—which includes philanthropic institutions and other non-governmental organizations—can bring about basic changes in values and rules, and thus unleash the market's enormous power to accelerate the transition to a new model and effectuate those changes efficiently without the stultifying and often corrupt hand of the state. There are leaders in the private sector who have started to change the ways their firms operate, and who recognize the serious challenge we face. But the "framework conditions" for a successful response to this ultimatum must be debated and forged primarily in the public sector.

Connecting the Two Ultimatums

The link between the environmental ultimatum and the WMD ultimatum is not obvious, particularly to those from the West, where the old industrial model developed and where technology has been seen as more boon than bane. But the link is fundamental, and it is this. Terrorism can be limited only if most people reject it, and if they are to reject violence proposed in the name of justice or change, they must feel that their present situation is not hopelessly unjust, that they have some prospects for dignity and self-improvement, and that they can influence those prospects through hard work and other peaceful means. That means they must have a stake in the system and some minimal sense of control over their own role in it.

If you live in a society that permits you to seek opportunity and has reasonably fair rules for allowing you to do that, then you will support that society and you will vigorously oppose those who threaten it. If you perceive that you are subjugated or discriminated against, or if the rules appear patently unfair to you, you will at best be neutral toward or unsupportive of the existing order, and at worst you will oppose it or support those who do.

The second half of the twentieth century has seen relatively few acts of internal terrorism in Western countries, and none to date carried out with WMD. This is because, in the main, Western societies have been seen by their citizens and immigrants to provide opportunities of all kinds, and to be fair—or getting fairer, which is more important. Anyone who would put a kilogram of plutonium in the reservoirs that supply New York City (hypothetical case) or who bombs a federal building in Oklahoma City (actual case) would therefore be seen as an abhorrent criminal or lunatic element, and would be treated as such by the legal system and by public opinion.

As a demonstration of the dynamic that can influence the marginalization of terrorism, consider the case of the suicide terrorist.

The mission of the suicide terrorist succeeds only if his work is applauded and celebrated, whether publicly or secretly, by those who are called upon to support his cause. Ten young men or women will step forward to take his place only if he dies a martyr and a hero. If he dies in obscurity, or is considered idiotic to have thrown his own life away in an unjustified act, no one will enlist in the cause, let alone step forward to take his place.

There is no way to prevent terrorism completely. The task is to marginalize catastrophic terrorism in the minds and hearts of human beings, and to make it as lonely, as difficult, as unrewarding, and as despised as possible. This requires giving people a stake in the global order that can lead them to condemn rather than celebrate terrorist acts; this means that this global order must be fair, it must be sustainable, and it must be inclusive.

What, more exactly, does that look like? Exploring, debating, and helping to answer that question is the kind of challenge at which the philanthropic sector could excel.

Today billions in the South do not have a stake in the global order, such as it is, and hundreds of millions in the North are ambivalent about whether they really desire a global framework and the global institutions this would imply. The actions of the present U.S. administration indicate that they have little interest in the path of sustainable economic development or in global standards of fairness and opportunity. But the deliberations of those who gathered in Philadelphia this winter suggest that the American people understand, at least on a general level, that sustainability and economic equity are important worldwide. Some business leaders and many NGOs also understand that addressing these issues—while they are complicated and daunting—is essential. If America's philanthropic foundations were to sharply ratchet up the resources and attention devoted to these questions, we would see that there are other players around the world ready to respond positively.

Globalization and Fairness

The present world economic system is organized around Western ideas and institutions. The primary engine of economic advancement on this planet for the past two centuries has operated through three interrelated drivers: the growth of industrial production and mass consumption, market capitalism within a framework of government regulation and minimum standards, and technological advances. This triad has benefited some people immensely and many somewhat. There are also many whom it has failed to benefit. But basically these economic drivers and the institutions that applied them have proved intensely powerful over the past two centuries, and have been either imposed or imitated in virtually all parts of the globe.

In recent years this Western industrial model has been good to the developed countries of the West and has powered successful growth in some countries in the East. It has been less evenly applied, and has to date a mixed record, in other nations, nations that now contain about two-thirds of the world's population. Recent findings suggest that the terms on which other nations have been integrated into the Atlantic economic regime (now termed "globalization" and, earlier, "the Washington consensus") may actually have contributed to a rise in inequality between rich and poor.[iii]

Today's industrial model, therefore, has two problems. First of all, unmodified, it leads to economic and environmental disaster. Second, its practical performance does not command the allegiance of billions of people who live either in poverty or on the precarious lower rungs of the middle class. The present pattern must be modified, therefore, in order to ameliorate both problems—to align economic activity with ecological realities, and to offer a reasonable quotient of opportunity to everyone on the planet. Only a modified economic pattern can insure that individual human effort leads to common success rather than general disaster, and can guarantee that everyone who is willing to work hard and take responsibility for their own future has reasonable access to the benefits of that model. These are the basic preconditions for a world community that the billions of people born outside the mainstream of Western economic progress may be willing to support and defend.

The gap on this planet between rich and poor, therefore, is a central element of the challenge before us. We have all heard the numbers and comparisons so often that we are numb as well as ashamed. The challenges before us do not require us to eliminate economic inequality or abolish poverty. The former is impossible and the latter will be a long time coming. What is needed is simply what all advanced societies already seek to provide their citizens: an offer of fairness and opportunity that is virtually universal, visible to all, and viable over the long term. Otherwise terrorism, the inevitable tactic of the dispossessed and the demonizers, will be tolerated by many who feel unjustly disadvantaged, and it will be supported by some who feel powerless, desperate, or intensely passionate about changing things rapidly. And a period of global terrorism, with increasing resort to WMD, will make of our earth a grim battlefield and a tragic charnel house.

Where Is American Philanthropy?

The key ingredients of strong philanthropy are imagination, disciplined innovation, the ability to spot talent, and tenacity. Philanthropy enjoys relative immunity from the three chastising disciplines of American life: the bottom line, the ballot box, and having the press walk up and down your back every day. In some foundations this immunity seems only to produce a kind of torpid contentment. For others it provides the space for truly daring and productive initiatives. The post-9/11 situation provides the backdrop for a searching self-examination on the part of American philanthropy: What are the biggest problems we face? How can philanthropies assist human beings of good will in working effectively to solve them?

The biggest practical objection to the argument that American philanthropy ought to address global inequities, terrorism, and environmental health is that historically American foundations have been chiefly concerned with domestic issues. But there are two good reasons to challenge the traditional preoccupations of American philanthropy.

The first is that in one important sense, the international challenge requires a search for quality and leverage, not quantity of effort. A few bold and effective foundations can make an enormous difference, and somewhere in the diverse and rich world of American philanthropy a few of those bold and far-seeing spirits are present. The second is that if the participants who attended the By the People forum in Philadelphia were indeed representative of the public, as its organizers took pains to assure, there is a broad awareness among the American people that international issues are now of crucial importance to them, and there are grounds to conclude that their basic disposition is that wherever possible the United States should approach these problems cooperatively through multilateral frameworks.

Rebuilding Our International Institutions

Meeting the new global challenges will require changes in our international institutional arrangements, in particular in the UN and the Bretton Woods institutions. It will be hard, at first, to get any kind of hearing for such a reconfiguration. The proposals of any single government in this regard will be suspect. The NGO sector, however, supported by foundations, is in a position to pull together the best ideas for reshaping global institutions and marshaling public opinion among the global elite to consider serious steps toward the modernization of our international institutional landscape. And efforts by some private companies to focus on the "triple bottom line" and other agendas that go beyond mere short-term profit suggest that there is a reservoir of interest and concern in the corporate sector that could be mobilized as well.

The world's present "international" organizations (UN, World Bank, IMF, WTO, NATO, et al.), economic regime, and military alliances are largely the result of institutions established by a handful of nations grouped around the northern Atlantic basin. The rules of the present global system are enshrined in and managed through a series of treaties, organizations, and multilateral arrangements—the foundations for which were put in place half a century ago. Few of these institutions and none of the political ideas and moral values that animated them arose in response to the two ultimatums before us. It should be no surprise that these Atlantic institutions as structured today are not adequate to deal with the deepest challenges we confront.

For three reasons, it will be difficult for the world to agree on the new institutional arrangements we need. First of all, such new arrangements will look even more like global institutions than the present Atlantic ones, and this may paralyze the U.S. government. Second, the new arrangements are likely to be philosophically offensive to large parts of the business community in the North. I believe that in the end business leaders will come around because the pragmatism of business will overcome its initial ideological reflexes; already some farsighted business leaders understand that the world economy will actually be stronger and more predictable under such new institutional arrangements. But initially, business opposition to these necessary steps will be intense and well financed. The third challenge for such new international compacts is that the nations of the South and the East are not likely to sign on to a mere cosmetic "updating" of existing institutions.

Under its present administration, the United States will be unwilling and unable to lead such an effort. Likewise China appears intent only on seeking to advance its own narrow national interest. If the NGO sector and foundations are needed to do the breakthrough thinking and ignite the public debate on modernizing the institutional landscape, where in the public sector could one hope to find sustained, powerful, and constructive leadership?

The Pivotal Role of Europe

One answer is Europe. The moral center of gravity in the world today is shifting toward Europe. There are many reasons for this, some historical and some accidental.

' Western Europe, for centuries the arena of some of the bloodiest violence known to the world, now has a fifty-year record of peace and structured dispute resolution.

' After spending five decades in the fitful process of building "the European project," Europe today is the only part of the globe with a successful form of supra-national government.

' Europe has championed and financed advanced positions on many large global issues, including protection of the environment, peace keeping, and aid to developing countries.

' Virtually no nation in the world fears that any European nation will bomb or invade it.

' The five largest countries of Europe,[iv] plus others such as Denmark, wrestle visibly and painfully with the difficulties posed by the presence of important and growing Muslim minorities. These countries are thus modern laboratories where both the tensions and the potential terms of mutual understanding between the West and Islam are tested and explored daily in concrete settings.

' Europe has supported the United Nations and other emerging patterns of global governance, while over the past two decades U.S. support has been episodic and ambivalent.

It is a curious situation: the continent that generated centuries of violence and bloodshed—from the Crusades to World War II—and that served as the cradle of the sciences that eventually produced modern weapons of mass destruction, is now well positioned to hold the moral balance of power among the community of nations and in global public opinion. This is a position of immense strength and importance, but one that Europe itself seems frequently not to recognize.

The picture of Europe playing a pivotal role in the future global agenda will surprise both Americans and some Europeans themselves. Many Americans see Europe as divided, clumsy and slow, and plagued by "group think"—long on rhetoric but short on coherent action. Some Europeans themselves cynically disparage the "European project," and doubt the ability of the European nations acting together to accomplish anything serious at all. Certainly the run-up to the war in Iraq gave us little reason to assume that Europe could act with coherence and cohesion on a major international issue.

But the picture is both more complex and more hopeful than that. Europe is certainly slow, and, like all governments and public sector confederations, it is often clumsy or divided. On the question of policies to control the spread of WMD, for instance, Europe has lagged well behind the United States—remaining reluctant to accept any serious role in the effort to dismantle or safeguard those that exist in Eastern Europe, and lax in the area of dual-use technology transfer (the transfer of technology with both commercial and military applications).

But in many arenas the United States is even slower. Two of these are environmental policy and economic equity, including efforts to narrow the growing gap between rich and poor. And compare contemporary European and U.S. performance in the following areas:

> access, cost, and coverage of health care;
> management of free trade obligations;
> effectiveness and scope of international development assistance;
> investment in and sound management of public infrastructure (transportation, water, sewage, etc.);
> national energy policies;
> campaign financing standards;

- national environmental policies;
- human rights policies;
- support for the elderly.

It is hard to run one's eye down this list and conclude that Europe is vastly more "clumsy and slow" than the United States. And over the past decade, this country has frequently been immobilized by internal divisions over issues ranging from economic and quality-of-life questions like health care and Social Security to ideological hot-button issues such as gun control, abortion, and capital punishment, and even with regard to self-evident needs like overseas assistance for family planning and women's health rights.

By contrast, the Europeans have acquired the practical experience and internal political latitude over the past five decades to lead in the building of the kind of new institutional arrangements that are necessary to meet today's global challenges. What is not clear is whether or how quickly they will do that.

Philanthropy and the New Global Agenda for Survival

Over the past quarter century, philanthropic institutions and NGO forces have been instrumental in the development of environmental and human rights agendas, both within the United States and around the world. What the world needs now is for the same energy, foresight, entrepreneurial ingenuity, and grit to be devoted to the elaboration of a popularly acceptable global agenda for survival. Much of this work could build logically on previous work in the areas of environment and human rights as it expands into such areas as action to prevent terrorism, dispute resolution, global minimum standards governing work and safety, and a universal opportunity agenda covering health, education, and family development.

Reasoning by analogy may be helpful. All the developed countries have already created large systems that provide—on terms that vary widely both by country and within country by individual —access to health, minimum income support, and opportunity (education, for example).

Our first challenge is to create a crude initial framework of an analogous sort covering the 4 billion poorest people on the planet and focusing particularly on the 2 billion presently living on less than one dollar per day. The cost of such a global framework of minimum standards must be borne jointly by the North and by the developing countries of the South themselves. This framework is completely feasible financially; so far it has not been feasible politically. The initial needs that can be addressed by such a framework are neither mysterious, nor—by standards of present global expenditures—are they very expensive. They include the following.

> ' Basic health services such as immunization, water treatment, family planning, community screening, and basic public health measures. This package may cost between $25 and $50 per person per year (3 billion people).
> ' Universal education, especially for young girls, through the age of fourteen or fifteen, at a cost of about $50 per student per year (up to 500 million youths not now covered).
> ' Access to clean energy at the household level (2 billion people). The provision of clean energy services can be largely self-supporting if subsidies for "dirty" energy are phased out.
> ' Food insurance against famine (1 billion people). This is a question more of logistics and organization than of cost.

It will also be necessary to remedy a persistently destructive situation that occurs throughout the developing world wherever natural resources are extracted from poor developing countries by multinational corporations.

What we need in resource-rich poor countries is a new kind of organization that would be capable of meeting three related challenges that contemporary institutions do not address effectively: environmental abuse, growing wealth disparity, and corruption. What is needed is the development of "national development trusts"—entities modeled after public authorities, responsible to elected officials but completely transparent and independently audited. Charged with managing the relationship with foreign extractive industries, a national development trust would be capitalized and staffed in part internationally, and be required to follow environmentally sound practices and to impose the same upon its multinational concessionaires. Such a trust would use the revenues generated by natural resource extraction to establish savings and investment accounts for the individual citizens of the host nation. The multinational corporations of the North would serve their own interests in supporting this kind of scheme; making contributions to an entity that helps create local wealth and sustainable development is surely preferable, for a host of reasons, to paying bribes to government officials, as they do now. Over the past decade, models for such trusts have been discussed for various countries, including South Africa and Chad. To date, American philanthropy has not been very involved in this promising idea, but I hope that will change.

The Stakes Are High

Whether or not the several approaches I have described in this essay seem, at this moment, to all of us, like the wisest choices is not the point. The point is this: we all—citizens, governments, and foundations—face in common the imperative to respond constructively to the crises of our times. And we are not responding. We are drifting.

The possibilities suggested in these pages constitute a broad and feasible agenda. Underlying this or any comparable agenda must be a moral core, a clear and widely appealing vision of fairness and hope that includes a practical opportunity stake for all, an economic model that can safely expand (both geographically and in time), and a set of norms backed by legitimate international force to restrain those who are today scheming to use WMD in pursuit of their hate-fueled ambitions.

Sadly, the United States is far from adopting such a position today. Indeed, in the eyes of a large part of the rest of the world, this country is currently the most visible and powerful supporter of an international system in which:

> ' the rich countries of the North gain in tariffs and trade protection a level of financial benefit from the poor countries of the South twice as great as what they extend to those countries in development assistance[v];
> ' the United States is by far the highest contributor to global environmental degradation and pollution, and is perceived correctly as the member of the G-8 least interested in doing anything about it; and
> ' those seeking to establish global cooperation on the environment and on WMD, and to extend the international rule of law, respect for individual liberties, and a level playing field—values which the U.S. government in its domestic political rhetoric swears it will defend to the death—often find that in the international arena the United States is their biggest opponent.[vi]

The United States needs to establish an international agenda that at once reflects its own historic values, serves its long-term interests, and commands respect around the world. Such an agenda has not existed since the fall of the Berlin Wall.

Because a war against terrorism is also a quest for the good opinion and moral support of human beings, to have even the slightest chance of success such a campaign depends upon the United States discussing and defining *in partnership with others* what is to be achieved, and how. The present message of the Bush administration's war against terrorism reduces far too easily to, "We are strong and we will do what is right." This is a dangerous and alarming message, particularly when spoken by the rich and powerful, and it smacks of hubris. Understandably, it sounds to others of different faiths, cultures, and perspectives more like, "We are strong, and we will do as we please because you cannot stop us."

The founders and early leaders of the United States hoped that this nation would be a beacon of democratic hope for the whole world. They consciously based the new republic's constitution and philosophy on a considered distillation of the wisest and most universally acknowledged principles of their time. Their ambitions did not run to military power or the ability to project superior force around the globe. Their dream was that America would be a model of democratic process, individual liberty, limits on the use of power of all kinds, and non-intervention in the affairs of others except in the case of self-defense. Their dream was to be the Athens of the community of nations, admired for its fairness and its ideals, not feared for its power. They would be troubled to see to what degree America has become not the Athens of our world, but its Sparta.

THE MORAL CHALLENGE to the United States is particularly acute today, and hence even for foundations that limit their activities to the domestic arena there is wide scope and critical need for intelligent engagement. If the actions and rhetoric of the U.S. government as it pursues the war against terrorism inflame both its foes and the undecided, if they confuse and alienate its friends, if they cannot establish plausible moral legitimacy in the hearts and minds of human beings around the world, then this nation will find itself alone and isolated and more vulnerable than ever. And when the agony of moral doubt deepens within our own borders and among our own people, then our democracy, like any other, will become paralyzed. The United States has had one such searing experience with an overseas military intervention based on flawed moral ground, and the scars from the Vietnam War persist to this day. Do its lessons survive as well?

Where are the American foundations in relation to these new historic challenges? The record makes it clear that philanthropy is capable of serious and effective engagement with all of the issues we have discussed here. The Pew Charitable Trusts, a foundation traditionally focused on domestic issues, launched its Pew Center for the People and the Press on a path-breaking survey of global attitudes about globalization, international cooperation and conflict, and the United States itself. The Hewlett Foundation funded the By The People initiative. The Gates Foundation has launched a broad and bold effort in the area of world health. And several American foundations have funded programs to identify and support a new generation of global leaders, such as the social entrepreneurs mobilized by the Ashoka Society. But these kinds of initiatives are rare and apparently unappetizing to the vast majority of American foundations. Something is missing. Is it understanding? Nerve? The conviction that one can be effective in the global arena? The American people have made real progress in "getting it" since September 11, but as I write in the summer of 2003, it is still not clear how American philanthropy will respond.

Before, We Said, "Never Again"; Now We Must Say, "Never"

Think back to the beginning of the period that led up to World War II. Think about how much the general public, and even the educated elite, did not know then about the application of modern technology and infrastructure to the organization of the instruments of death—both in the extermination camps and at Hiroshima.[vii] The gradual realization of the scope of these horrors impelled us to seek institutions and alliances that would prevent nuclear and other weapons of mass destruction from being used again. World War II was the dark stage on which slowly, and *after* the fact, we learned how far we had come in the terrifying convergence of the modern state, technology, and violence.

Some congratulate themselves on the temporary recession of the threat of worldwide nuclear war; others sense that today we are in fact a lot further down the road toward the possibility of terrible darkness and violence. But in terms of the great ultimatums, we still live in a time that is *before*. This is why the challenges we face are, in the temporal sense, ultimatums and not faits accomplis.

Think how much we already know today. About WMD. About damage to the environment. About the growing gap between rich and poor. Current trends point toward terrible potentials for destruction, toward events that we must never allow to happen—not even once.[viii] As we emerged from World War II and stood on the threshold of the second half of the twentieth century, we discovered that we had been naive about what could happen. But we learned. And we said, "Never again."

Today, on the threshold of the twenty-first century, we face global ultimatums.

Think of how much we now know about what *can* happen.

We know enough now to say, "Never."

---

i. A report on the By the People convention of 2003, and on the substance of those views, is available from the Center for Deliberative Polling at the University of Texas, Austin, Texas. See websites:
www.la.utexas.edu/research/delpol, and www.by-the-people.org.

ii. The Punjab, the Great North Plain of China, and the Great Plains of the North America.

iii. James K. Galbraith, "A Perfect Crime: Global Inequality," *Daedalus*, Winter 2002, 23-25 et passim.

iv.   Great Britain, France, Germany, Italy, and Spain.

v.   The World Bank, *Globalization, Growth and Poverty* (2002), 9 et seq.

vi.   For example, inter alia, United States opposition to the international treaty
      on land mines, the Kyoto Protocol on Climate Change, the International
      Court on Crimes Against Humanity, the Comprehensive Test Ban Treaty,
      and the Biological Weapons Convention.

vii. The extermination camps and Hiroshima are not presented here as moral
      equivalents. They are juxtaposed because they share something else: they
      both foreshadowed the character and the ruthless scale of organized violence
      in the modern world.

viii. This passage draws on the thinking of Pascale Weil, Publicis Consulting,
      Paris.

ANNA FAITH JONES

Doors and Mirrors:
Reflections on the Art of Philanthropy

ONE EVENING a few years ago I spoke at the opening of an art exhibit at the Boston Public Library. Sponsored by Dorchester Community Center for the Visual Arts, and underwritten by a grant from the Boston Foundation, the exhibit included many works by professional artists and other adults, but much of it was by children and teens completely new to art. These young people, from a part of Boston that includes some of the city's poorest and most troubled neighborhoods, had worked over a period of several months with trained artists to create life-size portraits of themselves that they had painted on hollow-core doors a local lumber company had contributed to the program.

The results were striking. Under the lights in the library, in the hush that daytime institutions take on after hours, the paintings stood in groupings in the four-story atrium of this great public building. All

Anna Faith Jones, who received her graduate degree in musicology from Columbia University, grew up with strong role models in an atmosphere of dedication to education and community service that has shaped her life and work. She is on the board of directors of the NAACP Legal Defense and Education Fund, the National Civic League, Public Radio International, and the Kettering Foundation. From 1985 to 2001, Jones was president and CEO of the Boston Foundation, one of the oldest and largest community foundations in the country.

over six feet tall, the images were full of bold splashes of color—reds, oranges, blacks, golden-greens—that seemed bursting with energy.

As I stepped up to the podium and looked out at those doors— nearly a hundred of them standing in that high, light-filled space—and as I looked from those radiant images to the smiling faces of the audience of families and friends gathered in support of the artists, I could see, I could feel, what it is that art does for individuals and for a community.

There, in those paintings, were the young people of Dorchester, presenting themselves to the world as they saw themselves. Simultaneously bold and innocent, the self-portraits conveyed a very different view of this community's young people than the one we see in headlines and on the evening news, where Dorchester represents the "inner city," a place of drugs and gangs and violence. These youngsters had freed themselves from other people's definitions to stand on their own, in their uniqueness and particularity, as large as life and as vibrant. They had discovered how to use art—not as experts, but as serious practitioners—to explore and celebrate their own identities, to create something that would tell the rest of us who they really were.

That sea of doors remains as an image in my mind today. Some of the doors stood alone, but many of them were hinged together, not only supporting each other but also intensifying the impact of each, so that the whole added up to more than the sum of the parts: a vivid metaphor for the way our individual lives are enhanced when we feel respected and supported by our communities.

The Boston Foundation's grant to the Dorchester Community Center for the Visual Arts was just one of many thousands made to nonprofit organizations engaged in everything from health care to housing to job training to education during the more than twenty-five years I spent as part of the foundation. Yet it captures the essence of what we were trying to do as a community foundation: build connections within the community that we saw as essential to freeing individuals to become themselves.

It seems to me that this is the primary mission of philanthropy in America, as it is the mission of the country itself: to make it possible for individuals to emerge from the constraints of history, from lives defined by poverty, by age or gender, by physical disability, by racial or ethnic discrimination, or by any other condition limiting the development of their innate potential. If philanthropy does a great deal of important work in this country today, none is more fundamental or more significant, in my view, than this work for individual freedom. It is the basis of our democracy.

What we tried to do at the Boston Foundation during my years there was to effect that freedom for individuals by leveraging the power of the community. We realized that no amount of "giving" could do for the community what the community could do for itself. We came to reject the notion that solutions could be superimposed on communities by outsiders. The grant to the Dorchester arts organization was minor in itself; its success depended on the impressive power locked within even the most economically deprived communities to lift individuals above their circumstances and transform their lives. With this small grant we tapped into the power present in the natural enthusiasm of children to express themselves; the power present in the desire of community elders, like the experienced artists who participated in this project, to share their knowledge; and the power that resounded in the applause at the end of my remarks that night, which lifted people to their feet—the remarkable power, the profoundly transformative power, of a community to recognize and celebrate the accomplishments of its individual members.

IN A MOMENT like that one at the Boston Public Library, it is clear that the money involved in philanthropy is, in an important way, secondary. It is essential as a means for fostering change, that is true, but it is not the change agent itself. Consumed as we all are with money in this business—the raising of it, the disbursing of it, and the often agonizing decisions that this involves—it is easy to forget that in the end this work is not about money. It is about people. Neither a community foundation like the Boston Foundation nor other, much larger philanthropic institutions have the power to change society. Only people have that power. A philanthropic organization attempting to bring about fundamental social change can do so only by getting the resources to the people who can make that change.

Because this is true, the relationship between philanthropic organizations and the people they try to help is of fundamental importance. It follows naturally, then, that successful grantmaking is based essentially on the ability of the grantee and grantor to communicate. Ultimately this is a process of getting to know one another. It is a responsibility shared by both parties, and we have to work at it. While we may automatically treat representatives of prestigious institutions with a great deal of respect, unfortunately the same does not always hold true in our relationships with those groups struggling on the fringes of society. Poor people in this country are too often seen as the objects of philanthropy rather than as the agents of change. The image we have of the poor makes a difference in what we do, and how well we do it. And the problem starts with seeing the poor as "them." This is an old issue, but a crucial one, and how to get beyond it remains an important challenge.

Remember the famous remark of the cartoon character Pogo: "We have met the enemy and they are us." At the Boston Foundation, we had a similar awakening, not so comic, but certainly parallel in that it brought us face to face with a startling reality. What we found out anew was that, in a critical way, the poor too are "us."

To tell you how we came to understand this basic truth and what the experience taught us, let me begin with a little background about the Boston Foundation and its purposes.

From its inception in 1915, the Boston Foundation had provided funds to charitable organizations throughout the metropolitan area to help the poor and needy. In effect, the foundation was Boston's "United Way" for several decades before the United Way itself came along. Every year it made modest operating grants to dozens of charities in Boston, and these charities provided social services throughout the community. During the Great Depression, when the demands on their services threatened to swamp these independent charities and their counterparts throughout the country, the federal government stepped in, and, in a new way in American history, the community as a whole assumed broad responsibility for the well-being of the citizenry.

In the 1950s and 1960s, as federal funding for social programs expanded, the role of the Boston Foundation changed. Increasingly, it was able to play a catalytic role, helping community-based agencies attract federal funding and adapt federal programs in areas of need, taking chances on experimental programs until they could fend for themselves, and providing the funds that would launch new efforts. In the 1970s, for example, the Boston Foundation provided funds to start several of the city's community health centers, an innovation that became a national model. In the early 1980s, it took the lead in new approaches to developing low-income housing, and these approaches were also widely imitated. Foundations like ours were playing a new part now, not just responding to the community's needs, but becoming a laboratory for social change and improvement.

But in the mid 1980s, when I became the head of the foundation— and I have to note here that the timing was exquisite —America was in full retreat from the goals and ideals of the Great Society programs. Those efforts of the 1960s and 1970s were deemed failures, and it became the practice to attribute poverty not to social and historic circumstances, but to the personal failings of individuals. To some of us, it seemed that the "war on poverty" had turned into something resembling a war on the poor.

In those years of the mid-1980s, the federal government took a giant step backward in its commitment to helping the needy. At the Boston Foundation, we felt the rug was being pulled out from under us. As cuts and more cuts were announced in Washington, we watched the principal source of social funding slowly diminish. Our grantees clamored for us to fill the gap, but we simply did not have the resources. Even accompanied by thousands of other "points of light," we could not begin to make up for the cuts in federally supported programs to aid the poor. With our minimal resources we struggled to find a new way to help.

At first we focused on what we understood to be the key areas of poverty. We provided what help we could, for instance, to mothers with small children, who were the first to suffer from the worst of the cuts. But soon we realized that our pockets were not nearly deep enough to change things through this kind of help. We needed to apply some new and creative thought to addressing the whole problem of poverty and to how, in the current era, we might be more effective in doing so.

We then did something so obvious, so straightforward, and so self-evident that we wondered afterward why it had not occurred to us earlier. We reached out directly to the poor and asked them what *they* needed, what *they* wanted. We convened a series of community hearings in which we asked several hundred Boston residents—primarily poor and low-income adults and youth, male and female, from a wide variety of racial and ethnic groups—to share with us their personal stories of the obstacles and indignities they faced in their struggle for economic mobility.

These meetings were not always easy, and we had moments of wondering what we had wrought. But listening to those voices from the community was an enlightening and indelible experience. In meeting after meeting, voices raised in anger and frustration also struck chords of dogged determination and tenacious faith and hope—in God, in family, and in the promise of our country's democratic way of life.

The people who so generously came to us and shared their experiences were hardly recognizable in relation to the representations of the poor and distressed neighborhoods we were hearing about in the media. They were as different from those stereotypes as the children of Dorchester showed themselves to be when they were given the opportunity to paint true images of themselves.

What we heard repeatedly in those meetings was a plea for dignity and respect, for opportunity, and for the chance to participate fully in the life of the community. When we asked what this meant, the participants said good jobs, decent housing, education for their children, and a habitable community in which they could feel respected and included. Most of all, these citizens wanted a say in getting these things for themselves. What they wanted, it was utterly clear, was no different from what the rest of us want. When we looked very hard at "these people," at their basic needs and deepest aspirations, at their goals in life and their hopes for their children, it was like looking in a mirror. The people we saw were remarkably like ourselves.

What did this mean for the Boston Foundation and how we conducted our business?

In practical terms, it meant dramatically changing our funding pattern. It meant redirecting our resources toward organizations more organically connected with the communities they serve, organizations with more community people on boards and staff, directly shaping and implementing policy. It meant drawing into the decision-making arena teenagers, elderly people, single mothers, the disabled, the jobless, the poor. Even if these people are struggling on the margins of society, even if their very problem seems to be their powerlessness, these are the people whose engagement and participation are most critical to successful social change. Such change cannot be imposed by politicians, or experts, or academics, or even well-intentioned persons such as those who run important philanthropic institutions.

In a democracy, social change occurs only through a process that is itself democratic, a process that involves people acting on their own behalf. We know this from the labor movement in this country, when people working twelve-hour days found time to organize for change. We know it from the women's movement, when women took to the streets and went to jail for the right to participate in society as voters. And we know it from the civil rights movement, when domestic workers, schoolchildren, obscure religious congregations—people from the so called powerless fringes of society—stood up for themselves and insisted on change.

At the Boston Foundation, we went about refocusing our funding in the community based on this renewed sense of who we were and who "the poor" were; we took care to direct our funds in a way that would energize people to come together around issues important to them, to work with their neighbors, to learn the process of advocating for themselves, to get their hands on the reins of their own lives, and to take control of their own destinies in the rebuilding of their own communities.

If we ask ourselves what philanthropy can do, what it ought to do, how it ought to do it, I believe this is the answer. And I believe this very deeply. Whether we work through indigenous institutions, churches, or other community organizations, or simply with a group of concerned citizens, I believe the best work we as community foundations in particular can do is to give the gift of respecting, believing in, and working with people, where they are, to help strengthen their capacity to change and improve their own lives.

THE NINETEENTH-CENTURY novelist George Eliot believed that successful communities depend on the ability of individuals to imagine in others a center of self equivalent to their own. The relationship we have with ourselves ultimately determines the direction of our lives. Philanthropy that aims to improve society must be rooted in that same fundamental identification with others, including those who may be leading very different lives. I think it is that belief that helps people discover how to take action in their own behalf.

The experiences of my own past are focused by these themes of identification and empowerment. I grew up in Washington, D.C., when it was a segregated city. My family lived on the campus of Howard University—my father was its president for many years—and the community there was something of a world unto itself, where black people occupied positions of authority and black leaders of the time came to study and to speak. In those days, Howard's classrooms held students who would become major figures in the civil rights era, and it was possible to sense their energy and determination even then. But we knew that beyond the enclosing walls of the university lay another world entirely, one in which we were rarely welcome. There were department stores in which we would not be waited on. There were theaters and restaurants from which we were simply excluded.

As one of the early black colleges, Howard had a lifeline to the federal government, which provided the bulk of its financial support. But that support was far from automatic; the budget request presented to Congress each year was always challenged by elected officials opposed to the kind of social progress the school represented. The core funding from the federal government was absolutely crucial to the university, success in securing it was no mean feat, and equally important to the school's survival was the public commitment that this money represented. That commitment was enhanced in important ways by support from high-ranking government officials, including President Roosevelt himself.

One gesture of that support stands out among my very earliest memories, and the full significance of it became clear to me only in subsequent tellings of the story by my parents. In the late thirties, the university put up a new chemistry building, and FDR accepted the invitation to speak at the dedication. My father then made a special request of the president: that he let the students see that he was crippled. The young people at Howard were struggling with a huge social disability, my father argued, and if they could see the president of the United States struggling with a disability himself, it would help them to see what they themselves might overcome.

When he arrived at Howard, FDR let himself be lifted from his car in full view of the audience gathered for the dedication. And then, with great difficulty, he made his way to the speakers platform. It was a gesture that must have cost Roosevelt a good deal. He had never made it before in his public life, as Doris Kearns Goodwin notes in *No Ordinary Time*, and would repeat it only one other time, at a hospital for wounded and crippled soldiers, during the war. For the audience at Howard that gesture seemed to erase the barrier between the privileged and the excluded; for a moment, there was that sense of fellow feeling that marks a community of shared understanding. It was a great gift. "If I can do this," he seemed to say, "think what you can do."

That belief in the innate power of all human beings, regardless of status, to act most effectively to develop their own potential—that's the critical thing, in my view. That belief was vital to my vision of the philanthropic mission of a community foundation, and it was vital to my own personal development. What the federal government provided, however unwittingly, through its support of the university, and what FDR validated in his visit to the campus that day, was not simply "help" for a group of people clearly in need of assistance; it was a recognition and support of the latent power of such a community to take charge of its own destiny.

Looking at Howard University in those early days, some people saw an institution operating on the remotest margins of society, an institution for permanent outsiders, run by a man whose own father had grown up in slavery. Others saw Howard, and all of black America in those days, as a deprived but potentially powerful community. For those of us within that community, there was no question that the ultimate hope for the future lay within the circle of our own community, in its institutions, and in the spirit of African Americans themselves.

For me, this community, these people, were a bastion against the ugliness of racism all around us. There was present a kind of strength that is bred in the bone, an inner strength borne of the knowledge of shared sufferings and shared beliefs. At moments, this power was something one felt as an almost physical experience.

I remember one of those moments very clearly. I can see myself now, as a very young girl, standing in an immense crowd of people, old and young, black and white, in front of the Lincoln Memorial. It was twilight and we were listening to the voice of Marian Anderson, the famous contralto. Denied the right to hold her concert in Constitution Hall by the Daughters of the American Revolution, she had won permission from the Department of the Interior to sing on the steps of the Lincoln Memorial. As her rich voice floated over us in the shadow of that powerful and symbolic statue of Abraham Lincoln, the crowd was hushed by the soaring beauty of the music and united by an overwhelming and collective sense of justice done in the face of senseless discrimination.

I look back on that experience as one of the defining moments of my life. It was on those same steps that Martin Luther King Jr. stood to proclaim his dream thirty years later. And there was that same stirring, the same sense of the spirit, the same sense of people melded into one by an experience. There is immense energy in people united in mutual understanding and shared commitment. At such moments the important "connective tissue" of community is realized. Rebuilding and strengthening the potential of this connection is the very essence of democratic community building.

It is when philanthropy reaches into and supports this fundamental power of people in a community that it can be most effective in bringing about social change. And from my own experience I know that there is no group of people in our society today who lack the ability to transform their own communal life. What philanthropy can do is to put a bit of ground under people's feet. And then, let them go. Ultimately we need to see ourselves engaged in a mutual learning and growing process with people in community—a relationship of partners working toward a more just and humane society.

DENNIS COLLINS

The Art of Philanthropy

AS A RECOVERING schoolmaster, I have always had a profound respect for those rare individuals who have mastered the
art of teaching, for those in the profession who manage to instill in
their students the habit of attention, the power of expression, the ability to assume a new intellectual posture and to enter quickly into
another person's thoughts—all qualities that William Johnson Cory, a
master at Eton, identified over a hundred and fifty years ago as essential characteristics of superb teaching.

Good teaching, in my view, *is* more art than science. And like teaching, philanthropy is also an art; those who manage to do it well possess
many of the same qualities and share many of the same values of good
teachers. Both activities are based on the optimistic view that we all
can learn, that society can improve, and that the love of humankind can
go a long way toward achieving ambitious goals. Much of the tradition
of philanthropy is deeply rooted in the belief that improvement and

Dennis Collins is a senior fellow at the Center on Philanthropy and Public Policy
at the University of Southern California. He took his graduate degree at Stanford
University and began his career as a teacher of modern languages (he is fluent in
French, Italian, and Spanish) at Occidental College, where he later became direc-
tor of admissions, then dean of students, and, currently, a trustee of the college.
Between 1986 and 2002, Collins was president and CEO of the James Irvine
Foundation, during which time he also directed that foundation's higher education
grants program.

social transformation depend on education, and on the nurture and development of both intellect and character.

In Search of Certainty

One more parallel between the work of a teacher and philanthropy: the nature of foundation work almost guarantees that certainty will elude us. Most problems we choose to address are human ones—embedded in people, their organizations, and their communities—and the inevitable human complications render the outcomes of our interventions unpredictable. It is perhaps because of that very inability to assure intended results that the art of philanthropy may today be considered somewhat old-fashioned and out of favor, being replaced by a new orthodoxy rooted in what William Ryan refers to as "hyper-rationalism" and "managerialism," which he claims are taking over the nonprofit sector, including philanthropy.[i] These new "isms" appear to be crowding out a more values-driven, mission-centered approach to philanthropy and replacing it with technically based, efficiency-driven, outcome-centered processes. In short, supplanting art with a pseudo-science that imagines metrics and matrices are reality rather than a set of useful but limited tools.

If that is true, we ought not to be surprised. The danger of becoming irrelevant in a market-driven society, where bottom lines and efficiency metrics eclipse non-quantifiable values and social missions, is very real. Foundations have never been very effective in documenting their achievements, in part because with regard to most social programs the problem of attribution, the difficulty in proving cause and effect, is so challenging. With the dramatic growth of market primacy and hyper-business thinking, it's no wonder that organized philanthropy has felt the pressure to improve its analysis. Unequipped as we have been to offer little more than anecdotes about our successes and impact, philanthropy has willingly, almost desperately, embraced the metrics of the for-profit sector, with its numbers, measurements, and narrow technical evaluations. Add to that the pace and scale of the electronic revolution, which make counting and recording almost second nature, and the rush to an outcomes-based philanthropy feels appropriately aligned with the new economy.

This shift in thinking has occurred during a period of historic growth for philanthropy, in which public and media attention has been drawn to a dramatic rise in the number of philanthropic institutions and to the total amount of tax-exempt assets they possess. The accumulation of such vast amounts of wealth in private hands, albeit for public purposes, has naturally rekindled curiosity about these organizations. Lawmakers, regulators, and watchdog groups alike have shown heightened interest in the ability of foundations to help solve society's problems. In the face of such potential scrutiny, "proof" of efficiency and organizational effectiveness is comforting, even at the risk of overestimating results and understating the uncertainty inherent in any such efforts.

One of the most pernicious consequences of this rush to proficiency is the impulse to avoid, if not eliminate, funding to address big, complicated, messy, seemingly insoluble problems, problems rife with uncertainty, risk, and inefficiency, and projects whose potential for failure is high. Indeed, a troubling feature of some of the "new" philanthropy is an enthusiasm to fund projects and activities that are easily quantifiable and highly visible, which may result in short-term "wins" but do little to change the underlying causes of the problems at issue.

Focusing on Learning

As we try to practice the art of philanthropy at Irvine, our efforts begin with listening, proceed to question asking, and almost always result in learning. We generally do this by bringing together those with the experience and knowledge to educate us about an issue or a problem.

The hallmark of these conversations is a spirit of open, joint inquiry as a way of tackling complicated subjects and questions to which no one person or group has the full answer. As discussions coalesce around specific topics, we often invite others to the table, people whose voices and perspectives deepen our understanding and lead us to still other resources. As a community of learners, we struggle with complexity and ambiguity as we begin to discern the contours and dimensions of a problem. But at the end of the process *uncertainty* remains.

Lest I give the impression that grantmaking as an art is devoid of rigorous due diligence, or that we have little interest in knowing whether we are succeeding or failing to realize our mission, I should note that we have invested heavily in tools, tactics, and talent to enable us to understand better the problems we work on and the approaches we use to address them. In fact, Irvine was one of the first foundations in the country to create an evaluation office and to train our program staff in logic modeling, theories of change, and methods of evaluation and assessment. But we have come to recognize the difference between attempting to prove results and invoke causation—where evidence is scant, margins of error are substantial, and the concept of social return on investment is fragile at best—versus trying to learn from our experience. It is on the *learning* that we have chosen to focus. And as we learn, we believe, we get better at practicing the art.

Just as good teaching requires subject mastery, field knowledge has been essential to our practice of philanthropy, not so much for the purpose of being able to debate or dissect discrete complexities, but rather to know enough to be able to discern possible entry points, seek out opportunities for intervention, and suggest alternate paths and creative connections. The level of knowledge required by program staff is clearly not equivalent to that possessed by the experts we consult, but at the very least it must be sufficient to enable us to map a field, ask intelligent questions, and devise a framework for understanding the essential issues and problems that the foundation wishes to address. As a multi-program funder with a strong regional presence, we have endeavored to connect and integrate our program interests to address problems as they present in communities, not as they are categorized in social science research. It is in such boundary crossing that the most creative solutions to public problems often emerge. As practitioners of this art, we have been reminded time and again of the importance of staying focused and valuing precise thought and expression while tolerating ambiguity and accepting the possibility and the lessons of failure.

The Power of Imagination

As important as cognition is to the reduction of uncertainty, as central as clear thinking is to effective problem solving, it is organized philanthropy's lack of imagination that reduces the power of its manifold good works. The reluctance or inability of foundations to "swing for the fences" with unbridled passion, to fund the extraordinary, is discouraging. It's a mystery to me why a field so unfettered by outside regulation, so well positioned to imagine the unimaginable and to dream the impossible dream, is disinclined to act more boldly. Pablo Eisenberg may have been right when he alluded to Oscar Wilde's famous description of English fox hunts ("the unspeakable in full pursuit of the inedible") in describing foundations as "the well-intentioned in full pursuit of the not-so-relevant."[ii] Benjamin Mays, the former president of Morehouse College, might well have been speaking of foundations when he noted that "not failure, but low aim, is the real sin." Self-stifled imagination and the pulled punch hold foundations back far more often than a lack of resources or inadequate know-how. Perhaps fear of risk inhibits imagination as much as lack of imagination inhibits risk, but we are far less likely to risk the big idea if we cannot first imagine it. While we know that making great art, like superlative teaching, derives from the power of creative imagination, there is little incentive today for program officers to explore the mysterious or embrace the ambiguous. To the contrary, hyper-rationalism and efficiency metrics move us inextricably to the opposite corner. Peter Karoff reminds us that "process should be a servant of intuitiveness, values, instincts, and passions—and not the other way around."[iii]

The Pursuit of Pluralism

Much of the angst about foundation effectiveness derives from the debate about why foundations should exist in the first place. Indeed, why should we care whether it's art or technical metrics, if we can't agree on the reasons for our legitimacy? Kenneth Prewitt, of the New School University, poses the question, "Are we to presume that foundations perform a social task or function that the state and/or the market cannot perform?"[iv] He answers by suggesting four plausible purposes for foundations—redistribution, efficiency, social change, and pluralism. Individually, Prewitt goes on to argue, the first three of these purposes are not sufficient bases for legitimacy, and although they combine to create a "non-trivial cumulative impact," even in combination they fall short of justifying the transfer of large amounts of money from the tax system into private institutions and private decision making about public well-being.

Only the fourth purpose, in Prewitt's view, gives large-scale philanthropy its legitimacy, and this is because foundations contribute in meaningful and essential ways to a pluralism without which there can be no open society. Foundations can buck conventional expectations because they are not dependent on the ballot box or a shareholder vote or any of the other consensus-forcing demands that are rightly placed on government and commerce. Their independence allows for social experimentation, for funding the unusual and the unexpected. By contributing to a pluralism of practice and thought, to a diversity of participants and views, foundations can make a significant difference in the degree to which tolerance and openness are valued principles in a democracy.

It follows, I think, that the pursuit of pluralism can best be achieved by ensuring that foundations not mimic the overdependence on metrics and matrices of the for-profit and political sectors. Precisely because foundations depend upon the delivery system of the nonprofit sector, they have a unique opportunity to diversify and expand societal thought and action without running the risk that the results will be imposed by government or mass-marketed by commerce.

New Standards of Accountability

One of the unfortunate, unintended consequences of the accountability movement in philanthropy has been the push to emphasize the measurement of results over an understanding of why we choose to intervene in various situations. Pseudo-science has propelled us into thinking of accountability as providing proof that things worked out the way we intended. The art of philanthropy requires a more spacious and nuanced concept of accountability, one that pushes foundations to greater openness about mission, our core values, and our partners, an accountability that communicates a clarity of purpose, unambiguous policies and procedures, and an openness to criticism and new ideas. The new accountability requires that we demonstrate our commitment to learn from our work, acknowledge our failures, and improve our practice. And above all, this commitment must derive from an authentic and demonstrable engagement in partnership. Not too long ago, in a feedback program we initiated to encourage critique of our own foundation, we learned that the quality of the relationship experienced by our partners and our program staff was considered as valuable, and in some cases more valuable, than the grant dollars received. Philanthropy is not a solo act. Standing alone we accomplish almost nothing. It is through partnership with grantees, and increasingly with fellow funders, that the promise of philanthropy can be realized.

I began my career as a teacher. Teachers share a trade secret, and it is this: high expectations increase the likelihood of high performance; if you expect me to hold myself to high standards of excellence and discipline, you increase the likelihood that I will act according to those standards. An accountability based on shared purpose, mutual respect, and honest and open communication will do more to ensure a vital and reflective philanthropic sector than thousands of published evaluations and documented best practices.

Charity is often confused with philanthropy. Charity can ameliorate social problems. Philanthropy, if done well, can help discover and elaborate solutions. Philanthropy seeks out root cause and leverages results; it inspires and promotes individual growth as it nourishes human welfare. In the grand scheme of things, foundations occupy a position of unusual privilege in society. Perhaps their greatest privilege is being well protected from almost any form of challenge or criticism. Neither the rigors of the marketplace, the fickleness of shareholders, nor the seismic effects of the ballot box disturb our privileged station. Even the distress and concern of failed grant seekers most often goes unspoken, for hope springs eternal.

Such immunity from criticism can have a corrosive effect on some in our field. They begin believing their own press, they talk more than they listen, and they become convinced that the quality of their contributions to the discussion are well above average. Focusing on what a privilege it is to receive a grant, they lose sight of what a privilege it is to be in a position to make one.

We can guard against such hubris and combat the occupational hazard of arrogance by acknowledging that our work is indeed an art, that it flows from a deep philosophical and ethical base, that its uncertainty represents opportunity, and that thoughtful efforts to improve practice should prompt our imagination and challenge our powers for creative problem solving. Again, it was Benjamin Mays who said it best: "The tragedy of life does not lie in not reaching your goal. It lies in having no goal to reach. It is not a calamity to die with dreams unfilled, but it *is* a calamity not to dream."

i.   William Ryan holds a fellowship at Harvard's Hauser Center for Nonprofit Organizations.
ii. Pablo Eisenberg is a senior fellow at Georgetown's Public Policy Institute.
iii. Peter Karoff is the founder and chairman of The Philanthropic Initiative, Inc.
iv. Kenneth Prewitt is dean of the Graduate Faculty of Political and Social Science, New School University.

SCOTT McVAY

The Philanthropic Tipping Point:
The Intimate, Albeit Frail, Connection
between Survival and the Work
of the Independent Sector

OVER THE LAST thirty years, we in philanthropy have dealt in "hope" and "opportunity," creating a place where people—whether they are working on vital social issues, in education or the arts, or for the well-being of animals—can bring their ideas and their dreams. But all along the way, as I have met with some of the finest and most dedicated of these workers, I have detected a concern that our society—and humankind as a whole—may be headed toward an abyss because our capacity for mischief has moved beyond a local context and is now planetary in its reach. A gathering undercurrent of evidence suggests that we may be undone by any one or a variety of problems in combination.

Scott McVay, past president of the Chautauqua Institution, knows whales as well as philanthropy and has published in *Scientific American*, *Science*, and *American Scientist*. Early on, he was a special agent of the Counter Intelligence Corps in Berlin. He is a recipient of the Albert Schweitzer Award and the Joseph Wood Krutch Medal from the U.S. Humane Society and has served on the boards of the World Wildlife Fund and the Smithsonian Institution. A graduate of Princeton University, McVay was executive director of the Geraldine R. Dodge Foundation from 1976 to 1998.

It is also true, as any one who reads a good newspaper can detect, that there is slippage in many of our institutions—in business, in government, in religious groups—that the touchstones of our world seem less steady, less reliable, less assuring than we thought in years past. Meanwhile, many, including Michael Lerner of Commonweal and the Jennifer Altman Foundation, have questioned whether organized philanthropy has had any lasting effect on human affairs.

What is at stake and how could philanthropy make a difference? In its ideal form, philanthropy is truly a sacred trust. After making a broad inventory of options and issues, and listening to key players, the grantmaker or philanthropist places bets on persons and organizations whose mission may improve the prospects for the human condition. The money given is modest compared to the size of the problems, but these precious dollars, wisely spent, can make a big difference.

One August evening a few years ago, when our family was vacationing at Lone Mountain Ranch in eastern Montana, a man known as Walkin' Jim Stoltz spoke to guests about his adventures trekking on foot along the Continental Divide from Mexico through the northern Rockies and deep into Canada and Alaska. He also sang songs inspired by these journeys, one of which included these lines:

> You get up in the morning,
>   shake the dew off of your mind.
> As the sun pours like honey
>   through the ponderosa pine.
> You're livin' every moment
>   as if you've just arrived,
> Because you know
>   what it means to be alive.[i]

In their cadences and their invocation of the pull of the trail, Stolz's songs are reminiscent of portions of earlier lyrics that chronicled life in the wilderness, like "The Law of the Yukon," "The Shooting of Dan

McGrew," and "The Cremation of Sam McGee," by Robert Service. But those were written in the context of the rush for gold on one of the last "frontiers" for Europeans in the New World, whereas Walkin' Jim and his songs are propelled by an urge to protect the wilderness and wild places that are vanishing as our society extends its imprint over the whole planet.

At the end of the evening, Jim turned to his attentive, appreciative audience for questions. "What was your closest call?" I asked. He said that one day, as he was walking a glacier field along the Divide, he fell and started to slip and slide toward a great chasm. The ice of the glacier was so sheer and unyielding that as he slid, downward, feet first, on his stomach, he could get no grip with his fingers. Rubbed raw by the effort, they left only faint trails of blood on the ice. Finally, though, he managed to turn on his back, and when he did the neck of an old guitar strapped to his pack dug in and began to slow him down. He came to a stop with his legs dangling just over the precipice. Jim told us that he rested there for fifteen or twenty minutes before extricating himself and moving on.

I think of this story often because today it sometimes seems that human survival itself hangs in the balance, held by something as slender as the neck of an old guitar. A host of daunting issues are unfolding, any one of which, or several in combination, could do us in. The world's human population has tripled, since my birth in 1933, to 6.3 billion souls; as we know, these numbers put the larger biological landscape, which gave us rise and provides our daily nurture, at risk. The nuclear threat is not abating, although attention to it within the philanthropic community has waned. Good work goes forward on development of alternatives to fossil fuel, like wind, solar, and geothermal power, but the energy issue is still a large and daunting one. Consumption as a religion, beautifully detailed in Alan Thein Durning's book *How Much Is Enough?*, is the root cause for our unsustainable, uncertain economy. Durning writes, "Lowering consumption is our part of the bargain." Meanwhile, growing contamination of the biosphere, of every living thing, has been described by hundreds of researchers and compiled in some twenty-seven thousand entries, to date, in a database created by Theo Colborn and her team at the World Wildlife Fund.

In 1992, a major United Nations conference in Rio de Janeiro addressed two huge issues: the loss of biological diversity and global warming. But the United States was a reluctant player, and progress on protecting both the planet's climate and its bio-diversity has been delayed for lack of leadership in our country.

Just ten years ago, Edward O. Wilson, then Frank B. Baird Jr. Professor of Science at Harvard University, published an essay in the *New York Times Magazine* entitled "Is Humanity Suicidal?" The pull-quote subtitle read: "If Homo sapiens goes the way of the dinosaur, we have only ourselves to blame." E. O. Wilson is perhaps the clearest voice from the life sciences on the stresses to our planet, and in this carefully reasoned article he noted both the way our living planet has evolved— through "the spread of large assemblages of organisms, from forests, grasslands and tundras, to coral reefs and vast planktonic meadows of the sea"—and the cataclysmic role human beings have had within and upon the planetary whole.

What Wilson calls "the Moment" will arrive when "the forests shrink back, . . . atmospheric carbon dioxide rises to the highest level in 100,000 years, the ozone of the stratosphere thins, holes open at the poles . . . and one species has gained control of the Earth, becoming a geophysical force through the sheer mass of protoplasm." For Wilson, the human species is, "in a word, an environmental abnormality." "It is possible," he says, " that intelligence in the wrong kind of species was foreordained to be a fatal combination for the biosphere. Perhaps a law of evolution is that intelligence usually extinguishes itself." Wilson acknowledges that this admittedly dour scenario is based on "what can be termed the juggernaut theory of human nature, which holds that people are programmed by their genetic heritage to be so selfish that a sense of global responsibility will come too late."[ii]

What Are the Links between the Gnarly Issues and Philanthropy?

Okay, what does philanthropy have to do with these great issues? Everything. Despite recent suggestions that organized philanthropy has become timid and self-serving, I believe that it *can* be a force for good in the future as it has been in the past.

"The Pigeon Feast," a short story by Haldor Laxness (an Icelandic author who won the Nobel Prize in literature in 1955) about a "pants presser" who comes into money and runs into problems when he tries to give it away, brilliantly captures the twin problems of philanthropy—the limitations of giving and the difficulty of making one's gifts strategically and wisely. But in his influential book *The Tipping Point*, business and science writer Malcolm Gladwell gives us a hint as to how they might be addressed when he describes how "little things can make a big difference."

> The problem, of course, is that the indiscriminate application of effort is something that is not always possible. There are times when we need a convenient shortcut, a way to make a lot out of a little, and that is what Tipping Points, in the end, are all about.

"Ideas and products and messages and behaviors," Gladwell writes, "spread just like viruses do." And as this happens, a "tipping point" may be reached that transforms "the ebb and flow" of fashions and trends into major social change. [iii]

Many of the reforms that have benefited our society—among them women's suffrage, civil rights, child labor laws, improved workplace conditions, ending the Vietnam War—have come about not overnight but because of the fervent and long-term efforts of not-for-profit groups, which today number over a million. These groups are fueled by giving, giving by individuals and by families and by foundations. But the choice of issues is crucial, and it may be true that too often the path of least resistance is taken, rather than the line of greatest advantage.

What are the elements of informed, effective philanthropy? I believe they are curiosity about the human condition, the imagination to see fresh options, *and* the courage to act on perceptions of how to improve that condition. These elements are uncommon individually, rarer yet in combination, but they are potent when joined together consciously and spiritually. For me, the real question is, How do we move beyond mere charity to more strategic philanthropy that can change thinking and behavior, especially with regard to major issues that affect both human beings and the planet itself?

Sometimes foundation leadership makes the difference. Years ago, for instance, Bill Moyers pointed out that without campaign finance reform we cannot have responsible governance because elected officials are forced to spend all of their time fundraising for the next election. (Tim Wirth described the problem eloquently in a 1992 article titled "Diary of a Dropout," published in the *New York Times Magazine* after he chose not to run for reelection to the U.S. Senate from Colorado.[iv]) Moyers made campaign finance reform a central issue for the Florence and John Schumann Foundation, and presented a strong case for it to a group of environmental grantmakers in Charleston, South Carolina, in 1996. A vital link was made. The McCain-Feingold legislation, recently upheld by the Supreme Court, is a step in the right direction, but money still has too great an influence on elections and governance.

Sometimes the answer is a book. Island Press, for example, publishes many books on environmental topics, and this literature extends and reinforces the impact of philanthropy and the works of nonprofit foundations and organizations in that realm. Books can do much to alter perception and behavior for the better, and perhaps the most prescient act of philanthropy during the last century was Andrew Carnegie's creation of 6,200 libraries, building in local support to sustain them.

It is also crucial to analyze past efforts and plan for the future as best we can. Jesse Perry, the architect of the "Green Revolution" programs for the Rockefeller Foundation acknowledged during a brown-bag lunch at the Dodge Foundation that perhaps they had been working on the wrong problem. Then retired, he was beginning to think that, instead of focusing on more bountiful crops for food, perhaps the foundation should have spent more of its money on assisting couples or women in ways that would encourage them to have fewer children. Such support would have been less expensive than the Green Revolution. I admire Perry's willingness to reassess a program, a highly touted program, that he had shaped from the outset.

The art of strategic, creative philanthropy, then, lies in knowing the issues well, identifying promising change agents, and then deciding to act on one or two or three issues. The undertaking by Pew in consort with the Rockefeller and MacArthur foundations to address the energy issue is a good example—very astute and telling. Together these three foundations created the Energy Foundation, which has made substantive contributions over the past fifteen years, building on the early work of the Natural Resources Defense Council in California and the Conservation Law Foundation in Boston. And the ultimate gladiator in the energy arena is still Amory Lovins of the Rocky Mountain Institute—a foundation-supported entity. With his twenty-six books and his regular meetings with leaders in industry and government, here and abroad, Lovins is a persisting, nimble, and original player.

Early Signals and Early Lessons

I entered the foundation field in May 1972 as the first executive director of the Robert Sterling Clark Foundation in New York City. Within the first month, I heard Paul Ylvisaker, then with the Ford Foundation, cautioning a gathering of grantmakers against the hubris of our work: "Who would return your calls if you weren't giving money away?" A year later, in San Antonio, Bill Moyers suggested two tasks for philanthropy:

> One, you can help people take on the spoilers of society one-by-one. ... Second, you can continue to bet on excellence. ... I still believe in the touch of one life upon another; single out people with capacities and give them a boost.

Soon after, the Council on Foundations moved to Washington, D.C., from New York City, a surprise, since at the time 40 percent of all organized philanthropy was concentrated in New York. This left a lacuna with regard to cooperation and networking, and so the Foundation Luncheon Group was formed. Arch Gilles, then with the John Hay Whitney Foundation, drew three hundred grantmakers to a lunch with Nelson Rockefeller, who was then planning a run for the presidency. Arch also drew three hundred for a lunch with Ralph Nader, a classmate of mine from college, whose issues then, as a citizen advocate, had broadened beyond the dangers of cars that were "unsafe at any speed." The convening power of foundations—one of their most useful assets—was palpable.

Another collaborative group was the New York Regional Association of Grantmakers, formed through the impetus of Herb West of the New York Community Trust and John Coleman of the Hartford Foundation, who authored *Blue Collar Journal* when he was president of Haverford College. I had the pleasure of putting together the first board of twenty-one, composed of old hands and new faces, conservatives and liberals, one from New Jersey and one from Connecticut, some from business and family foundations, and, of course, independent foundations large and small. Together we began to address some of the major concerns we all shared: how to choose areas of concern, how to evaluate promising programs, and how to make the best use of our financial resources. Here are a few examples of what I learned in the process.

The Jesse Smith Noyes Foundation was exemplary in the choice of issues it tackled, such as sustainable agriculture, toxics, reproductive rights, and encouraging enduring communities. The credo of how they worked, written by Edith Muma, is the finest I have encountered.

One memorable event was hearing David Rogers, the first president of the Robert Wood Johnson Foundation, speak in the basement of the Ford Foundation; his program people, he said, would be out on the road at least three days a week to listen, learn, and map the territory of possibility in grantmaking in health and health care.

The Hewlett Foundation in California was then in its first year, and I invited Roger Heyns, its first president (and former chancellor of the public university system in California) to come to New York and to tell us about his unfolding plans. Roger said that certain fractions of their income were going into education, the arts, population, and the environment, and that 15 percent was being set aside for "things we haven't thought of yet." This is an excellent idea—one I have not heard before nor since.

Another memorable insight came in 1975, at Rockefeller University, when I invited Philip Morrison, then a professor of physics at M.I.T., to address New York grantmakers on what we should be thinking about in the next twenty-five years. Morrison had been the reviewer of all science books for *Scientific American* for a quarter of a century. Imagine. Well, this consummate man of science spoke only of the arts, beginning with glassmaking in Murano, Italy, in the twelfth century and moving swiftly on to our own day. The last part of his remarks was devoted entirely to Christo, who had recently created his "running fence" in California, but many of whose great works—like the umbrellas in California (yellow) and Japan (blue), and wrapping the Reichstag in Berlin—were yet to come. His presentation taught me that scientists and engineers can often be our guides in understanding the value of the arts to society's efforts to imagine our future.

As a grantmaker, the undertaking I'm proudest of from my days at the Robert Sterling Clark Foundation, where our mandate included supporting culture and the arts, was a nationwide effort to support liberal arts colleges in a program called Building Bridges across the Moats, which encouraged active engagement in their communities. For this program, I visited seventy-five colleges, from Maine to Oregon, from Minnesota to North Carolina. Warren Wilson College, located northeast of Ashville, North Carolina, provides a good example of how our money was spent. The college has an organic farm on which students work fifteen hours a week, and its student population included then 22 percent from abroad; the Clark Foundation grant supported a beautifully conceived program that sent these international students into the Ashville public schools to share insights and stories from their own countries.

Forming the Blueprint for the Dodge Foundation

One day stands out in my mind as the most important of all to the formation of the essential scaffold of the Geraldine R. Dodge Foundation's program for giving: July 26, 1976. That was the day I invited our charter board of trustees to gather and hear from leaders familiar with program areas under consideration and to interact with them informally.

That day Paul Ylvisaker, then dean of the Graduate School of Education at Harvard, spoke of the spirit of philanthropy that works steadily at what seems to be unworkable, that chips away at impossibilities, that over time produces answers. Paul urged us to be "both prudent and bold." He believed that foundations could achieve "fantastic leverage with public bureaucracies," which we later discovered to be true, especially during Tom Kean's eight years as governor of New Jersey.

John Esty, an educator with the Rockefeller Brothers Fund, spoke to us of the great promise of experiential and age-integrated learning. As if peering into our future, he suggested we make grants to school principals, who bear the responsibility for creating a climate for excellence in learning. Julius C. Bernstein, former superintendent of schools in Livingston, emphasized the efficacy of mini-grants to teachers, grants that have an impact out of all proportion to the dollars expended, an idea that was, as he drolly put it, "doomed to success from the start."

Governor Brendan Byrne spoke to us about the necessity of preserving the Pine Barrens, a unique one million pristine acres astride an aquifer holding 17 trillion gallons of water—the only dark spot in a wash of light between Boston and Washington as seen from a satellite at night. The governor also spoke of the need to develop a cultural identity for New Jersey, which has a wealth of artistic talent.

Ralph Burgard reminded us that 30 percent of our state's citizens or their parents were born in another country, offering possibilities in the arts such as the amazing evening on August 12, 1998, at Liberty Science Center, when we gathered people from India to Zimbabwe to China to say, often from memory, poetry from home that they treasured. And he spoke, too, of festivals, little knowing that ten years later we would fashion the Dodge Poetry Festival, the largest gathering of poets and poetry lovers in North America.

Our final presenter that day was Lester R. Brown, founder and president of the Worldwatch Institute, who had been a tomato farmer as a youth in South Jersey. His ideas and writings on building a sustainable society helped guide our efforts to tackle a brace of critical issues.

We listened hard to all these wise voices, and then, in the fall of 1976, we published and distributed widely a statement of policy, priorities, and guidelines. One-third of the Dodge Foundation's resources would be concentrated in the arts, the welfare of animals, and local projects in Morris County—a focus suggested, although not mandated, by Mrs. Dodge in her will. The remaining two-thirds would be placed in two exciting areas that offered many giving options: pre-collegiate education and critical issues, that is, issues related to human survival. With a declared interest in programs and people, we would not consider proposals for capital purposes, endowment, or deficit operations. This strategy has fared well, but words can only hint at the joy of the journey, the grand companions discovered along the way, and the sense of hope for the future.

During my years at the Dodge Foundation, I often wondered what it would be like for Geraldine Rockefeller Dodge to return to Madison and travel about, meeting folks whose dreams we had nurtured with her resources. Barbara J. Mitnick's book about Mrs. Dodge, written for the twenty-fifth anniversary of the Foundation in 2000, suggests that she would be pleased with how her legacy lives on, and I believe that is true.

Three Dodge Foundation Initiatives

THE POETRY INITIATIVE. By the end of my first decade at the foundation, I had learned that sometimes a good philanthropic strategy is a matter of being a niche player in an under-addressed arena. Take the example of the Dodge Foundation's poetry initiative. Before we began this program, I think it is safe to say, none of our nine capable trustees had an active interest in poetry. But noting that only 7 percent of all giving in America went to the arts, and that of that sum, less than 2 percent went for writing and poetry, I reasoned that we could have a disproportionate impact with our gifts.

Looking through the larger lens of life on earth, it may well be that among mammals generally (circa 4,000 species), primates specifically (circa 260), and the great apes in particular (5), our distinguishing feature as a species is language. Until quite recently some six thousand distinct human languages existed on Earth, although that number is rapidly shrinking with rampant globalization and the morphing toward English and Chinese as dominant languages.

Language, although it may also be written, is an oral proposition. The music, resonance, and cadence of language, a living thing, is a basic connector within every tribe, essential in communicating what it feels like to be alive, where we come from, where we are going. Each of us is defined by our stories. A champion storyteller—Sappho, Homer, Lao-tzu, Dante, Cervantes, Shakespeare, Goethe, Dostoyevsky, Shaw, Dinesen—conveys the essence of an age and the timelessness of the human continuum. Great poets can convey in an epic or a haiku the feelings of us all and articulate our infinite yearnings along our brief journeys through the world. Language, I would say, is a crucible for human understanding.

In the fall of 1985, I presented the trustees at Dodge with two ideas for verbal arts initiatives, one for poetry and one for theater, that in each instance would engage practitioners (poets and playwrights) as well as devoted teachers. The trustees chose to support the poetry proposal first, and the drama idea was approved a year later. On the last day of that year, in the late afternoon, I called on Jim Haba, an associate professor of English at Glassboro State College, and invited him to be our poetry coordinator. It was a wonderful conversation beside Jim's wood-burning stove and a couple of cats. The dream was given loft because of Jim's love of poetry, his desire to encourage teachers to "befriend" poetry, and his ability to conceive of poetry, offered with grace and conviction, as existing in places often apart from the confines of academia.

This endeavor was one of those things that unfolded just right from the outset. To identify teachers, I wrote all public school English teachers in New Jersey, asking how the teaching of poetry could be given a boost and inviting them to submit their visions for a poetry festival. Based on scores of responses, Jim and I gathered fifteen teachers in my home in Princeton on a spring Saturday. Each teacher had been asked to bring a poem close to his or her heart, and the reading of those poems electrified the first hour. Whitman, Dickinson, and Shakespeare were represented, also Neruda, Issa, and even the efforts of an unknown student or two. Laughter, joy, cognition, and emotion splashed through the living room. Five hours flew by, and we had the good counsel of a new coterie of superb teachers who would not stand alone again but would be joined with colleagues in a teaching and writing adventure for years to come.

Throughout, we knew that respect for teachers' wisdom and expertise leads to lively learning by both teachers and students. What counsel could we gain from poets themselves? On another spring day, Jim and I traveled to New York to meet with poets Galway Kinnell and Stanley Kunitz, who cheered us on. The choice of Waterloo Village for the locus of the Dodge Poetry Festival was ideal, due to the rural character of the place, nurtured into its present configuration by Percy Leach and Lou Gulandi. It offered many venues for events in tandem, as well as one great green tent for featured poets.

I felt it was essential to capture the events and readings of the festival on film for broad distribution, and that goal has been amply fulfilled. At the time of the first festival, in the fall of 1986, an ambitious series of films on poetry called *Voices and Visions* was being completed, and I invited its executive producer and director, Lawrence Pitkethly, to make a film for us for PBS. That film, *Poets in Person*, was aired in 1987, and although women poets were underrepresented, it captured some of the flavor of poets in action. At the next festival, in

1988, filmmaker David Grubin documented the spirit and content of the gathering, involving Bill Moyers as narrator and interlocutor in a six-hour PBS series called *The Power of the Word*.

In 1994, Moyers put a major effort into another PBS series, eight-hours long, *The Language of Life*, and an accompanying book. In 1996, Juan Mandelbaum, an Argentinean filmmaker based in Boston, did an enchanting three-hour series, *Poetry Heaven*, also for PBS. In 1998, Moyers did another splendid seven hours, *Fooling with Words*, and again a fine book. Each series had an accompanying guide for teachers nationwide. Altogether, some twenty-five hours of poetry on film reached public television audiences (an estimated seventy to eighty million viewers). The Dodge Poetry Festival and these films helped to transform the public's view of contemporary poetry from one of remoteness and suspicion to something closer to what's expressed by these lines from William Carlos Williams's "Asphodel, That Greeny Flower":

> My heart rouses
> > thinking to bring you news
> > > of something
>
> that concerns you
> > and concerns many men. Look at
> > > what passes for the new.
>
> You will not find it there but in
> > despised poems.
> > > It is difficult
>
> to get the news from poems
> > yet men die miserably every day
> > > for lack
>
> of what is found there.

The Dodge Poetry Festival (now a biennial event) became, as Malcolm Gladwell would put it, the "connector," the place for poets from around the world to come to meet informally and encourage one another. Nine U.S. poets laureate have sung there. Throngs responded to the ruminations of Rumi as conveyed by Coleman Barks accompanied by the Paul Winter Consort. (Today the thirteenth-century Persian poet Rumi is the fastest-selling poet in America—500,000 books to date—and the number one poet on Afghani radio.)

"I have never believed that poetry is an escape from history," Adrienne Rich has stated, "and I do not think it is more, or less, necessary than food, shelter, health, education, decent working conditions. It is as necessary." And in thinking about how desperately poetry is needed in these troubled times, consider the amazing poem "Wage Peace," by Judyth Hill:

> Wage peace with your breath.
> Breathe in firemen and rubble,
> breathe out whole buildings
> and flocks of redwing blackbirds.
> Breathe in terrorists and breathe out sleeping children
> and freshly mown fields.
> Breathe in confusion and breathe out maple trees.
> Breathe in the fallen
> and breathe out lifelong friendships intact.
> Wage peace with your listening:
> hearing sirens, pray loud.
> Remember your tools:
> flower seeds, clothes pins, clean rivers.
> Make soup.
> Play music, learn the word for thank you in three languages.
> Learn to
> knit, and make a hat.
> Think of chaos as dancing raspberries,

imagine grief as the outbreath of beauty
or the gesture of fish.
Swim for the other side.
Wage peace.
Never has the world seemed so fresh and precious.
have a cup of tea and rejoice.
Act as if armistice has already arrived.

THE CHINESE LANGUAGE TEACHING INITIATIVE. The story behind our Chinese language initiative is enlightening. In 1982, some in America already sensed that China, with one-fifth of the world's population, would become a huge economic force, and twenty-one years later, in a March 2, 2003, article for the *New York Times*, Daniel Altman wrote:

> To hear the alarmist tell it, the emergence of China as an economic super star is bad news that is only growing worse. Their familiar cries—China has an unlimited supply of cheap labor that threatens American workers, China stacks the deck against foreign companies that invest there, China will destroy American manufacturing—were recently reinforced with a new one: last year for the first time, China probably bested the United States as the world's top choice for foreign investment.

Back in 1972, during Richard Nixon's historic encounter with Mao Tse-tung, the United States did not even have its own Chinese-language interpreter. Today, however, some two hundred schools, both high school and elementary, offer Chinese language instruction daily to twenty-five thousand students. How did this language revolution come about? In 1982 Bill Rockefeller, then the president and chairman of the Dodge Foundation, and I met with Ted Sizer and John Esty in Boston to consider undertaking an educational initiative of national import. After reviewing some forty previous educational grants made by the Dodge Foundation and considering what idea or path might be truly strategic and important, we decided that an exploratory grant to St. Ann's School in Brooklyn Heights to teach Chinese could be a bell-wether for a national initiative.

We chose Chinese—and Mandarin in particular—in part because Mandarin Chinese is the most commonly spoken language on Earth (far more common than Hindi, Spanish, and English, the other leading languages of the world), and to further understanding between East and West. As Ernest Boyer has pointed out, "We study Western civilization to understand our past, but we need to study non-Western cultures to understand our future."

After a meeting during which we heard advocates for Japanese, Russian, and Mandarin Chinese language studies, the trustees chose the last as our focus. Professor T. T. Ch'en of Princeton University and Timothy Light of Ohio State University were crucial mentors in those early years. We invited principals at nine hundred leading high schools from coast to coast to compete for grants, asking them each to design a five-year plan and make a commitment to imbed Chinese in their language offerings.

In 1983, twenty schools were funded, another twenty in 1984, and a final cohort of twenty high schools was added in 1987. Beyond its financial support, the foundation brought the teachers together every summer, typically at Middlebury College (a major venue for summer language study), but also at Ohio State, Northfield-Mount Herman School, the Beijing Language University, and Honolulu, to build curricular solidarity and collegial spirit. Spurred in part by prescient parents, another two hundred and forty schools jumped on the bandwagon in the meantime.

The tipping point of that initiative was generated by splendid leadership and networking, by parents' ambitions for their children, by constant training and cultivation of teachers, and by good timing. As Gladwell explains, the success of such "social epidemics" is based, in part, on individuals, "the involvement of people with a particular and rare set of social gifts."[v] One of the rare and gifted people who propelled the Chinese language initiative was Wei-ling Wu, a language teacher from West Windsor High School in New Jersey. Wu is a master teacher who inspired an entire network of colleagues, and led with grace and persistence an initiative to teach Chinese to elementary school students—an enterprise that is very different pedagogically from language teaching in high school—in leading schools in the Garden State. Her resilience, wit, and diplomacy helped make the whole national initiative click.

Chih-Wen Su and Lucy Lee and their colleagues from CLASS (Chinese Language Association of Secondary Elementary Schools) deserve praise for gaining approval of Chinese language learning as an Advanced Placement examination of Educational Testing Service.

Today Chinese language instruction in America is flourishing, with some fifty thousand students at both the university and pre-collegiate level pursuing Mandarin, a study that takes young Americans inside Chinese culture, its long history, literature, and art, even the cuisine and calligraphy that are essential to the Chinese way of life. These culturally literate citizens will be far better emissaries for us than those without the insights that come only with study and respect for other ways of knowing.

I would very much like to see similar initiatives now across America to introduce or strengthen the ties of our citizens to other languages and cultures. The world of Islam, to cite the most obvious example, includes at least 1.2 billion people located all over the world, but very few American college students—fewer than five thousand—are studying Arabic, its foundational language.

OUR FATE IS CONNECTED TO ANIMALS. Until recent centuries, human beings understood that our well-being is inseparable from the health and well-being of the creatures with whom we share the planet Earth. Compared to the immensely successful dinosaurs, whose reach through time was one hundred times longer than ours has been so far, it was only "the day before yesterday" that we began to distance ourselves, physically and emotionally, from other animals.

Still, a sense of the oneness of humanity with the rest of the natural world is found in diverse cultures throughout history and in every language, occasionally touching poetic heights, as in this quote from Chuang Tzu (369-286 B.C.E.):

> I do not know whether I was then a man
> dreaming I was a butterfly, or whether I
> am now a butterfly dreaming I am
> a man.

Over two millennia later, Indian Nobel Laureate Rabindranath Tagore (1861-1941) directed our attention to the consequences of our interference with even the tiniest of the magical parts of the animal kingdom:

> The butterfly flitting from flower to
> flower ever remains mine,
> I lose the one that is netted
> by me.

A central tenet of Geraldine Dodge's life, and an animating force of the foundation that bears her name, is the prevention of cruelty to animals, a principle that rests on the knowledge that our care of animals, especially those we are in close contact with, shapes who we are, and what we become.

Through research on our relationships with companion animals, we verified what one could readily intuit, namely that their effect on human health, in this lonely world, is profound. Dodge funding in the early 1980s at the University of Pennsylvania School of Veterinary

Medicine supported a study that demonstrated that a person's blood pressure goes down steadily (for fifteen minutes) when petting a dog, caressing a cat, or even looking at a fish tank (which may explain why many dentists today have fish tanks in their offices).

In 1996, after twenty-one years of backing projects and programs to advance the welfare of animals, the Dodge Foundation launched a new initiative aimed at encouraging resourceful and talented veterinary students to pursue projects that had humane consequence along the continuum of animals—from companion animals to livestock to wildlife. (The first two categories are growing as rapidly as the third is being depleted.)

Our conviction that the best ideas would come from the students themselves was borne out in the quality, character, and freshness of the proposals we received. The majority of veterinary students at that time were women, and perhaps that accounts for the gentle, caring strategies that were developed. Pioneering professors of veterinary medicine in Canada, the United States, and Mexico were indispensable mentors to the students and participants in several exhilarating fall gatherings where research was reported and further lines of inquiry suggested. The veterinary students' reports were subsequently posted on the Dodge Foundation website.

The undertaking—*the Frontiers of Veterinary Medicine*— would not have succeeded as admirably as it did without the leadership and moral authority of Mark Jerome Walters, a journalist and veterinarian, and one of our program officers. We are also gratified that four other funders collaborated in this North American initiative, which continues to alter the field of veterinary medicine in ways more telling than we could have imagined at the outset. Each year a major figure—among them Franklin Loew, Patricia Olson, Temple Grandin, and Jane Goodall—joined in to cheer these accomplished students on. The singer and song writer Dana Lyons has often attended as well, to entertain students with his audacious ballads, including "I Am an Animal" and "Cows with Guns."

A Baker's Dozen of Other Dodge Foundation Initiatives

SUMMER EDUCATIONAL OPPORTUNITY AWARDS FOR TEACHERS. For twenty years, the foundation has given $5,000 summer awards to twenty-five public school teachers annually to pursue educational dreams of their own design, often with astonishingly positive results.

PROVISIONAL TEACHERS (ALTERNATE ROUTE). Of thirty-six educational initiatives undertaken by Governor Tom Kean in New Jersey, the identification and support of hundreds of recent college graduates as teachers, and of those who come to teach from other lines of work, may have had the greatest impact. The Dodge Foundation gave added support to the top twenty-five of these provisional teachers, persons whose lifework suggested they were superbly qualified for this high calling.

THEATRE PROGRAM FOR TEACHERS AND PLAYWRIGHTS. Following our time-tested strategy of "seining" for talented teachers, we arranged many occasions when drama teachers and leaders from the theater in New Jersey could connect as peers. Recognizing that the origin of all theater is the play itself, the program evolved into opportunities for teachers to write and perform plays themselves.

ARTIST-EDUCATORS. A non-verbal arts initiative was undertaken to identify and back visual artists of skill, joy, and originality who also teach. A good teacher alone can do much, but the foundation's program sought to link up artist/teachers with kindred spirits across the state and provide opportunities to meet in the lofts and studios of major artists, and to travel to the Storm King Art Center and museums in New York and Washington, D.C. The program continues to flourish.

CELEBRATION OF TEACHING. For a decade (1986-1996), Ruth Campopiano and Peter Schmidt cochaired the foundation's national initiative Celebration of Teaching, which encouraged able high school students to enter a profession that allows one to be creative, to challenge, and to be challenged. With the expenditure of a million dollars overall, and the active collaboration of State Teachers of the Year, thousands of young people in all fifty states were reached, and many have indeed become teachers.

SCHOOLS ATTUNED. In 1987, the trustees wanted to undertake an initiative of national consequence for youth who struggle to learn. Physician Mel Levine, at the University of North Carolina at Chapel Hill, was invited to devise a strategy that would, in time, go to scale at the national level. The All Kinds of Minds program, wherein no child is humiliated and every one encouraged to build on natural strengths, has done just that. Dr. Levine—a man who understands through keen observation the seemingly infinite variety of ways children learn—is the author of *Keeping a Head in School*, *A Mind at a Time*, and *The Myth of Laziness* and is currently instructing twenty thousand New York City teachers in his methods.

LANGUAGE PROGRAMS. The foundation also lent support to the teaching of three other languages besides Chinese: Russian, through a new four-part language textbook written by teachers in Russia and the United States; Spanish, through the development of secondary school materials to supplement *Destinos*, a fifty-two-week PBS college telecourse, developed by WGBH, which immerses students in interactive learning (1991); and Japanese, through distance learning by SERC (Satellite Educational Resources Consortium) from an instructor in Nebraska by satellite to students nationwide.

A PASSION FOR TEACHING. The foundation's encouragement of excellence in learning, teaching, and school leadership has sparked a number of wonderful publications, among them *A Passion for Teaching*, a book published in 1999 by the Association for Supervision and Curricular Development. The book features forty-two teachers chosen nationwide who have remained passionate about classroom teaching for many years. It contains enthralling essays, artwork, poetry, and portraits of each teacher by photographer/educator Kit Frost.

WOMEN'S STUDIES. Over the years, the foundation found many ways of backing women leaders, educators, artists, and activists—among them Carol Gilligan, author of *In a Different Voice*, and Peggy MacIntosh, with the Women's Studies program at Wellesley College—thus contributing to the valuing of women historically and currently as nurturers, relationship builders, and often as the souls of community.

TEACHERS OF THE RAIN FOREST. Beginning in 1985, the foundation began sending public school teachers on Earthwatch expeditions to the tropical rain forest and planning spring and fall gatherings; these teachers, numbering more than three hundred today, know the issues and have become environmental leaders in their schools and communities. They now have their own, highly motivated group, Teachers for Biological Diversity.

PRINCIPALS' CENTER FOR THE GARDEN STATE. After years of funding able teachers to help them pursue their dreams, the foundation also began to identify and encourage principals who, ideally, are the principal learners in their schools. A Principals' Center for the Garden State was created, led initially by Mary Lee Fitzgerald ("the only viable unit for real change is the individual school"), former state commissioner of education, and housed at the Carnegie Center for the Advancement of Teaching at the invitation of Ernest Boyer on the Princeton campus.

Today more than five hundred principals are active members, and they find many ways to share their knowledge.

DOMESTIC VIOLENCE. Partnering with DiAnne Arbour of the New Jersey Battered Women's Service, the foundation addressed the issue of domestic violence just as the gravity and extent of the problem was beginning to be recognized. We backed training for police, physicians, educators, judges, attorneys, therapists, clergy, and members of other occupations. The documentary *Battered Wives Shattered Lives* was produced, funded by Warner Lambert, and aired nationwide by New Jersey Network, drawing ten thousand phone calls in the first hour.

CHILDHOOD CRUELTY TO ANIMALS: A PREDICTOR OF TROUBLE TO COME. A path-breaking study by Stephen Kellert and Alan Felthous revealed a high correlation between childhood cruelty to animals and violent behavior as an adult. The study is now imbedded in the working understanding of judges who confront adolescent boys whose aggressive behavior has brought them before the court. Frank Ascione of Utah State University has since extended the body of knowledge about this tragically predictive behavior.

NEW JERSEY ANIMAL ASSISTANCE PROGRAM. The foundation's annual assistance to scores of New Jersey animal shelters and humane groups that address companion animal overpopulation and abandonment through humane education, responsible pet ownership, and low-cost sterilization has helped create one of the strongest support networks in America.

From Giving to Giving

What I never dreamt when I was in the swim of philanthropy was that in so-called retirement I would continue to serve in a position of consequence for an institution with national clout. Since 2001, I have been president of the Chautauqua Institution, located in western New York.

The Dodge Foundation legacy has continued in my life as many of the leaders with whom I was privileged to work before have been woven into a tradition, and an institution, known to some as America's Utopia. I never dreamt that I would be given the chance to continue to recognize and honor and bring together people of achievement in so many shapes and stripes across education, the arts, religion, and recreation. And I have been blessed with a joyous marriage of forty-five years to Hella and granted buoyant health and energy for this new calling, a calling I never imagined nor sought.

Poet Laureate Stanley Kunitz, at ninety-six years, wowed our audience at Chautauqua in 2001 with these most appropriate words:

> Though I lack the art
> to decipher it,
> no doubt the next chapter
> in my book of transformations
> is already written.
> I am not done with my changes.

The next summer, the poet Pattiann Rogers reminded us that

> The family—weavers, reachers, winders
> and connivers, pumpers, runners, air
> and bubble riders, rock-sitters, wave-gliders,
> wire-wobblers, soothers, flagellators—
> brothers, sisters, all there is.
>
> Name something else.

i.   From his song "All Along the Great Divide".

ii. Edward O. Wilson, "Is Humanity Suicidal?" *New York Times Magazine*, 30 May 1993.

iii. Introducing the central concept of his influential book *The Tipping Point*, Malcolm Gladwell writes, "*The Tipping Point* is the biography of an idea, and the idea is very simple. It is that the best way to understand the emergence of fashion trends, the ebb and flow of crime waves, or, for that matter, the transformation of unknown books into bestsellers, or the rise of teenage smoking, or the phenomena of word of mouth, or any number of the other mysterious changes that mark everyday life is to think of them as epidemics. Ideas and products and messages and behaviors spread just like viruses do." Gladwell, *The Tipping Point: How Little Things Can Make a Big Difference* (New York: Little Brown and Company, 2000), 7.

iv. Tim Wirth, "Diary of a Dropout," *New York Times Magazine*, 9 August 1992.

v.   Gladwell, *The Tipping Point*, 33.

JOEL L. FLEISHMAN

Simply Doing Good or Doing Good Well:
Stewardship, Hubris, and Foundation Governance

IT IS IMPOSSIBLE to disagree with the proposition that the philanthropic sector is better off today than it was a decade ago. There are many more foundations than there were in 1993, and even with the losses that many of their endowments have suffered, foundations have larger asset pools now than they did then. Moreover, there is a whole new breed of newly wealthy individuals, some of whom are practicing philanthropy with the same zeal, energy, and self-confidence that characterized Andrew Carnegie.

In addition, community foundations, an American invention of almost a century ago, have soared into orbit. Their experimentation with donor-advised funds offers new choices of philanthropic vehicles to families, individuals, and corporations. Although many community

Joel L. Fleishman is a professor of law and public policy at Duke University, where he teaches a course on philanthropy and voluntarism and directs a research program on impact measurement and strategic choice making by foundations. He came to Duke from Yale, where he was associate chairman of the Center for the Study of the City and Its Environment, and associate director of the Institute of Social Science. From 1993 until 2001, he was president of the Atlantic Philanthropic Service Company, a component of Atlantic Philanthropies.

foundations were initially nervous about competition from financial institutions that copied the donor-advised fund concept, there is little evidence of erosion of the community foundation donor base. Indeed, it seems that the donor-advised analogues established by Fidelity and other financial services firms have tapped billions of donor dollars that would not have gone into community foundations in any case, and thus their giving vehicles have actually expanded the philanthropic pie. Finally, there has also been a great deal of other promising experimentation with various multi-sectoral solutions to public problems.

Sunsetting and Strategic Philanthropy

There are, however, signs that not all is well in the world of philanthropy. Many of the founders of the more recently established foundations have incorporated sunset provisions into their bylaws, requiring them to spend themselves out of existence within a specified number of years. That is not necessarily a bad thing for society, but it is different from what most large foundation creators have done heretofore. On the one hand, limited foundation life is good for society because the near-term benefit of an endowment that will be entirely spent in solving problems over a specified number of years is significantly greater than that of an endowment from which only the income will be devoted to comparable purposes for all eternity. That an increasing number of donors are choosing to limit the lives of their philanthropic assets and focus them on solving problems in the short run contains hints of the problems inherent in organized philanthropy as we have known it. If one takes at face value what such donors say when explaining their motivation, one can quickly understand the seriousness of the issues they are raising. In the past it was commonplace to acknowledge that many, perhaps most, foundation creators were at least partially motivated by their desire to create a monument for themselves that would last for all time. When a donor creates a foundation that will pass out of existence in a short time, however, he or she thereby underscores the conviction that benefiting society is more important to them than achieving eternity for themselves, or than controlling one's beneficiaries from the grave. The act of sunsetting one's foundation, therefore, gives added credibility to one's explanations for doing so.

Some such donors say that they are moved to focus the activities of their beneficence on the short run simply because they are convinced that the immediate problems facing society are profound and require the application of as many charitable dollars as quickly as possible. In other words, they believe that it is better for today's philanthropically inclined wealth accumulators to put their dollars to work solving today's problems, and to let tomorrow's wealthy individuals solve tomorrow's problems. A choice based on that motivation does not imply a criticism of perpetual foundations, but only a personal choice in giving style. It is worth noting that the donor of Atlantic Philanthropies feels so strongly about the validity of that motivation that he has announced that not only will Atlantic spend itself out of existence within ten to fifteen years, but also that he and Atlantic plan to seek to persuade other philanthropists to follow his example by sunsetting their foundations as well.

Other wealthy individuals who have announced sunset policies for their foundations appear to be motivated less by the desire to benefit society in the near term than by their lack of confidence in what will happen to their philanthropic assets once they depart this world. To put it plainly, they simply don't trust their successors, whether close friends, family members, business associates, or professional foundation managers, to be faithful to the purposes and values that led them to establish the foundation in the first place. Where did they get that idea? Partly, I think, this view arises from the different giving styles between foundations guided by living donors and foundations whose donors are long deceased. Where donors are still alive and in control, their foundations appear to be energized by their engagement in what has of late been called "venture philanthropy," and these foundations often act more quickly and more nimbly than those without living donors, and more economically too. Some donors, therefore, sunset their foundations because they believe that presidents and program officers of the long-standing private foundations are less dedicated to economy of operation and efficient grantmaking than their counterparts at institutions where living donors are looking over their managers' shoulders.

The rush to strategic philanthropy—giving that is tightly focused on defined problems with the intent to solve them—is another recent development, and one that might be potentially troubling, although not necessarily so. The idea that a philanthropist should be strategic in selecting his or her objectives is hardly new. It is inherent in the conception of philanthropy as an attempt to achieve systemic solutions to public problems rather than simply to alleviate their symptoms, as traditional charity is thought to do. Moreover, some of the founders of the great American foundations, especially Andrew Carnegie, were nothing if not strategic philanthropists. One cannot read Carnegie's *The Gospel of Wealth*, even if one disagrees with some of his choices or the paternalistic manner in which he formulates them, without marveling at his clarity of vision and purpose. There is no doubt that he was, about a hundred years ago, a strategic philanthropist.

There are dangers inherent in a tightly focused approach to philanthropy, however, and they are the same as those that attend any strategic choice. Selecting a strategy necessarily forces the strategist to opt for some courses of action, sometimes only one course, over others. In philanthropy, this means that one thereby trades off the breadth of a more diverse grantmaking program for the focus of narrower targeting. Being strategic, in other words, necessarily requires making a bet that a particular approach will work, and therefore it also requires performing a serious risk assessment before choosing among approaches. Properly formulated, a strategic choice forces one to identify, up front, the outcomes and, if possible, the social impacts that the strategy aims to achieve. Precise identification of outcomes and impacts is the most demanding part of being narrowly focused, and all too often this indispensable stage in the process is given short shrift or even neglected altogether.

None of these characteristics of strategic philanthropy is bad in itself so long as the majority of foundations do not plunge into this style of decision making to the exclusion of all other forms of philanthropy. In fact, in principle, strategic philanthropy can be a gale of fresh air, a much to be desired alternative practice. Without doubt, a more strategic approach enables foundations and philanthropists to increase their chances of achieving the kind of systemic change that philanthropy at its best can achieve, and being more strategic undoubtedly increases one's bang per philanthropic buck, because the focus that is the essence of strategy forces attention to be paid from the beginning to the outcomes one is seeking and the criteria by which one intends to measure them.

Nevertheless, I have the uneasy feeling that strategic philanthropy is being overdone by some foundation leaders who have embraced it as a new mantra, a cure-all for the criticisms that trustees and others have expressed about the way foundations tend to operate. It is true that large foundations are not subject to any of the forces of accountability that constrain—and motivate to much higher performance—both the for-profit sector and many of the grant-seeking not-for-profit organizations. It is true that foundations have almost always been unwilling to evaluate rigorously the social impact of their philanthropic dollars. It is true that foundations have been shamefully unwilling to share their assessments of their successes and failures with those on the outside. But an overdose of strategic philanthropy will hardly cure any of those imperfections in accountability, with the possible exception that strategic philanthropy requires more in the way of gathering data about the impact of a given effort. And another danger arises from that very requirement—the danger of making grants only to projects that lend themselves to easily measurable outcomes. If foundations engage in strategic philanthropy to the exclusion of all other approaches, pursuing only easily evaluated courses of action, they will inexorably abdicate their wider role as providers of the social venture capital on which our society depends for its renewal. Unless one is exceedingly careful, being relentlessly strategic almost always precludes the tentative exploration and seeding of new, and sometimes conflicting, ventures that have been the source of some of our most important social innovations.

To my mind, the analogy frequently made between for-profit venture capitalists and social venture capitalists—the foundations and wealthy individuals—has in fact been overdrawn. For-profit venture capitalists assume ahead of time that they will sow many more seeds than will sprout. They go into a mix of ventures only after calculating the risks each entails, and with this knowledge they are willing to undertake very significant risks. Typically, they expect eight or nine of out of every ten investments to fail, and one or two to succeed mightily, more than making up for the losses. How many foundations have officers and trustees who would be comfortable with a record of one or two wins out of ten tries?

It is more than a little bit arrogant for those with philanthropic resources to think that they can, acting alone, make a detectable, measurable difference in solving huge social problems, yet that is often what strategic philanthropy is thought of as meaning. Making a measurable difference solely by one's own actions is very different from a strategy of joining with other foundations in a group effort and/or working through a network of existing nonprofits in order to make a measurable difference, and, more often than not, that has been the way foundations have chosen to make their impact. Unless a foundation switches from being a grantmaking to an operating foundation, it must necessarily give its funds to other organizations that are working on solutions to some part of the problem that the foundation cares about.

Typically, foundations have chosen to support scholars, scientists, advocates, and grant-receiving organizations as instruments for implementing their strategies. They have usually sought to identify major social problems, both domestic and international, and then have chosen to work with the most promising people and organizations already at work in their areas of concern. When existing organizations do not seem adequate for addressing a particular problem, foundations sometimes create new ones. Whatever their course, foundations rarely seek to solve major social problems alone, preferring to catalyze partners to work with them. Most foundations recognize that a bit of humility is appropriate when grappling with major social change.

However, in the process of choosing strategies, a foundation can be tempted to assume that its strategy has the potential, in fact, to solve a major social problem. Such hubris is inappropriate in an arena that calls for humility. So while I underscore that effectiveness and efficiency require grant-seeking nonprofits and foundations to become much more strategic than they have been historically, I would argue that their success in doing so depends upon being modest in making their choices and humble in the way they implement them.

The Context: Charitable Giving in the United States

Americans are the most voluntarily charitable people in the world, giving both money and time to nonprofit organizations at a much higher rate than citizens of any other country. In 2002, the most recent year for which data are available, total charitable giving by Americans amounted to an estimated $241 billion, of which foundation giving constituted only 13 percent, or nearly $28 billion. The remaining $213 billion came from individuals, given either while alive or in bequests at death, and from corporations, which accounted for about $8 billion. Total giving by Americans, therefore, constitutes about 2 percent of the gross domestic product of $10 trillion.[i] The country closest to the United States in national charitable effort is the United Kingdom, whose citizens give approximately 0.7 percent of GDP to charity. Americans are also generous with their time; sixty million Americans are estimated to give five hours a week each year as volunteers, with an imputed value of some $200 billion.

Why do Americans give so generously? What motivates us to make charitable giving a fixed part of our lives? Some do so out of religious obligation analogous to tithing—approximately 38 percent of all charitable contributions are given to religious congregations or institutions—but religious obligation extends far beyond this to encompass education, food for the hungry, housing for the homeless, medication and treatment for the ill, and other forms of relief for the needy. Some people give for philosophical or emotional reasons, or to "give back" to institutions from which they themselves have benefited. Still others give because they have been richly blessed by fortune, and they would prefer to share their wealth with society. Many give to help solve social problems they care about deeply, especially protecting human rights and civil liberties, conserving natural resources, cleaning the environment, and discovering cures for particular illnesses. Many give to strengthen institutions that uphold values, that give meaning to their lives—in the worlds of music and art, for instance—and to broaden the access to such values throughout society. And, yes, some give to acquire that social cachet that arises from being known as a significant donor to prestigious institutions or events. Most Americans, then, give either from a sense of obligation or to advance or defend the interests they care about. In general, however, it is only foundations and a small number of very wealthy people who define their charitable giving as intended to bring about measurable, fundamental change in society.

All of those dollars go to a wide variety of nonprofit organizations, which are registered with the Internal Revenue Service and accorded tax-exempt status by the U.S Internal Revenue Code. The usually accepted figures on U.S. nonprofit revenues put the total at around $800 billion in 2001, but estimates range from a low of $448 billion to a high of about $1 trillion. Based on what we know about the sources of nonprofit revenues, the latter figure seems more accurate: when we sum up the $241 billion of charitable contributions, the approximately $400 billion in support of nonprofits by government, and the approximately $400 billion in fees for services provided by nonprofits, the $1 trillion aggregate seems persuasive.

Foundation Influence on Nonprofits

Because foundation giving is the largest institutional component of aggregate charitable giving, and because foundation giving occurs, with rare exceptions, in grants much larger than gifts by individuals, foundation influence—on grant-seeking organizations, on public policy research and advocacy, social service delivery, and all areas of public interest activity—is far greater than the influence of individual donors, even though their number, and the number of dollars they donate, is larger.

While virtually all organizations are understandably grateful for the grants they receive from foundations, many of them, perhaps even most, are not entirely happy with the ways in which foundations and their program officers deal with them. The most frequent complaints are about these issues: program officers who are inordinately slow responding to proposals and making decisions on those proposals; institutional unwillingness to support initiatives that pose significant risks; boxing grantee requests into specific project grants instead of providing more flexible, and more needed, general operating support;

enticing grant seekers to undertake initiatives that are not their highest priorities (perhaps not even in their strategic plans); micro-management by program officers who frequently second-guess grantees and sometimes attempt to impose their own judgment about how to run grantee organizations; high-handed treatment by program officers of successful grantee officers who are insufficiently deferential; and not being forthcoming about why a proposal has been turned down. Some of the dissatisfaction grantees feel has been empirically documented for the first time in recent surveys done by the Center for Effective Philanthropy, but much of the unhappiness suggested by critical comments in the press and anecdotal references by executives and trustees of recipient organizations is yet to be substantiated.

That there is much criticism of foundations is not to be doubted, however, when so many foundation officers themselves give voice to the unhappiness experienced by recipient organizations. With a very large share of many nonprofit organizations' budgets coming from foundations, and with the especially critical role individual foundations play in starting up new organizations or sustaining them in the early years, there is not the slightest doubt that the decision-making style of foundations and their giving criteria affect grant-receiving organizations very substantially. How foundations make their choices of program areas to support, how they formulate and implement grant-decision criteria, and how they allocate, or choose not to allocate, funds to grant recipients—all these decisions have critical effects on individual not-for-profit organizations, and inexorably on the not-for-profit sector as a whole. What I find most distressing is the opacity of those decisions; virtually all foundations operate with their cards held very close to the vest, and even now there is no empirical data exploring or explaining the nature and extent of this particular problem. I will revisit this theme often as this essay continues.

First, a few words of background. Foundations come in many sizes, shapes, and natures, and it is misleading to generalize about them as if they were all the same. The largest aggregations of capital are in the private foundations, most of which—like Ford, Rockefeller, Carnegie, Kellogg, Robert Wood Johnson, Lilly, and Pew—are at least a half-century old, but some of which, like Gates, Moore, Weinberg, Soros, Hewlett, and Packard, are of comparatively recent vintage. Among private foundations, the largest number are family-dominated entities and generally they behave quite differently from private foundations that are not family dominated, even if they were originally family foundations. Among the family-dominated foundations, those whose donors are still alive and serving on the boards are very different in character and operating dynamic from those whose donors have passed from the scene, and foundations in which descendants of donors outnumber non-family members are quite different from those that have made the transition from family to non-family private foundation status. In addition, community foundations, which have surged in numbers and assets in the last decade, are entirely different in governance and decision making from the private foundations, whether family influenced or not. Each community foundation is itself a hybrid of a private family foundation, with its nest of donor-advised funds, and a community-serving public charity with its pool of discretionary or donor-restricted funds and usually a publicly representative allocation committee or advisory panel.

Corporate foundations are yet another, and entirely different kind of foundation, almost always both controlled by the officers of their parent corporations and dependent on them for continuing financial contributions. There are also, of course, non-grantmaking foundations, such as operating foundations, but as these entities do not generally make grants, they are excluded from this discussion. It is the private foundations in all their forms, each with its own individual form, culture, and history, to which my comments in this essay apply.

The criticisms I have to offer here are very much in the nature of a lover's quarrel, and I want to underscore in the strongest possible terms my belief that foundations play a hugely beneficial role in American society, and that, on balance, they play that role remarkably well. They are not perfect, of course, but neither are any human beings or any of the other organizations they create. I believe deeply that foundations do far more good than harm, and that such harm as they do can be attributed mostly to operating inefficiencies and the consequent waste of assets, assets which they are morally obligated to steward wisely.

Foundations play an indispensable role in the continuous refreshment and refurbishment of the not-for-profit sector in particular and of American society in general. Foundations are the holders of America's primary pool of social venture capital, and they have provided the wherewithal for countless, largely undocumented, changes for the better in our society. Often behind the scenes, and often without fanfare, they have conferred enormously valuable benefits on all Americans. That they have been able to do so is a direct result of their freedom from both government and the for-profit sector. That independence from government and from any external control over their policy and grantmaking decisions is indispensable to their fulfillment of their important role in U.S. society. The fact that foundations have shortcomings must not lead us to doubt their profound and continuing value or to embrace corrective measures that would circumscribe their autonomy.

It is that autonomy that breathes life and power into what I will call our American polyarchy, by which I mean a pluralistic society composed of many power centers independent of one another. I have no doubt that it is this characteristic of our society—the proliferation of countless points of view on all issues, the proliferation of countless independent sources of initiative—that is the bedrock of our nation's vitality, vibrancy, power, and enduring strength. And this invaluable polyarchy rests, in part, on the independence and autonomy of America's foundations.

The Question of Accountability

Most of the shortcomings of foundations arise out of the context in which they operate, an environment that is all but devoid of forces for accountability, forces that might be conducive to better performance in general and to paying more heed to the needs and desires of their stakeholders, their grantees, in particular. As William Bowen wrote in *Inside the Boardroom,* "Market-driven forces play a relatively weaker role in determining outcomes in the not-for-profit sector, [and therefore] effective governance is potentially more important in this sector than it is in the for-profit sector." Consider for a moment the wide range and significant influence of those forces for accountability that are at work in the for-profit sector. For-profit corporations have several bottom-line metrics, such as profit or loss and stock price quotes, by which the performance of their executives and boards may continually be measured. Not-for-profit organizations have none. For-profits can be policed through suits by shareholders and the threat of hostile takeovers. Not-for-profit organizations face nothing comparable. The directors of for-profits are elected and removable by shareholders, while directors of most not-for-profits select their successors. The directors of membership not-for-profits are elected by members, but, as with for-profit corporations, the existing board members and the chief executive choose the slate to be submitted for approval.

For-profits also face the continual scrutiny of financial analysts as well as business reporters and editors of magazines, newspapers, and television programs. Except for the oversight of the *Chronicle of Philanthropy,* not-for-profits are subject to no such regular examination. Nonprofits do not face questions from controlling shareholders or large institutional investors, nor do they typically have investor representatives on their boards. While publicly traded for-profits are subject to close supervision by the Securities and Exchange Commission and the stock exchanges on which their securities trade, not-for-profits are subject to no such oversight. By comparison, the supervision that the Internal Revenue Service and state attorneys general provide to not-for-profits is as light as the brush of a feather.

What is true of not-for-profit organizations in general is true of foundations to an extreme extent. Grant-seeking nonprofits have a variety of stakeholders who exert significant influence on their decisions and the manner in which they make them. All not-for-profits that earn revenues by providing services to customers, such as hospitals, private schools, universities, arts and performance organizations, and not-for-profit newspapers and journals, have to pay attention to their customers. Universities have students, faculty, alumni, townspeople, and the press constantly looking over their shoulders, ready to pounce on anything that threatens their interests. Hospitals have patients, relatives of patients, health insurance firms, government regulatory agencies, and the press always alert to problems and irregularities. Social welfare organizations, which typically receive most of their revenues from one level of government or another, regularly have to justify their actions to the agencies that support them.

It is foundations alone that are effectively accountable to no one. This absence of accountability might sound like an appealing aspect of freedom, of the autonomy we spoke of before as being key to the ability of foundations to play an important role in society, but in truth it creates a cocoon-like environment that removes incentives for its inhabitants—program officers or senior management—to act toward others in accordance with normal standards of behavior. Although many foundation officers have internalized healthy standards by which they govern all of their relations with others, there is nothing in their professional environment to encourage qualities such as responsiveness, deference, and courtesy. Even in my own role as a senior officer of a large foundation, in attempting collaborations with my counterparts in other foundations I encountered many examples of what can only be called rudeness, including repeatedly unreturned e-mails or phone calls and a variety of truculent, tardy, or astonishingly rigid responses.

I can only conclude that it is a lack of accountability that tempts some in positions of power at foundations to engage in arrogant behavior ranging from the minor sin of discourtesy in failing to respond to letters of inquiry or return phone calls either in a timely fashion or at all, to an arbitrariness and indulgence in whim in approving or rejecting proposals.

Furthermore, such lack of accountability also permits some foundations to share with the public only such information about their work as they, in their own judgment, choose to share. No matter how many press releases are churned out, foundation transparency doesn't really exist. Annual reports, frequently of glossy, professional design and featuring touching photographs, are often published, but they are rarely self-critical and almost always filled with self-praise for what foundation managers regard as their successes. These reports usually contain little in the way of evidence that a careful reader might use to judge whether or not the successes they boast of are indeed successes, and, with one exception that I know about, foundations never report publicly on their failures. (That one exception is the Casey Foundation, which has publicly reported on *one* of its failures.) Instead of acknowledging difficulties and disappointments as evidence that they are pushing the envelope by experimenting with solutions to social problems that do entail the risk of failure, which is what social venture capitalists ought to do, foundations cover them up and thereby force others who seek to solve social problems to reinvent the wheel without the benefit of learning from the mistakes that others have made.

Perhaps worst of all, lack of accountability in this field allows foundations to get away with not coming to grips in a systematic way with any kind of stringent measurement of the impacts of their grant-making. Some of the large foundations do employ credible evaluation procedures, but what they measure, by and large, is outputs and outcomes rather than social impacts, and, in any event, the sharing of such evaluations is limited to insiders. Outsiders never get the benefit of what a foundation learns about how it has spent its resources.

No one has yet proven that such behavior by foundation officers is widespread, and certainly I cannot. But I can point out that the absence of forces that would demand accountability from foundations is unquestioned, and that where there is no incentive to behave responsibly, decently, and indeed in a genuinely stewardly fashion, many individuals will not do so. Alas, human beings are fashioned, as Isaiah Berlin observed, from crooked timber.

There are critics, such as Mark Dowie, who would transform foundations from "essentially private" to "unremittingly public" institutions.[ii] Dowie has proposed, for example, adding to foundation boards persons appointed by elected officials, up to perhaps a third of board membership. That is what the French do, but, as we all know, the French foundation sector is hardly known for pioneering, creativity, or independence. Mark Dowie has also proposed breaking up the largest foundations, in a move that would be analogous to the breakup of monopolistic corporations. In my view, and that of most observers of the nonprofit sector, such steps would undermine the very freedom that is the source of foundations' unique value to American society.

The primary dilemma in facilitating accountability is figuring out how to encourage better, more stewardly behavior by foundations without circumscribing their autonomy. No reasonable person can support government regulation or supervision of foundation goal setting or decision making (other than with regard to foundation actions that may be illegal). It is possible, however, for foundations themselves to create mechanisms for accountability, practices and protocols that could provide incentives for responsible behavior. One such mechanism is the "anonymous customer survey," which a dozen or so foundations are already using regularly to obtain the views of grantees about how well the foundations they interact with are carrying out their responsibilities. Another such mechanism is to survey expert or influential opinion in the program areas in which a foundation operates. The Robert Wood Johnson Foundation has been utilizing both of these methods for some years. It would also be a welcome innovation if foundation boards themselves were to conduct self-assessments on a regular basis and to engage outside consultants to evaluate their performance periodically as well.

A few organizations are doing pioneering work, research that compares the performance of a large number of foundations over a variety of indicators relating to the way they conduct their grantmaking, and this research may well help us develop important tools for increased accountability. As reports on comparative foundation behavior are made public, what foundation could long tolerate being at the bottom of the rankings on indicators such as turnaround time, helpfulness to grantees, and courteous treatment of all the people they deal with? These mechanisms are only a few examples of steps foundations themselves can take if they are willing to sacrifice their sense of being all-powerful for the sake of accountability.

Why should they be moved to do so? The short answer is, in order to avoid the possibility of government intervention of one sort or another. There will be hearings on foundations at some point, and foundations will be hard pressed to provide convincing evidence of the social benefits they are supposed to confer on society in return for the generous tax advantages they enjoy, benefits that most of us who are

involved in the foundation sector believe that foundations do in fact
provide.

The Question of Social Impact

If, however, one searches for published evaluations, crisp analysis, or
hard data on foundation accomplishments, one quickly comes up short.
There is very little persuasive research on the impact of foundation
grants either in achieving their particular objectives or in benefiting
society in general. Institutional histories of foundations exist, along
with a scattering of books by outside historians (including some
excellent ones by Ellen Condliffe Lagemann, Stanley Katz, Barry Karl,
and Stephen Wheatley), but there are few works that systematically
scrutinize the accomplishments of foundations across the board. The
dearth of objective research on foundations by scholars and made
available to social scientists, the public, and the press is another, and
very important reason that foundations have so little accountability.

This lack of objective data leads many to the erroneous conclusion
that foundations do not have any measurable impact on society. Anyone who has followed the field for any length of time—and my direct
experience as a petitioner, consultant, strategy advisor, or board member goes back forty years—has his or her own list of foundation-initi-
ated grants that he or she believes, but cannot prove with data, have
had significant beneficial social impacts. My list includes, but is hardly
limited to: the Carnegie Foundation for the Advancement of Teaching's "Flexner Report," which led to the radical reform of medical
education in the United States; the creation by the same Carnegie
Foundation of what became TIAA/CREF, now one of the largest
pension funds in the world; the groundwork laid by a Carnegie commission for the establishment of the Public Broadcasting System by
Congress and the White House; the fostering of the "Green Revolution" by the Rockefeller and Ford foundations; the founding of several

environmental law research and advocacy centers by recent law graduates in the late sixties, with support from the Ford Foundation, whose efforts led to congressional enactment of the Environmental Protection Act and other federal environmental protection legislation; the significant support from the Ford Foundation for the creation of community development corporations (CDCs) in poverty-dominated urban and rural communities all across the United States; the establishment of university-based international and area studies programs with support from the Ford Foundation; the creation of the Local Initiatives Support Corporation by the Ford Foundation; and the creation of the National Community Development Initiative under the leadership of the Rockefeller Foundation. My list could go on for several more pages, but what is striking about it, even in abbreviated form, is that with the exception of the Flexner reforms and the Green Revolution programs, none of the other achievements I could cite as being initiated or supported in a major way by an American foundation has been adequately analyzed and documented in published writings. When foundations are asked to justify themselves by pointing to persuasive data, therefore, they are usually unable to do so.

At the same time, politicians and commentators of both right and left continue to polemicize about the inordinate influence that foundations have on public policy, which suggests that foundations must be doing some things that have a significant impact on society, perhaps even things that are worthwhile.

Partisans of the right used to attack foundations as being dominated by liberals and lefties, so, starting in the seventies, they began to set up their own foundations, which in turn supported conservative think tanks like the American Enterprise Institute, the Cato Institute, and the Heritage Foundation, in addition to university-based centers of research, public interest law firms, journals of opinion, and individual scholars. They made quite an impression on public discourse and public policy, which consequently became much more diversely robust than in the sixties and earlier.

Meanwhile, the left-leaning foundations and social activists have become exercised by what they perceive to have been the achievements of the right, and have set out to emulate the strategies employed by their right-tilting counterparts. The main lesson they seem to have learned is that targeting grants according to ideological leanings—ideological strategic focus—is the only way to make a difference. That seems to me to be a serious mistake. I am more inclined to agree with the sentiments expressed by Jonathan Fanton, president of the MacArthur Foundation, in a speech to the Commonwealth Club in San Francisco in December 2003.

> I do not like the prospect of an ideological arms race in philanthropy, nor do I think the field is helped by such labeling. MacArthur is often grouped with liberal foundations, but that is not a welcome stereotype. MacArthur is a complex organization with Board and staff members who hold diverse views. But its members are united in a belief that ideas matter, good research and reasoned discourse can improve public policy, and that the public interest is well served if we engage challenging issues. We believe democracy works best when the public has a vigorous discussion of policy options based on good information and a hearing for all points of view—hence support for research, policy centers, documentary films, and public television and radio. We are not afraid of controversy and are willing to take risks to stimulate a good debate. We are constantly alert for new ideas, fresh perspectives on persistent problems, issues not yet formulated, technologies not fully employed, voices not widely enough heard.

What those on the left who have adopted a deliberately ideological policy have missed is that short-term strategic focus can have only short-term consequences, and that if they wish to make a significant public policy difference in the United States, they will have to adopt long-term strategies that incorporate data that scholars, public policy makers, politicians, and the press can count on as scientific and reliable. In my view, it was the long-term, knowledge-building strategies of those on the right that gave them the power to persuade the public, and not the intrinsic appeal of the superstructure of action-oriented initiatives that rested on that knowledge base. My main point, however, is that while both left and right assume that foundation initiatives have a major impact on society, there is very little documentation proving that this is the case.

If one means by "impact" the conferral of a benefit on those who directly receive foundation grants, there is no room for argument. Scholarships enable students to attend college. The endowment of professorships enables individual faculty members to be appointed to fill those slots. Donor-funded buildings enable universities to have new classrooms, laboratories, and libraries for students to use. Scientists who receive funding explore promising avenues of research, making scientific discoveries or identifying dead ends. Musical compositions get scored and performed. Books and articles get written. The question is, How do any of these things affect the rest of us?

Direct recipients almost always benefit, but how can we determine whether, on the scale of comparative social benefit based on worthiness and need, a given program is the best means available for doing wider social good? Until better measures of social impact can be devised and put into use, it will be difficult if not impossible for foundation trustees and officers to make the most responsible of all possible choices among competing objectives within the constraint of funds available to them.

Moreover, if what are thought to be philanthropic successes were to be seriously analyzed, it might be possible for foundations and other influencers of social policy to better shape initiatives in other areas by utilizing the strategies and tactics of these earlier successes. If, for example, and as I suspect, it turns out after careful exploration that the

Local Initiatives Support Corporation (LISC) is a huge success, there may well be other problem areas that lend themselves to the very same approach. LISC was created initially with a $25 million grant by the Ford Foundation to generate credit-worthiness information for inner-city and rural community organizations, information on which banks and insurance companies might safely rely in lending funds to start businesses and build housing. It has since built upon that Ford grant to attract billions of government and for-profit dollars and a national network working in about sixty cities. It seems to me that LISC has already achieved so much because its founder, Mike Sviridoff of the Ford Foundation, identified a niche in which foundation support could leverage many times more money from financial institutions and the federal government than an original grant could possibly have supplied.

Strategic Choices and Subjective Preferences

Unless foundations are bound by rigid restrictions established by their donors and embodied in the provisions of their constitutive documents, they are utterly free to direct their grantmaking programs with total discretion so long as their actions are within the scope of the Internal Revenue Code. Some foundation trustees may choose to respect clearly articulated donor intentions that are not binding, but few foundation donors articulate specific guidelines for their successors to follow, and, in any event, successor trustees are not legally bound by informal expressions of intent. If a living foundation donor serves on the foundation's board, his or her views will almost always determine program direction, but family squabbles among multiple family donors or different generations of a family may muddle the clarity of focus and make choosing strategies a bargaining process, either polite or acrimonious.

These realities underscore the role that personal subjective prefer-ence plays in structuring foundation grantmaking programs and in choosing which organizations that apply will receive grants thereafter. Unlike those of grant-seeking organizations, the strategies that foundations choose are determined solely by the subjective choices of their trustees. Grant-seeking organizations are, almost always, created to benefit society in quite specific ways—to achieve particular specified objectives and/or to serve particular specified stakeholders. While the trustees of any such organization have great latitude in defining the scope of activities that serve that objective (universities have even been known to field quasi-professional athletic teams as part of their educational mission), they are obliged by law to serve a specific charitable purpose, and numerous court cases have tested whether a particular organization's purpose is indeed a legitimate charitable one.

Grant-giving foundations, on the other hand, are totally free in choosing the purposes to which they give their money, so long as those purposes qualify as "charitable, educational, scientific" or meet other vague generalities specified by the Internal Revenue Code. There is no case law, so far as I know, which has held a foundation's grantmaking decisions to have fallen outside the legal boundaries of their trustees' discretion. There are, however, many examples of foundation grants that have been successfully challenged by legal or administrative authorities as being contrary to statutory law, such as foundation grants to encourage partisan voter registration or voter mobilization, and foundation grants intended to influence political elections. There have also been legal or administrative agency challenges to foundation expenditures that seemed arguably to constitute illegal personal benefit or are in violation of state or federal law, but, to repeat, there are no court decisions which otherwise constrain in any way the discretion of foundation trustees.

Against the background of the most minimal of constraints, the trustees of most foundations, large and small, are utterly unfettered in the administration of their grantmaking programs. In my opinion (and again without supporting hard data), these trustees have by and large served the public interest, as they have viewed it, faithfully and well. Their practice has essentially been to pick and choose among available options—in other words, "You pays your money and you takes your choice." There's nothing wrong with that approach. Indeed, I do argue that the unfettered freedom of donors and their foundations is one of the glories of America's civil society sector.

It is both true and inevitable, however, that such subjectivity in giving means that a foundation's philanthropic decisions will not necessarily be based on objective standards of comparative social need, even if we were miraculously able to make that calculation with any degree of confidence. Rather such decisions represent another example of Adam Smith's "invisible hand" working to benefit society in the absence of any precise public interest criteria. The likely consequence, therefore, is that most foundation giving will continue to benefit those whose needs most closely reflect the values and perspectives of the socio-economic elite, as represented by the individuals who sit on most private foundation boards, rather than the needs of those who are less well off and their advocates.

This is not at all to suggest that many, perhaps most, of the private foundations do not strive to implement programs intended to help America's less well off citizens. A cursory examination of grant programs will quickly dispel that misperception. It is rather to suggest that, because of the lack of empirical data, no one knows whether such programs really do benefit those whom the well-meaning foundation trustees intend to help or whether there are other, better ways of serving them. Yet, I believe, to curtail the independence of foundations by, say, government-appointed foundation trustees or tighter government regulations would be to go much too far. The costs society would incur from restricting trustee discretion—constraining the freedom of donors and trustees to follow their view of the public interest—would be severe, and would, I believe, profoundly undermine the vitality and robustness of America's social and philanthropic sector.

At the same time, the freedom that foundation trustees enjoy has too frequently enabled them to make their decisions based on pure whim rather than a careful exploration of alternative approaches to their good works, including seeking ways to maximize the social impact of their grants. It is true that some foundations do a better job than others at objectifying the inherently subjective process. They do research and conduct "contextual" or "environmental" scans, survey expert informants, and otherwise try to identify society's most pressing problems within the arenas of their interest. The good consequence is that careful analysis and sampling of opinion will yield strategies that focus on what many others regard as worthwhile objectives, as well as a widely shared logic model of how the desired outcomes can be brought about. The bad consequence is that such exploration of the views of others can merely encourage the herd mentality of which foundations have long, and justifiably, been accused, recently embodied in programs characterized by trendiness, chic, and political correctness.

In the end, most foundation founders, unlike their successor trustees, make their first and most basic decisions—about the area or areas on which they wish to spend their hard-earned or inherited money—based on long-held personal values. The biographies of John D. Rockefeller Sr., Andrew Carnegie, Alfred P. Sloan, Andrew W. Mellon, and other major donors make it clear that, although these philanthropists employed advisors to help them formulate strategies, their own objectives were the guiding, indeed driving, principles behind their philanthropic endeavors. In hindsight, one can fault Andrew Carnegie, for example, for rigidity and paternalism, but one cannot deny the lasting effects of the libraries his values and instincts led him to build, the teachers' and professors' pension system his foundation created, the scientific discoveries of the Carnegie Institution in Washington, or accomplishments of the other institutions which he founded.

Living donors do not usually ask themselves in what way they wish to benefit society: their hearts, and sometimes their minds, have already told them. *La cœur a son raison que le raison ne connais tout*— the heart has its own reason that reason does not know. The living donor himself or herself, therefore, *is* the strategy, and usually has no difficulty making strategic choices. Moreover, such donors, having acquired the assets (or at least having the disposition of them), are fully entitled to deploy their money as they will. The problem lies with their successor trustees, stewards of the money of others, who may be less confident of their values or feel unjustified in spending someone else's money based on their own subjective whims. This very human circumstance is yet another reason that balancing essentially subjective choice with careful strategic analysis is necessary, and why it comes in so handy.

Conclusion

Philanthropy in America is thriving as never before in its history. As is always the case with thriving enterprises, the more they thrive, the more challenges they face. It is hardly to be expected that American philanthropy would differ. Those of us who are dedicated to maintaining the freedom and robustness of the not-for-profit sector in general and foundations in particular have an obligation to help philanthropy face its challenges successfully—and now, before actual threats to that freedom materialize, is the time to be resourceful and imaginative in figuring out the best ways to offer our help.

i. The figures in this paragraph are estimates made by the AAFRC Trust for Philanthropy and published in *Giving USA*, 2002. It is impossible to square them with the overall figures on the nonprofit sector's gross domestic product generated by the Bureau of Economic Analysis, which reports that the nonprofit sector's share of GDP in 2001 was $448 billion.

   See www.bea.doc.gov. Other reputable estimates of nonprofit sector revenues run as high as $1 trillion. If BEA figures are accurate, then charitable giving would constitute almost 50 percent of nonprofit GDP, which we know cannot be the case, as both government and fees for services rendered constitute about four times the size of charitable contributions as a percentage of nonprofit revenues.

ii. Mark Dowie, *American Foundations: An Investigative History*, p. xxxix.

BRUCE SIEVERS

Philanthropy's Blindspots

L IKE MOST people who have had the privilege of working in philanthropy, I feel very fortunate to have been able to spend a career in a field that offers the rare opportunity to connect resources with important social needs. Few other professions—and I believe philanthropy *is* a profession—allow one to simultaneously engage in worthy causes, occupy a unique listening post in society, and interact daily with smart, committed people who are seeking to improve the human condition.

This privilege is accompanied, however, by a significant weight of responsibility, and by a worry about whether one is using those precious resources to achieve the highest benefit for society. Philanthropic foundations are peculiar in that they lack a natural feedback loop to provide guidance or a check on their behavior. This is both their virtue—the freedom to pursue goals outside the constraints of the market or the political process—and a temptation to vice, in the form

Bruce Sievers is the author of "If Pigs Had Wings: The Appeals and Limits of Venture Philanthropy." He did graduate studies at the Freie Universität Berlin and Oxford University and holds a Ph.D. in political science from Stanford University, where he is a visiting scholar and lecturer. Sievers currently serves as a senior fellow with Rockefeller Philanthropy Advisors. He was the founding executive director of state humanities councils in Montana and California and served as executive director of the Walter and Elise Haas Fund, a private foundation in San Francisco, from 1983 to 2002.

of a potential arbitrariness that can accompany unchecked power. This condition engenders endless internal discussions about philanthropic goals and strategy, and these days the pages of philanthropic publications and websites are full of deliberations about methods to increase leverage, grow return on investment, enhance effectiveness, improve evaluation, measure outcomes, strengthen organizational development, and so on.

My concern is that most of these discussions bypass an essential dimension of philanthropy. What is lacking in most modern critiques of the field is attention to the broader purposes and assumptions that underlie the entire nonprofit enterprise. Philanthropy has an unfortunate tendency to import models from other social realms as guides to its own behavior. It also has a parallel tendency to seek to reduce serious reflection about its actions to a critical analysis of its means alone. The result is what philosopher Donald Schon describes (in discussing the epistemologies of other professional fields) as a kind of "selective inattentiveness" to important features of the social worlds in which foundation officers, like other professionals, operate.[i] The effect of this inattentiveness in modern foundation practice is a reduction of philanthropic vision from a 3-D world of multivalent human goals, including social change and collective action, to a 2-D world of efficiency and effectiveness.

As I have experienced the evolution of the field over the past three decades, I have become increasingly concerned about the conceptual fads that periodically sweep through the foundation world. In the currently popular rhetoric of foundation meetings and publications, as well as much of what is written in the popular press, the centerpiece of the philanthropic enterprise appears to be the effective management of resources and efficient administration—as if cost-benefit analysis were the most important element of the philanthropic enterprise and its role in shaping a healthy civil society.

I want to suggest some of the limitations of this current mind-set and point out how it may be steering the field away from areas critically important to the future of society. If, as I would argue, philanthropy is primarily about building upon the values and institutions of civil society to engage critical social needs and promote human growth, then it is important for us to approach our work more as students and champions of the human condition than as cost accountants or social engineers.

The Business Model

Because conceptual models play a profound role in philanthropy, it is important to understand their power and limits—where these models illuminate and where they create blindspots—and to move beyond areas of limited vision to the broader possibilities of the philanthropic imagination. In his essay "The Evolving Role of American Foundations," historian Jim Smith insightfully characterized successive eras of philanthropic development in the United States, tracing how the dominant models in the field have corresponded to evolving modes of understanding the natural and social worlds; thus Smith describes the philanthropic model of the early years of the twentieth century in terms of "germ theory" (find the single cause of the disease/social illness and attack it), an approach that was later followed by models influenced by physics, equilibrium theory, and so on.[ii]

Although today we have a better understanding of distinctions between the conceptual models of the natural and social sciences, the search still seems to be on to find a quasi-scientific basis for intervention in the social world, and in recent years, economic analysis has become a popular interpretive framework for understanding the workings of society. Based on this trend, philanthropy has most recently adopted a species of the "business model" as a guide. This model— actually an odd hybrid of economic theory and practical business precepts—has now risen to a position of prominence in philanthropic practice similar to that held by the germ theory model of a century ago.

The business model dictates that the proper way to look at philanthropy is as a system in which inputs (primarily money, but also expertise, technology, and other resources) are processed through entities (nonprofit organizations) that are seen as analogous to business firms to create outputs of social value. The analogy is between a business investment—in which funds are directed to various operational functions, such as production, sales, and management, with the outcomes of products, market share, and, ultimately, profit—and a philanthropic "investment" in which charitable dollars are directed to the operating activities of nonprofit organizations, with the outcomes of services, impact, and, ultimately, social value.

Clearly, some aspects of the model do work for philanthropy. Like business, philanthropy involves an allocation of money toward a desired goal. Also like business entities, nonprofits (as the recipients of philanthropic dollars) carry out their missions through a variety of organizational functions—management, public relations, information systems, service delivery, and so on. Both kinds of entities have to deal with personnel, technology applications, marketing, and the myriad other practical requirements of making an organization work. Both business and nonprofits deal with the realities of budgets and providing services or products as efficiently as possible.

Unlike businesses, however, philanthropic and nonprofit organizations operate in two worlds. One of these is defined by instrumental objectives such as financial stability, numbers of people served, inches of press coverage. The other world, however, is defined by different end goals of human action: education, artistic expression, human advancement, personal security, freedom of thought and action, concern for future generations, and preservation of cultural and environmental legacies. The latter are often described as public goods, that is, goods to which access cannot be limited and that carry costs that cannot easily be individualized.[iii] These ends are the goals and aspirations of the human experience and are not reducible to the same kinds of categories that define profit margins and make for the most efficient production of widgets.

It is this mission-driven dimension that separates the world of the nonprofit from the world of the for-profit in a fundamental way. "Mission" is even too limited a word to capture all that is entailed in the nature of the nonprofit enterprise; it suggests a single-mindedness of goal that belies the multi-dimensional character of any activity aimed at ameliorating or enhancing the human condition. "Purpose" or "aspiration" might better describe the goals of organizations that operate in the social sphere. Within their broad purposes, organizations certainly adopt specific tasks, but the point of the overall effort lies beyond these instrumental vehicles. As Peter Karoff points out in the opening essay of this volume, it is poetry rather than metrics that often best captures this dimension of human experience.

Some advocates of the business model have proposed the concept of "social return on investment" (SROI) as an equivalent of profit in the nonprofit arena. But beyond some rather crude calculations about theoretical public dollars saved, SROI does not and cannot adequately account for the complex and intangible human dimensions of what nonprofit organizations seek to accomplish. The meaning and import of a ten-year process of policy development, a shift in public consciousness, a spark of understanding brought through the arts, or the transformation of a single human being in a youth development program simply cannot be captured by a sheet of SROI figures.

The drive to find nonprofit equivalencies to business concepts like "market share," "going to scale," "deal flow," "branding," "burn rate," "value chain," and so on, is, I would suggest, for the most part similarly misguided. Although sometimes useful analogues can be found (e.g., funding resources for nonprofits are a close counterpart to for-profit capital markets), they usually mislead more than they enlighten.

Take the currently popular term "measurable outcomes," for example. This phrase has become something of a mantra in the foundation world. *Of course*, the argument goes, who can object to seeking to measure the results of one's work? If businesses can set quarterly earning targets, why can't nonprofits set achievement targets by which the results of *their* efforts can be measured? The answer is that they can, to a degree, but neither the time horizons nor the precision of such business-derived goals may be really meaningful to the larger mission of a philanthropic organization. Such targets may distort an organization's program or actually cause more important, intangible aims to be overlooked. For instance, an educational organization may measure test scores, but thereby steer teachers to "teach to the test," ignoring the broader purposes of a good education, a tendency widely documented as a result of standardized testing programs. Or an ethics organization might be distracted by reporting conference attendance numbers or column inches of press coverage, when its actual mission is to be concerned with discovering new insights into, for example, the use of technology in sustaining life.

These days, the need to satisfy funders' desires for numerical targets has become something of a joke among nonprofit organizations. Many set their targets artificially low in order to insure a final report that will look good. Foundation program officers become willing accomplices in this strategy, so that they can show the results of their grants to their CEOs, who in turn can take glowing reports back to their boards. And for what? To satisfy some generally perceived need to provide language and numbers that equate with reassurance that something important has happened as a result of funding.[iv]

In order to achieve measurable outcomes, the next step typically taken by foundations is the narrowing of program focus. With more tightly focused programs, so the logic goes, a foundation can target its resources in such a way as to maximize impact and better assess (through metrics) its progress toward objectives. And it is a natural next step that the foundation becomes more proactive, setting its own agenda rather than responding to diverse requests from others engaged in the fields in which it operates. The ultimate consequence is foundation-driven, narrowly conceived programs that pursue narrowly defined objectives.

All of this may sound compelling until one asks what the ultimate result is of this kind of "strategic philanthropy." The model suggests that human action can be understood in terms of linear, sequential steps that can be orchestrated in predictable ways to arrive at a goal, like the engineered stages and components of an industrial production process, as in, say, the impressively efficient production line of an auto assembly plant. But most sophisticated social analysts, Donald Schon among them, posit a very different model of social change, one that is stochastic (non-linear, incapable of precise prediction), self-referential, and multi-variant. The "selective inattentiveness" that accompanies the business model makes foundations averse to this kind of complexity, leading them to insulate themselves from diversity within the fields in which they operate and to bypass vital areas of social concern that do not fit easily into a linear framework of analysis. (More on this below.)

The entire enterprise exemplifies what the philosopher Alfred North Whitehead called the "fallacy of misplaced concreteness"—the attempt to reify one aspect of the human condition extracted from the complex interdependent framework in which it exists. In the case of foundations, the primary source of this error is the disjunction between their central resource—money, which is countable—and social objectives, which generally are not. There is a natural inclination to ask, How much social value can we buy with this money? The proper response, in my view, is that this is the wrong question: rather than seeking to conjure something that would satisfy the "biggest bang for the buck" requirements of a buyer, those involved in philanthropy ought to pursue the kinds of success appropriate to social organizations.

Two examples illustrate how imposition of narrow business model objectives on social organizations can create distortions in mission through unintended consequences and redirection of purpose. In the first case, a micro-credit lending organization operating in Bangladesh began with the radical mission of improving the lives of impoverished women by helping them to become small-scale entrepreneurs. Although it has had great success in this effort, in recent years the organization has increasingly begun to emphasize growth, bottom-line performance (high rates of debt repayment), and competitive rankings with other lenders. Studies by two researchers have criticized this trend, noting that the "target-driven preoccupation with growth, and the differing pressures of the expansion process, appear to be diverting organizational priorities away from development of 'others' (women), to development of 'selves' (the organization)," and that this market-driven model in turn "increases tension and frustration among household members, produces new forms of dominance over women and increases violence in society."[v]

A second example is the practice by many donors of using simple financial ratios (in particular, the ratio of administrative to program expense derived from Guidestar or similar sources) to evaluate non-profit organizations. Although inspired by an understandable desire to avoid expending philanthropic dollars on "unnecessary" overhead expenses, this practice ironically often has counter-productive results. By failing to comprehend the nature of nonprofit organizational budgeting, it can steer organizations in dysfunctional directions. It ignores several realities of nonprofit life: that the line between administrative and program functions (especially in small organizations) is typically blurred, making categorization of such expenses a judgment call; that different blends of such expenses occur at different points in the life cycles of organizations; and finally, that there is no demonstrated relationship between low administrative expense and overall program success. Furthermore, to the degree that organizations seek to accommodate perceived pressure from funders to reduce administrative expenses (to look good in ratio comparisons), they may actually undermine their own long-term success by reducing their fundraising capacity or their ability to attract outstanding employees. The drive to meet narrow financial tests thus frequently undermines the true organizational mission.

Of course, avoiding rigid metrics cannot be a rationale that excuses sloppy thinking or poor organizational management. It is legitimate to ask about the hoped-for accomplishments of funded organizations, and it is entirely fair to apply critical analysis to both the means and ends of nonprofit activity. To be valuable, however, such an analysis must reflect an appreciation of the full nature of the social mission involved, and not merely consist of a brute calculation of the most easily measurable features of nonprofit work.

Neglected Social Agendas

Philanthropy's drive toward the adoption of narrowly targeted guidelines, foundation-driven agendas, measurable outcomes, and concrete deliverables—in sum, the application of the "high impact" business model to philanthropy—has the ironic result, I would suggest, of actually *reducing* the potential social impact of foundation dollars. The reason is that techniques that are designed to increase management and control can actually steer people working in our field away from areas in which they have the greatest potential for achieving significant social change. The complexity, size, and downright messiness of some social issues deter funders who seek quick, tangible results from their investments. If effective grantmaking is thought to be validated primarily by precise increments of numerical change (test scores or numbers of clients reached), foundations are unlikely to find such validation when they work on issues of large-scale social change or transformation of values. Consider the civil rights movement, for example. Inspired in some part by the publication of the hugely influential *An American Dilemma*, by Gunnar Myrdal (funded by the Carnegie Corporation in the late 1930s), this movement catalyzed a transformation of values in American society. Triggered by a growing realization of the clash between ideals and realities, this profound evolution of understanding and canons of social behavior could scarcely have been predicted or evaluated through statistical analysis alone.

Similarly, the women's movement, the environmental movement, rise of the conservative agenda in American political life, and the movement toward equal rights for the gay and lesbian communities, all aided by significant philanthropic support, have transformed American life in ways that lie beyond any calculations of "return on investment." Of course, we also believe that there *have* been calculable returns on investments in these issues, but the point is that these movements have recast the American moral landscape, resulting in enormous changes in the way society functions and understands itself, with consequent changes in policy. Commitment of philanthropic resources to these issues was not merely a matter of analyzing increments of inputs and outputs; it was a moral engagement with wooly, unpredictable issues that called for deeply transformational action.

So what are the equivalent issues today? Although there are many candidates, I would propose five issues with especially profound significance for the current and future state of the world that are largely ignored by contemporary philanthropy. They are neglected not because they are unimportant but because they are diffuse, value-laden, change-resistant problems that do not lend themselves to straightforward cost-benefit calculations. Like the historic efforts cited above, they call for deep social change.

The Mass Media

Increasingly, we have learned that modern mass communications play an extraordinarily powerful role in determining the way populations throughout the world perceive the problems their societies face and engage in action to address them. Commercial radio and television in particular shape public consciousness to a degree unimaginable in earlier eras. But the combined force of commercial interests, governmental power, and ideological agendas mean that this power is often exercised to the detriment of balanced public education or rational debate on issues.[vi] This effect takes place in both Western democracies and authoritarian political systems. In the United States, the market-driven nature of the media has steadily reduced coverage of public affairs to sound bites, polling numbers, slogans, and cartoonish talk-show jousts.

Only a few foundations have directed significant resources to media issues, principally among them, the Pew Charitable Trusts, the Freedom Forum, and the Benton, Knight, and Bertelsmann foundations. (The last four of these originated in the media business itself.) Other foundations media involvement does not generally extend beyond establishing communications departments to publicize their work and that of their grantees. And the majority of the funding that does emerge from the media-oriented foundations is directed either to policy work or to public radio and television production. These are useful, but limited, arenas for affecting one of the most powerful forces in modern society.

Given the obvious and pervasive influence of commercial media on the setting of social agendas, this situation seems puzzling, until one considers how difficult "problems of the media" are for contemporary philanthropy to address. The media involve heavily value-laden social structures, posing fundamental questions of legitimacy to grantmakers. Who are foundations to weigh in on the autonomy of the media, with its long-defended First Amendment protections? Further, as huge and complex institutions, the enterprises that make up the media do not lend themselves easily to tidy deciles of measurable outcomes. Beyond measuring audience numbers (typically the "deliverable" offered up by media projects), deeper issues of the formation of public opinion are extremely difficult to assess.

Nevertheless, radio and television channels are the primary sources of information about public affairs for the world's population. Whether and how issues are covered determines what the world's citizens know about everything from local education to issues of war and peace. Media coverage dictates our very comprehension of issues and, to a large extent, shapes public sentiment about what should be done about them. Indeed, every field in which foundations operate is fundamentally influenced by the way it is covered in the media. So it would seem incumbent upon philanthropy to engage the large-scale media in significant ways, despite challenges of size, complexity, and measurement of impact.

What can foundations do? As in other arenas of profound social significance, many areas of the media could be positively influenced by foundation ideas and resources: the attitudes and skills of media professionals, program quality, relationships between the media and community groups, and standards of practice. There are many practical funding opportunities to pursue improvements in these areas, a few of which are already being explored by foundations. To name several: creating advanced training opportunities for journalists from commercial radio and television, providing better content for stations, developing exchange programs for journalists and nonprofit sector professionals, "seeding" issue ideas for inclusion in the plots of popular dramatic series, working with grassroots organizations on media strategies, and making issues experts accessible to media outlets.

The Political Process

The serious and accelerating erosion of the American political process is a matter of apprehension for anyone concerned about the well-being of modern democracy. The profound dysfunctionalities of the system that sets public agendas—a system that includes election campaigns, candidate selection, education of office holders, the information base of the electorate, and state and federal budgeting processes—combine to create a toxic brew of negative forces at work in the policy-making process. Exemplified by the circus-like atmosphere of the recent California gubernatorial recall election, our entire political system is increasingly controlled by money and narrow interests, and this reinforces the cynicism of an already skeptical electorate.

Foundations have traditionally been wary of involvement with the political process, because of both the legal requirement to avoid partisan electioneering and a desire to retain the civic credibility that emanates from being perceived as politically neutral agents.[vii] Yet foundations can uphold both principles while still actively engaging with structural features of the political process. A remaining concern—that the political process is cumbersome and messy—can also deter foundations from involvement if (as in the cases noted above) they see their work as confined to narrow, predictable arenas with the goal of producing precisely measurable results. Involvement in the political system requires a long-term commitment and an acceptance that the results of one's efforts may be unpredictable and modest.

A few foundations—notably Carnegie, Schumann, Surdna, Cummings, and Kettering—have weighed in on specific elements of the political process: voter participation, campaign finance reform, citizen education on issues, and improving public infrastructure. However, given the magnitude of the problems and the vital role of the political process in determining the future well-being of American society, it is remarkable that philanthropic support for this work lies mostly at the margins. Journalist Mathew Miller laments the fact that "the big center-left foundations . . . shrink from engaging on larger questions of tax and spending policy that would affect [social welfare] on a national scale."[viii] At a minimum, it is vital for foundations to contribute to improving the workings of our political process and the quality of information available to the public.

Civil Society

Modern liberal democracy rests in large part on a foundation of "civil society," the set of institutions and values that occupy the civic space between the individual and the state. Although writers from divergent political and philosophical viewpoints vary in their descriptions of civil society, they are in general agreement that a healthy civil society is essential to the effective functioning of the modern democratic state.[ix] Civil society fosters commitment to the democratic ethos and enables free operation of the network of voluntary associations that undergird democratic government.

There is strong evidence of the deterioration of civil society in America in recent decades. Political scientist Robert Putnam has studied the closely related concept of social capital—"social networks and the norms of reciprocity and trustworthiness that arise from them"— and has provided compelling documentation of the decline in membership in civic associations and in levels of social trust over the past several decades, leading to a conclusion that "we have been pulled apart from one another and from our communities over the last third of the century."ˣ Low levels of social capital are strongly correlated with poorly functioning political processes.

Despite the centrality of social capital to their work, however, foundations pay relatively little attention to the fundamental elements of civil society. Much more needs be done to strengthen nonprofit sector organizations and the values of civil society. Greater support for research, sector-wide associations, technology applications, financing vehicles, and professional development are a few of the ways in which the nonprofit sector can be strengthened. Programs that promote civic education, the development of social trust, civic participation, community service, respect for individual rights, tolerance, and concern for the commons are among those that can help build the value structure of civil society.

Since philanthropic organizations are part of this network of voluntary associations, it would seem natural that they would understand the importance of strengthening civil society, but their interests are typically drawn to more concrete problem areas. Again, a few foundations (notably Ford, Skoll, Kellogg, Packard) have allocated significant funding resources to these issues, but the total represents only a tiny sliver of the philanthropic pie. A grant category for "Citizenship and Civic Participation," with which I had experience at the Walter and Elise Haas Fund, revealed to me how promising this field is, but our foundation, like most others, devoted only modest resources to this area. Civil society work remains a blindspot on the philanthropic horizon.

Contemporary Ethical Challenges

A fourth arena with the potential to make a vital contribution to civic life but largely ignored by foundations is that of professional ethics. We did not need the Enron debacle to illustrate that ethics are central to a good society, but the case reminds us that non-ethical choices have profound effects in all realms of professional activity and policy making. In a society overly focused on bottom-line outcomes, ethics can seem esoteric—until the destructive force of ethical lapses make their appearance.

Business, medicine, science, law, journalism, education, and other professional fields have enormous influences on society but retain a significant (and necessary) insulation from regulatory processes. Consequently, their primary accountability to the public is through self-defined ethical standards. Yet the evolution of these fields constantly raises new ethical dilemmas that push the boundaries of traditional approaches and pose ever new social policy conundrums.

A prime example is the field of medicine. As scientific and technological advances have vastly increased our knowledge of and control over life, troubling questions arise about what to do with that knowledge and control. Who should have access to genetic information? At what cost, both financial and personal, should a life be extended? How can we resolve the conflict between our individual right to choose the manner of our death and society's concern to protect all its members?

These questions now pervade our everyday life, touching all families, yet few foundations, including the large foundations primarily concerned with health care, are addressing them. Because ethical issues can be seen from many different perspectives, they are complex and in some cases seem unresolvable, and they are therefore unappealing to foundations seeking demonstrable results. But there is enormous potential for supporting intellectual work on these issues: assisting people working in the fields of medicine and medical research—and professionals in other fields as well—to develop ethical standards, engaging the public in addressing these questions, and disseminating information to wide audiences. The Wallace Alexander Gerbode Foundation, the Greenwall Foundation, and the David and

Lucille Packard Foundation are among the very few that have broken a path for support of ethical analysis and advocacy.

Inter-Cultural Understanding

A fifth field that has enormous consequences for society worldwide but resists short-term quantitative measurement is that of inter-cultural understanding. Despite heightened awareness in the United States since 9/11 of the critical need for improved understanding across cultures, relatively little has been done, by either government or philanthropy, to advance this goal.

There is a history of foundation support for some aspects of inter-cultural education; indeed, the plan published in 1949 outlining the future of the Ford Foundation program in this arena stresses an overriding commitment to the realization of "democratic ideals" and includes a section explicitly devoted to "the development among the peoples of the world of the understanding and conditions essential to permanent peace."[xi] And Ford's record of substantial support of fellowships for foreign study (both in the original foreign scholars program in the 1950s and 1960s and the modern incarnation of the International Fellowships Program initiated by Susan Berresford) represents an admirable model of investment in this field. Other foundations, such as the Trust for Mutual Understanding, have also supported exchange programs and academic research in the international arena in important ways. Much less has been done, however, to advance inter-cultural and global understanding at the K-12 level and among the general public. Indeed, civic education is the forgotten piece of the education reform movement.

Most of the modest allocation of foundation dollars to international work—about 11 percent of total funding in 2002—is directed toward specific problems in areas of population, the environment, health, and economic development. Although programs in these areas are clearly important, indeed crucial, they do not address or touch only indirectly on the issue of improved *understanding* across cultures; both within the United States and abroad, the fundamental tasks of improving access to information about other cultures and fostering an appropriate appreciation for cultural differences receive only the tiniest fraction of foundation support.

This is not to imagine that education and information alone will overcome the cleavages that divide the world's cultures. Fundamental differences in values, traditions, economic situations, worldviews, and prescriptions for social behavior will continue to separate national and ethnic groups. Nevertheless, improved understanding across cultures is a necessary, if not sufficient, condition for progress toward a saner, more peaceful world. One example that holds promise for the future is the modest program initiated by the Daniel Pearl Foundation to bring journalists from other countries for year-long residencies at the *Wall Street Journal*. Another, the domestic program Facing History and Ourselves, has long provided a superior model of education designed to improve understanding of cultural diversity in this country and worldwide. But such programs are for the most part small and poorly funded. Without a great deal more effort in this area, there is little prospect of countering the disastrous consequences of ignorance, xenophobia, suspicion, and fear that haunt the worldviews of many human beings on this planet.

The Bottom Line

An objection the reader might raise to my list of neglected areas in foundation funding is that many other areas of human endeavor could be named as similarly worthy of greater philanthropic support. After all, there are many important causes in society, and since foundations cannot do everything, they must make difficult choices. Accordingly, they are led to focus their resources on areas where they have determined they can have the "greatest impact."

There are two flaws in this argument: 1) the establishment of fundamental priorities, in my experience, is often less a matter of rational analysis about impact or social importance and more a matter of personal donor interests, legacy, and subjective board member perspectives; and 2) when impact is considered, it tends to be assessed, as described above, on the basis of narrow, short-term criteria rather than in terms of larger social agendas.

I am advocating that we consider increased efforts in the five areas noted precisely because they are so often systematically overlooked by foundations, and they are overlooked because they do not fit neatly into the current fashion for tangible, short-term, measurable results. All five share this same difficulty of assessment, and all five are profoundly important to the future well-being of world society.

At its best, philanthropy is about the transformation of the human condition—a transformation that does not lend itself to a simple, linear conception of the process of social change nor to a unidimensional measuring rod. The seductively simplistic concept of the "bottom line"—whether single, double, or triple—as a means of judging the results of our work is ultimately limiting. We should resist it. Philanthropy's true power lies in its ability to engage complexity and vision, and to do so the philanthropic community has to understand its role in the transformation of society as being more like a conversation than a measured production process. To sustain, energize, and expand this conversation is to realize the full potential of the philanthropic imagination.

i.   Donald Schon, *Beyond the Stable State* (London: Temple Smith, 1971), p. 14.
      Much of Schon's work is devoted to understanding the complex nature of
      social learning—a process in which both collective goals and processes for
      achieving them undergo constant revision as societies learn—and an accom-
      panying critique of reductionist approaches to understanding human agency.

ii.   Jim Smith, "The Evolving Role of American Foundations, " in *Philanthropy
      and the Nonprofit Sector*, edited by Charles Clotfelter and Thomas Ehrlich
      (Indiana University Press, 1999).

iii. See, for example, Burton Weisbrod, "Toward a Theory of the Voluntary
      Non-Profit Sector in a Three-Sector Economy," in *Altruism, Morality, and
      Economic Theory*, edited by Edmund S. Phelps (New York: Russell Sage,
      1974); and Henry Hansmann, "Economic Theories of Nonprofit Organiza-
      tion," in *The Nonprofit Sector: A Research Handbook*, edited by Walter W.
      Powell (New Haven: Yale University Press, 1987). One way of characterizing
      the difference between for-profit and nonprofit objectives is to observe that
      for-profit firms seek to exclude "economic externalities" (e.g., the ultimate
      costs of air pollution, etc.) from their cost accounting to the highest degree
      possible, while nonprofits seek to bring exactly those "externalities" back into
      the equation.

iv.   In this context, the comments of John Glass, a full-time evaluator in a family
      services organization, are typical: "I spend more time gathering and entering
      data (that has some meaning, but not as much as a focus group/interview)
      that is what the funders require, but doesn't really translate well for our pur-
      poses" (posted on ARNOVA listserv, 14 June 2002).

v.   Rosamund Ebdon, "NGO Expansion and the Fight to Reach the Poor: Gen-
      der Implications of NGO Scaling Up in Bangladesh," *IDS Bulletin* 26, no. 3
      (1995), 49-55; Aminur Rahman, "Micro-Credit Initiatives for Equitable and
      Sustainable Development: Who Pays?" *World Development* 27, no. 1 (1999),
      67-82.

vi.   There is a long history of documentation of the negative impact of television
      in particular on civic attitudes and participation. Daniel Boorstin, former
      Librarian of Congress, described television as "the next great crisis in human
      consciousness." See Joel Swerdlow, " A Question of Impact," in *The Wilson
      Quarterly* 5: 1 (Winter 1981), 86–99; Daniel Hallin, "Network News: We
      Keep America on Top of the World," in *Watching Television*, edited by Todd
      Gitlin (New York: Pantheon Books, 1986), pp. 9–41; James Fallows, *Breaking
      the News: How the Media Undermine American Democracy* (New York: Pan-

theon Books, 1996); and Pippa Norris, "The Impact of Television on Civic Malaise," in *Disaffected Democracies: What's Troubling the Trilateral Countries?* edited by Susan Pharr and Robert Putnam (Princeton University Press, 2000), pp. 231-251. There is general agreement among scholars and critical commentators that there is a strong correlation between heavy television watching and low levels of social trust and civic participation, and that the media have more to do with fundamental agenda setting than they do with particular attitudes on specific issues.

vii. An exception to this pattern was the coordinated action by a number of conservative foundations over the past three decades; they have invested more than $70 million to advance the conservative agenda in policy and advocacy, an extraordinarily successful strategy by their own account. See Robert Kuttner's description of this strategy in "Philanthropy and Movements," *The American Prospect*, 15 July 2002.

viii. Matthew Miller, "Shaping the Debate: Where Are the Center-Left Foundations?" Tribune Media Services, 30 July 2003 (www.dpage@tribune.com).

ix. There is a vast and growing literature on civil society that encompasses a range of definitions and constructs. From this literature emerge a set of predominant characteristics—voluntary associations, a legal structure, a system of free expression, individual rights, tolerance, pursuit of the common good, and philanthropy—that I describe in a forthcoming book as a composite set of key defining qualities of modern civil society.

x. Robert D. Putnam, *Bowling Alone: The Collapse and Revival of American Community* (New York: Simon & Schuster, 2000), pp. 19, 27.

xi. *Report of the Study for the Ford Foundation on Policy and Program* (Detroit: Ford Foundation, 1949).

MICHELE COURTON BROWN

Making the Case for Corporate Philanthropy:
A Key Element of Success

THE FINANCIAL challenges facing corporate America in the early 1990s produced an important change in thinking about corporate philanthropy. As business units were increasingly asked to articulate how their function supported the company's overall business objectives, similar questions were posed to officers in charge of corporate giving. The result was a movement to "strategic philanthropy." As defined broadly by the corporate community, strategic philanthropy is an approach to giving that links a company's business strengths with community needs. At Bank of Boston, then at Fleet, we found that by aligning our philanthropic programs with the business strengths of a company, we were able to unleash the power of our expert employees and to have far more impact in the community. As an added benefit, our

Michele Courton Brown is senior vice president and director of the Charitable Asset Division at Columbia Management Group. Prior to that, she served as director of corporate contributions at BankBoston. A constant advocate for good corporate citizenship, she has also served on numerous nonprofit boards, including those of the Center for Women and Enterprise, the Museum of Afro-American History, the Boston Symphony Orchestra, and City Year. From 1999 to 2002, Brown was president of the FleetBoston Financial Foundation, which contributed over $25 million annually to charitable endeavors.

employees—our most important constituents—developed stronger connections to the company as well.

Many of the companies highlighted in Michael Porter's important article "The Value of Corporate Philanthropy" (published in the *Harvard Business Review*, December 2001) have found ways to serve the needs of the community while simultaneously addressing their business-specific objectives. In fact, some company outreach efforts are providing tangible returns on the investment of company resources, especially in the form of targeted training programs that reap huge direct benefits—better qualified new hires for their companies, for example, or better informed consumers.

In tandem with this movement to strategic philanthropy, many companies, banks and financial services companies in particular, embraced "emerging markets" as growth markets. In order to reach urban and ethnic markets, substantial marketing resources were dedicated to building brand and product awareness. As companies began to make inroads in these markets, they also began to see their community outreach efforts as a powerful tool to strengthen company/product loyalty. Thus a virtuous cycle linking corporate citizenship and business development emerged.

By way of example, Fleet saw a tremendous business opportunity in increasing our market share in urban areas by getting our online banking services to more people in those areas. Our greatest challenge was in addressing the "digital divide." In response, Fleet developed a program called Community Link, which provided free computers and free Internet access to low- and moderate-income customers. There were several key elements to the program: 1) free access to both technology and the Internet, 2) a computer training curriculum that incorporated financial literacy education, 3) a partnership with community-based organizations to offer the computer training in urban neighborhoods, and 4) an investment in a neighborhood-based website to ensure that relevant local information was available. Our goal was simple: by providing access to technology, making program participants feel comfortable using computers, and ensuring relevant community re-source–based content, we could create an environment among the participants that maximized use of these new technological tools. Fleet's foundation participated in the effort by funding the creation of a curriculum that provided financial literacy and Internet usage. We then partnered with community-based groups to provide training to the recipients. The results: more than three thousand customers have received their computers and training.

The Greater the Risk, the Greater the Reward

I have long believed that good philanthropy nurtures both proven and new ways of addressing societal needs. We took the approach that we wanted to maintain a balanced portfolio of grant relationships, and that meant stepping up and stepping out by becoming early funders of nonprofit organizations that, we are proud to say, have grown into national models. During the height of the "dot com" boom, many of us used terms like "social venture capital," and we sought "social return of investments," but ultimately, we were playing a different role in corpo-rate philanthropy during that time: we were becoming greater social risk takers. What did this mean for us? We made contributions to peo-ple and organizations who were not necessarily "proven commodities." We applied our business acumen in evaluating the viability of these start-up nonprofits, who all embodied that wonderful combination of vision and sound business planning. We also redefined our role as grantmakers. Realizing that making early gifts wasn't enough, we opened our Rolodexes and introduced potential funders to these pro-grams. We also reached within our organization to lend our support through volunteers, board members, and, occasionally, an executive loaned to help propel these emerging groups forward. This way of

thinking required us to bring all of our resources to the projects chosen, and even with that enormous investment of time and capital we
needed to be prepared for the possibility that some good concepts
might not work in practice. In that case, we accepted the learning that
was generated from the experience—and applied its lessons to other
initiatives.

The results have been amazing. We have seen local ideas morph into
national programs serving exponentially more people than we could
have envisioned in the early days. And not only has it been satisfying to
see that many of the organizations we supported have so successfully
developed their funding bases, we can now look for new opportunities
to lend our unique corporate brand of community support to others.

Diverse Philanthropy/New Voices

One of the wonderful transformations in corporate philanthropy over
the last decade was the growth of diversity among corporate givers.
Specifically, there are more women and people of color serving in all
levels of community relations and as corporate foundation staff. Today,
among the nation's largest corporate foundations, a sizable number are
led by a woman or a person of color. Many more have broadly diverse
senior and middle-level staff and trustees. How did this change corporate philanthropy? As an African-American woman working in this
field for nearly fifteen years, in the beginning I frequently found that
my perspective on community needs and priorities was a unique one at
trustee meetings. While no one can speak for an entire segment of the
population, I often felt that I could bring a viewpoint that otherwise
would not have been heard in strategic discussions about community
needs and opportunities.

It has been well documented, for instance, that people of color have
led efforts to support faith-based community organizations. Fleet and
JP Morgan Chase are just two of the companies that saw the strength

of these organizations and were early and leading supporters of church-based community development corporations (CDCs) and after-school programs. I have also witnessed greater corporate support for programs specifically focused on the needs of women and girls. With broader views and experiences brought to the decision-making table, there appears to be a greater appreciation now that "one size fits all" solutions will not be as successful as solutions that are more closely tailored to the special needs and interests of a given community. Furthermore, corporate foundation decision makers have become more willing to take risks, risks that in many cases have reaped significant rewards for the community in question.

Increased diversity in corporate foundation staffing in our foundation enriched not only direct grantmaking but the execution of funding strategies as well. During site visits, we ask how the staff composition of nonprofits compares to the population served by them. We have adopted anti-discrimination policies for grant recipients. We fund the production of bilingual resource materials. We are better and more thoughtful grantmakers because we have the benefit of many different backgrounds and experiences influencing the decision-making process.

The More Collaboration, the Better

Collaboration is not a new concept in giving circles, although in the 1990s, in many communities, there still remained "silos" separating corporate giving from family and private foundations, community foundations, and public sector support. As a result, we frequently "peacefully coexisted" on the funding lists of nonprofits—our joint investments in the community occurred by dint of similar funding interests, not as a planned consequence of shared thinking. Happily, this has become less and less the case over the past ten years, as illustrated by the following two examples from my own experience.

In the mid 1990s, our local United Way sought to bring a program called Success By Six to Boston. FleetBoston Financial Chairman and CEO Chad Gifford agreed to serve as founding chair of the initiative. Very quickly, he attracted more than fifty leaders from business, the public sector, academia, and community groups to develop a statewide agenda for children and to participate in a campaign to champion the needs of children. The results are impressive: the passage of universal health care access legislation for the Commonwealth of Massachusetts, the creation of an "affinity" license plate that generates revenues for child care programs across the state, and an award-winning public awareness campaign on Boston's ABC affiliate, WCVB-TV. These successes would simply not have been achieved if all of the participants in this campaign had continued to do our work in separate silos of influence and energy. Only by joining together through the leadership group could we mobilize networks and relationships statewide to raise the funding and galvanize the support of key constituents in order to reach our goals.

Recently another collaborative, the Boston After-School Partnership for All, brought together fourteen funders, ranging from Harvard University, the Boston Foundation, companies such as Fleet and Verizon, and private foundations, to pledge $25 million targeted to increase the number of affordable, academically rich after-school slots in Boston by 17,000 over five years. While the full results won't be known for some time, this promising initiative has already drawn national attention. Its focus has less to do with the amount pledged, and more to do with the fact that an engaged, diverse funders' collaborative has been created. The members of this group are driven by a mutual desire to establish a mechanism for shared learning and investment that will have a ripple effect in other aspects of their individual funding programs.

Empowered Employees Make Great Company Ambassadors

Even in today's increasingly challenging job market, companies actively seek to attract and to retain the best and brightest employees. Consistently, employees cite compensation, benefits, and work environment as among their top criteria for joining and staying with a company—and increasingly they also state that it's important to them to work for a company that they see as committed to good corporate citizenship.

In 1996, the FleetBoston Financial Foundation launched an employee-led giving program. Through the sponsorship of our company's Office of Diversity, seven employee-run resource groups were created around areas of interest and concern: a working parents group;a group for Latino, Asian, and black professionals; a "women's interest network"; a group that focuses on disability issues; and a gay and lesbian resource group. All of these groups were given a funding allocation, and their members were provided with basic grantmaking training. Each resource group then reached out into the community to conduct site visits and to make grants within their area of affinity or interest. Most of the grants were to small nonprofits, and in numerous instances resource group members also became involved as volunteers and as board members. Since the program's inception, our employees have made over three hundred grants to more than a hundred organizations. The employees who have had the chance to participate in identifying promising nonprofits, conducting site visits, and making grant awards have stated that their commitment to the company has been strengthened by the experience of representing Fleet in the community.

In 2000, recognizing that the merger between BankBoston and Fleet would result in the largest bank divestiture in U.S. banking history, FleetBoston Financial Foundation launched its Fleet on Board program, designed to provide employee training on nonprofit board governance and to subsequently identify nonprofit board placement support. Through this program we offered a series of workshops, in partnership with Board Source, the premiere board training organization in the country, to literally hundreds of employees across the country. We also reached out to the nonprofits we had funded over the past five years and invited them to consider Fleet employees as they embarked on their board development activities. And, instead of the more traditional process of fielding board placement inquiries on an ad-hoc basis, we asked each organization to share with us their mission, priorities, definition of "good" board membership, and time and financial requirements, as well as the specific sets of skills they needed in new board members; then we undertook a similar, mirror exercise with employees interested in finding board opportunities. While this whole process was more labor intensive than those we'd followed in the past, we found that the matches it produced were more successful because both the employee and the nonprofit had a clearer set of expectations of one another from the start. The added benefit: Fleet gained greater stewardship of our philanthropic investments because our colleagues were actively involved with these organizations.

In another move that went well beyond more traditional ways of engaging employees in philanthropy, the FleetBoston Financial Foundation made a commitment of $4.5 million to six cities to help expand an economic development priority in each. By engaging our local executives in the planning and execution of these grants in each market, powerful and effective internal and external relationships developed. While the grants given by the foundation provided the financial fuel to move these projects forward, the business expertise that Fleet people lent to them underscored, in a tangible way, our commitment to community development. In the process, Fleet's corporate citizenship leadership position was enhanced as our working relationships were strengthened with local government leaders, broader business constituents, and funders. To date, Fleet's initial investment of $4.5 million has attracted nearly $12 million in additional public and private funds directed to the projects we have supported.

Global Strategies

My experiences in global philanthropy—Fleet has operating foundations in Argentina and Brazil—have been among the most interesting of my career. First among the strategies that have worked for us overseas is the belief that effective global philanthropy must be led "in country" by people who live in and know the culture well— that we couldn't simply transport U.S. programs to global markets without modifying them based on an understanding of the social and political dynamics of the places in which we were operating. With that in mind, we supported the innovations that led to our Export School in Argentina; to Travessia, an outreach program for street children in Brazil; and to the Boston School, which, among other things, provides distance learning opportunities for employees and community partners in Brazil.

My colleagues in South America have demonstrated the importance of combining leadership with innovation and an appreciation of cultural mores. Given the different roles that non-governmental agencies play around the world, I am grateful to have been given the chance to learn from them some of the requirements of a nuanced approach in corporate citizenship around the world.

Owing to my long-standing involvement with City Year, a national youth service program, I also serve as a founding board member of City Year South Africa and as a selector for the Clinton Democracy Fellows Program. Participation in these efforts to bring national service models abroad has been an incredibly enlightening experience, one that has again reinforced in me both a sense of possibility and a better understanding of the challenges of melding a program that has evolved in a U.S. context with the immediate needs and priorities of a different culture. Balancing the need to integrate "ideals" with "idiom" will be our goal as we move forward.

Ongoing Challenges

MEASUREMENT ANGST. Now that we have moved out of the economic boom of the 1990s, companies feel greater pressure than ever before to quantify corporate giving accurately and to measure its impact. In quantifying corporate giving, many companies underreport donations that are funded through business units or across geographies. When this happens, we are leaving equity on the table because, by and large, those contributions are not leveraged or represented as part of a company's commitment. To remedy this situation, the Committee to Encourage Corporate Philanthropy recently invited twenty or so companies to participate in a new effort to evaluate their overall giving. The results may lead to a more consistent methodology for recognizing the depth and breadth of a company's commitment to community.

In terms of evaluation, the limitation of resources available for this process continues to be a challenge. We have seen some useful tools emerge, most notably the Boston College Center for Corporate Citizenship's "measurement standards." Unfortunately, however, many companies do not have the resources to make this type of in-depth analysis a priority. Hence we are not able to fully measure the individual or aggregate impact of business philanthropy. Without simpler and more affordable ways to assess how well a company's social investment is paying off, it may become increasingly difficult to maintain leadership giving levels.

TRANSPARENCY. With information so readily available over the Internet, our constituents are able to make their own assessments of our success at being good corporate citizens. This means that we are subject to greater scrutiny by the community, government, customers, advocacy groups, and shareholders. The issues of corporate governance and corporate social responsibility have taken on more prominence. Accordingly, we need to be mindful of the interconnectedness of business and community, and to ask ourselves how this mindfulness affects a company's actions across labor practices, legislative priorities, business ethics, consumer confidence, and media relations.

CORPORATE GIVING MEETS CORPORATE CITIZENSHIP. Over the last several years, a number of my colleagues in the field of corporate philanthropy have expanded their roles to include a much broader conception of "corporate citizenship." As the issues of business ethics, corporate governance, environmental responsibility, fair employment practices, and community relationships converge, it will be interesting to see how corporate giving, which started in many companies as an offshoot of community relations, will be transformed by a new set of priorities.

And the Journey Continues

Recently I moved to the other side of my company's philanthropic universe, and I now have the exciting opportunity to bring my expertise to more than 3,500 private foundations under management at Fleet's asset management arm. I am quite stimulated by the new challenge of meeting the investment management and philanthropic services needs of a diverse set of customers, and at the same time I have become even more aware of how critical private philanthropic resources are for society. It is from this perch that I reflect on the strengths and weaknesses of corporate philanthropy.

Corporate philanthropy's inherent strength is its potential to apply the discipline of the market economy to the issues of civil society. In today's tough business environment, a corporation has no choice but to approach its philanthropy from the perspective of its business interests. While that may sound like a conflict of priorities, it is in fact where things get interesting. The truth is that the needs and expectations of shareholders are aligned in substantive ways with the needs and expectations of employees and communities with regard to critical issues facing society in a number of arenas—education, health care, economic development, and persistent poverty among them.

One major observation I would make in this connection is that, as a whole, the corporate community has not fully grasped how powerfully their collective actions already influence society's values and mores. Those influences can be both positive and negative. Some aspects of corporate influence in regard to globalization—destructive environmental policies and insensitivity to indigenous cultures in particular— are examples of negative influence. This is a unique time in history, one in which the lines separating the domains of the market, government, and the nonprofit sector have become blurred. Richard Parsons, the CEO of Time Warner, has said that the multinational corporation has de facto assumed many of the responsibilities previously held by the nation state.[i] It is within that context that the opportunity for corporate leadership extends far beyond the business objectives of individual companies.

It all comes down to leadership from the top, and it has become clear to me over the past twenty years that too few CEOs have understood the opportunity as I have been articulating it in these pages. A second vulnerability of corporate philanthropy can be traced to the vagaries of the market and the inevitable ebb and flow of corporate fortunes: all too often the commitment to stay the course in a "down market" just isn't there. A third is that sometimes corporations are really just "talking the talk" when they should do more "walking"; some of the current trends in corporate philanthropy are not based on thoughtful analysis of social needs but are instead thinly disguised public relations and marketing ploys. That's disappointing, but my experience is that all the important stakeholders—the market, the consumer, and employees—will see through that kind of veneer and that, increasingly, they are putting pressure on companies to take their citizenship and community responsibilities more seriously.

On the positive side, business enterprises, and especially large corporations, have an enormous influence on society, and they also have unique strengths that no other actors in the arena of philanthropy possess. Several are referenced in this essay, among them human resources departments that include people with a wide variety of professional skills; networking, access, and convening capacities; the availability of social investment capital; and sheer buying power. Corporations have the capacity to galvanize literally thousands of people in support of a cause while at the same time acting as brokers between employees and community organizations. In that latter role, corporations have generated increased societal interest in a broad array of community needs. Whether it's the Avon Breast Cancer Walk, Home Depot's long association with Habitat for Humanity, or Fleet's company-wide volunteer program, both employees and customers have raised money and consciousness for great causes. Corporations also bring management and financial skills to the nonprofit and NGO community, from experience in strategic planning and marketing, to innovative schemes for revenue generation to augment fundraising, and the skills to help negotiate "mergers and acquisitions" arrangements between nonprofit organizations. Corporations, perhaps more than any other circle in the realm of organized philanthropy, can leverage all of these multiple resources.

So, after a decade plus of working in corporate philanthropy I feel the power of possibility and of a potential that is still to come. My

FleetBoston experience in these realms has been a good one, and as the very institution itself is poised to go through a new chapter,[ii] I am excited for what that potential portends.

---

i.   Richard Parsons, speaking at the 2001 World Economic Forum in Davos, Switzerland.

ii.   As of this writing, FleetBoston is in the process of being merged into Bank of America.

DAVID FORD

Ruminations upon Ruminations:
From Inside the Corporate Garden

CORPORATIONS range from McDonald's to Ben and Jerry's, from the New York Times to American Express to Merck. Some take social responsibility very seriously and their philanthropic programs emerge from the very heart of the corporate mission. Others give just a little, when they feel they have to, and without a lot of thought. In the last twenty years, however, many corporations have become better at giving money wisely—at figuring out what they want to enable through their gifts, measuring the effect of what they fund, and adjusting their strategies as they go along.

Almost twenty years ago, after nearly a decade at Rutgers University, where I directed a center on workforce issues, I was selected to direct Chase Manhattan Bank's philanthropic program. I entered the white-shoe world of one of the largest banks in America with great

David Ford is executive director of the Richard and Susan Smith Family Foundation. Between teaching English at an inner-city high school in Milwaukee through Vista and becoming president of the Chase Manhattan Foundation for ten years, he traveled extensively and studied in Asia and Europe for two years. He has been on the boards of the Independent Sector, the Council on Foundations, Associated Grantmakers, and the NY Regional Association of Grantmakers (where he is also a past president). A graduate of Colgate University and the University of Wisconsin, Ford was president of Lucent Technologies Foundation from 1998 to 2002.

trepidation—and a beard. I later learned that the latter item was a topic of some discussion during the hiring process, and that apparently my candidacy was saved when one of the folks involved in the search said, "Well, it really is just giving money away, so what the hell."

For my part, I expected that everyone at Chase would look the same and think the same. But aside from a regrettable lack of racial and gender representation at top levels, there was as much diversity at Chase—diversity of opinion at least—as at the universities and community action agencies where I had worked before. Indeed, the bank's philanthropic program encouraged a wide range of social experience among its officers.

David Rockefeller, responsible world citizen that he is, had set up Chase's rather unusual corporate responsibility program early in his tenure as chairman, in the 1970s. What made the Chase program unusual was that senior officers, in surprisingly large numbers, were involved in deciding where the money went. In 1988, when I started, the Corporate Responsibility Committee (chaired by the bank chairman) was composed of sixteen of the bank's most senior officers, and it met four times a year to review all the philanthropic contributions to be made by the institution, including new recommendations that had been forwarded to it by one or another of nine subcommittees. Yes, *nine* subcommittees. There was a subcommittee on the arts, another on human services and community development, another on education, yet others on public policy, neighborhood grants, and so on. Cumulatively, more than sixty-five of the bank's officers, both senior figures and up-and-comers, inhabited these subcommittees, each of which also met four, or more, times a year.

During my first two years at Chase, I spent 30 percent of my time in committee and subcommittee meetings, about 30 percent of my time preparing for them, and the balance meeting with groups to explore possible contributions and representing the bank in the community.

Some of this activity was a waste of time, and in fact within a couple of years we had reduced the number of subcommittees to four, to limit the time spent feeding and caring for them. But, as David Rockefeller had intended, participation in the committee process had succeeded in encouraging Chase officers to take an interest in the larger world. Most of the sixty-five officers became involved in the causes and groups we funded, and most of them served on boards of directors of particular groups, or volunteered in other ways on their behalf. So, once it was streamlined a bit, this elaborate process was a good use of time for the officers, and for the communities we served.

Because so many Chase leaders were avidly involved in our contributions process, I thought our program budget would be protected even if the bank suffered financial reversals. I was wrong. When the international debt and real estate crises of the late 1980s hit, there were still sixty-five senior officers who knew our budget exactly. And it's hard to hide from that many senior officers. Nearly all were of the opinion that if the bank was suffering, and their own operating budgets were suffering, the community would have to suffer too. Twelve million dollars in annual giving quickly became $7 million. Still, after a year in which the bank lost a billion dollars (which used to seem like a large loss), and in a period when some thought it might not continue to open its doors from day to day, our corporation did keep contributing money (if less of it) in useful ways. The late Tom Labrecque, then our fine chairman, knew that the whole nonprofit community was also suffering economically, and he believed that we needed to do all we could to keep the most important groups afloat.

By 1996, when Chase underwent a shotgun merger with Chemical Bank, and Chemical's leadership team took the larger role in the new institution, our intensive corporate responsibility committee system went out the window. The Chemical folks didn't think they had the time to invest in such falderal.

A new, more customary system was put in place—with staff making decisions up to a certain level, senior management review above that level, and, finally, a very small board of the bank's most senior officers reviewing only the most major grants. Frankly, the quality of the grants made under this regime was just as high as it had been under the previous one. The difference was and is today that notably fewer managers who are preparing themselves for the highest positions in the bank spend any significant time learning about the nonprofit community.

During those eight pre-merger years, Chase made more than two thousand philanthropic contributions a year to nonprofit groups in New York and ten other states where it had a significant presence, plus grants to similar organizations in about fifteen other countries, many of them developing nations that were important to the bank. Many of these contributions were quite small—$1,000 to $5,000—and many of them were grants made in response to a specific request. These were useful grants that fertilized the economic roots of the communities served by Chase and bestowed a kind of "good housekeeping" seal on the funded organizations, encouraging other donors to contribute to them as well.

Beyond those grants, I took particular satisfaction in sculpting "impact" grants, significantly larger grants we made to a few organizations in each of our issue areas, to help achieve some significant social progress. Some examples are the Chase Active Learning Grants Program, which has provided more than $2 million in grants to teachers in most of New York City's middle schools and to middle schools in a dozen other cities around the country. These grants enable teachers to develop curricula and programs that encourage students to learn by doing, as well as through more typical "sit-in-their-seats" pedagogy.

Another designated impact grant area is the Chase Faith-Based Community Development Grants Program. Over the last seven years, this program has provided churches and other faith-based institutions with $3.8 million dollars of start-up funds to create child care centers, special needs housing initiatives, and income-generating projects. Strategic grant programs such as these give donors a better sense—if not a precise measure—of the impact of the efforts they fund. The donor knows that, absent the gift, the project would not occur.

IN 1998, WHEN I MOVED to Lucent Technologies as president of the Lucent Foundation, Lucent was one of the most wonderful companies in the world in which to have the job of "giving money away." From a philanthropic vantage point (and many others as well), Lucent was a stunning organization. The year I arrived, the contributions budget was $26 million. Within two years, we hit $60 million, and we believed that our budget would continue to gain at more than 20 percent a year forever. For well more than a decade, large corporations like G.E. and Wal-Mart had grown consistently at more than 20 percent a year. Why not Lucent? we thought—and funded at a level of 1.5 to 2 percent of these ever-growing earnings, our philanthropic program would be a wonder to behold. We all know how this particular chapter in the history of the technology economy ended, but before I give the details, let me reflect on the strengths—the continuing strengths—of the Lucent program.

Because Lucent is a business-to-business company, it does not experience nearly as much pressure as retail companies feel to build their public relations image through giving. Nevertheless, the members of the Lucent leadership team with whom I worked believed that a successful corporation has a responsibility to help the larger world develop. They had already decided that they wanted to focus on youth development to the exclusion of most other projects (with the exception of some modest funding of broad-based projects in communities around the world where the company had a major employee base).

Within youth development, we agreed that it would make sense for Lucent to pay particular attention to increasing the quality of and young people's access to science and math instruction and, based on the relative diversity of Lucent's workforce, to encourage young people to be open to the cultures, values, and ideas of other people with backgrounds very different from their own.

We set up a series of grant programs, and, working with a network of more than a hundred Lucent public relations colleagues from around the world, we selected and invited hundreds of nonprofit organizations to apply for grants that would be awarded on a competitive basis. Those invited to submit proposals included science museums (for programs to bring students into the museums to work on serious projects that might spark their interest in science), universities (for school-reform partnerships with local school districts), community groups (for projects promoting tolerance and openness to diversity), and school districts (for access to state-of-the-art science and math curricula).

About 10 percent of the most promising proposals we received were selected for grants that averaged $150,000 per year and lasted for three or more years. Because we expected Lucent's growth to continue without pause, we weren't shy, as many companies are, about making multi-year commitments. Organizations from outside the United States received almost a fifth of the grants. In addition to selecting international winners in the grant programs mentioned above, we also entered into a highly effective collaboration with the International Youth Foundation (IYF), an organization based in Baltimore. Lucent contributed more than $15 million, over four years, to IYF's very capable in-country partner agencies for use in a dozen nations, including China, Thailand, Japan, India, Australia, the U.K., and Germany. Funded projects focused on education reform, developing and supporting teachers, and inspiring excellence in science and math.

We took program evaluation seriously, using outside evaluation houses (the Heldrich Center of Rutgers University and the Conservation Company), which cost almost 5 percent of each program's budget. In addition, staff from almost all of the projects—from all over this country and as far away as South Africa and Indonesia—were brought to New York for annual meetings with each other, Lucent Foundation staff, and various experts in their fields, to share information about issues and help them make their programs even more effective.

We also developed the Lucent Global Science Scholars Program, which selected sixty graduating high school seniors from the United States and sixty first- and second-year college students from twenty other countries, naming them as some of the most outstanding science and math students in the world. Each of these young people received a $5,000 scholarship plus a weeklong trip that took them to Lucent headquarters for meetings with Bell Labs scientists and to New York City for fun. When possible, they also received at least one summer internship at Bell Labs or another Lucent research facility. It was the company's hope that some of these outstanding young scientists and mathematicians might come to work for Lucent eventually, and so a portion of the expenses for this particular program came from direct corporate rather than philanthropic funds. Sadly, with the huge decline in Lucent's fortunes and workforce, this program has been reduced to less than half of its original size; happily, it does continue.

In 2000, Lucent's philanthropic budget was $60 million, and then, in early 2000, Lucent's "bubble" burst. As I write, in 2003, almost a hundred thousand employees have been laid off or retired, and the philanthropic budget has diminished to less than $10 million. Lucent faces excruciating circumstances, and some would say that the company shouldn't give a dollar to anything other than its own core operations and business development. But commitments were made in the good years, and at Lucent, leadership meets its commitments. Its leaders still care about philanthropy, and I would expect that the company's programs to encourage young people will expand again with the company's fortunes.

Despite the fact that market realities have sorely limited the efforts of some donors, there have been trends or bents that have enabled others to become more effective. Philanthropy is a very complex field, and in the last decade hundreds, perhaps thousands, of smart and good-hearted people have entered the business of helping wealthy people and institutions give away their money in ways that serve society and local communities wisely and well. In addition to the plethora of consultants and attorneys who now advise the wealthy on their giving, such organizations as the regional associations of grantmakers, the Council on Foundations, and the Association of Small Foundations provide those services capably and usefully.

For major corporations, the contributions council of The Conference Board, of which I was chair for one year, brings together sixty of the contributions leaders from America's largest corporations for several meetings each year. From a corporate perspective, this gathering is the towering sunflower in the garden of philanthropic professional development and networking. Leading the philanthropic program of a corporation is an odd job. Corporations are in business to make money, not to give it away (though quite a few of them have been letting it slip away in the last couple of years). Each of the corporations represented on the council has tens of thousands of employees, and almost none of those employees have any idea what it's like to be on the philanthropic side of the business. So while each corporation's philanthropic program emanates from that corporation's character and business purpose, the leaders of these programs often have more in common with each other than with just about anyone else in their own companies.

In my experience, this part of the philanthropic garden is like a good university: by cultivating the educational and networking services available from these several sources, an interested student can get any degree or sort of knowledge out of it that she or he is willing to put the energy into acquiring.

Community foundations in particular can play an important role in helping donors, including corporations, understand their communities and address their communities' needs. I have seen three community foundations fairly close up, the New York Community Trust, the Boston Foundation, and the Foundation for the Mid-South (this last because a friend, George Penick, runs it). These three play absolutely vital roles in helping other donors understand the needs and opportunities present in their communities.

To cite one stunning example, thinking back on what the New York Community Trust, in collaboration with the New York City United Way, accomplished in the aftermath of September 11 still makes my spine tingle. In the midst of chaos and horror, by noon of September 12 they had managed to set up a Web-based system through which individual, corporate, and foundation donors could immediately contribute money to relief efforts. They arranged for IBM to install a powerful computer system on the morning of September 12, and the Council on Foundations had sent a broadcast e-mail and fax out by early afternoon. I made a personal contribution to test the system, and the system worked. That very afternoon we were able to inform tens of thousands of Lucent people that there was something concrete they could do to help just a bit. The Fox Network later maligned the Trust and the United Way for holding some of the collected funds to meet the longer-term needs of families of victims and affected organizations in New York and Washington, D.C., but in my opinion these two community organizations saw a need and met it—representing our sector at its best.

"Collaboration is an unnatural act among unconsenting adults." That line gets a knowing chuckle when said in seminars, because

although even in the absence of a crisis organizations do try and try
again to collaborate and add value to each other's work, in my experience (and that of others, apparently), most organizational collaborations don't last very long. Along with Ralph Dickerson, then head of
the United Way of New York City, I cochaired the Strategic Alliance
Fund, in which some twenty donors invested several million dollars
toward helping human services organizations develop collaborations
with other nonprofits to build new cooperative programs and/or save
administrative money through purchase of joint services. The fund did
help develop several quite useful projects, but after a cycle or two the
donors moved on to other projects. Based on current resource constraints and the lessons learned from earlier attempts, my guess is that
collaboration is an aspect of the art of philanthropy that we will need
to get better at in the next decade.

CORPORATIONS, OF COURSE, can have hugely beneficial effects on our
cultural, social, and environmental systems even beyond the effects of
their philanthropic largesse. In a much earlier incarnation, JP Morgan
Chase funded the building of the Erie Canal. Although Chase didn't
finance the canal as a gift, it surely had substantial, largely positive,
effect on mid-nineteenth-century commerce and life in this country. In
the 1950s scientists at Bell Labs, now part of Lucent, invented the
transistor. All the money that Lucent could have given in a hundred
years (even if it hadn't suffered an economic implosion) would probably not have had the societal effects of that one discovery.

   But the positive effects corporations have in the course of doing
business hardly diminish the importance of their strategic philanthropic programs. Consider the charitable grant of $50,000, or even as
little as $1,000, given to a capably managed reading program to pur-
chase books for kids and/or adults. This is not a particularly "strategic" grant, but it enables an organization to encourage people to read.

Hard to argue with that. On the other hand, $50,000 given to the same organization each year for five years to enable it to 1) develop a business plan, 2) build a better fundraising system, 3) hire a volunteer coordinator, 4) purchase online reading remediation tools and train the staff and volunteers how to use them, and 5) update its computer system—that would be good grantmaking at its strategic best. Hopefully, the reading program would be permanently strengthened by such a strategic grant and, over time, be enabled to serve a significantly greater number of people even more effectively.

Peter Karoff, an expert in the field, suggests that helping to build the capacity of a single organization, if it leads to the detriment of other important players in the system, can serve to mute the overall social gain. But essentially, I don't see a problem here. In truth, organizations tend to build themselves one at a time, and while I do have an interest in funding strategies aimed at strengthening an entire community, that is a very tall order. Three or four attempts I have seen at close range over the past twenty years have not taken deep root, including a serious attempt on the part of Chase Manhattan Bank to help the nonprofit network of Fort Greene, Brooklyn—where Chase had built an operations facility with six thousand employees—to grow and prosper. I would say, rather, that if the leadership of a particular organization is clever or lucky enough to gather the right support to grow better or faster than its peers or competitors, so be it.

Finally, I want to look at what we can expect from philanthropy, corporate or otherwise, and what the limits are. What about those critics, for instance, who charge that corporations are not doing their fair share for society?

People who give substantial amounts of their own money away, or who go to work for people and organizations that are generous, have big ambitions—they want to cure the ills of the world. But of course there are limitations, beginning with the funds available.

Even with the substantial increases in philanthropy of the last decade, total charitable giving in the United States has remained constant at 2 percent of gross national product. My guess is that close to half of that goes to support the religious activities of churches and other faith-based institutions, and half of the remainder goes to colleges, universities, independent schools, and hospitals. So only somewhere around .5 percent of GNP is available for all the charitable giving toward other social causes—for use both in this country and abroad.

We have a right to expect a great deal from the philanthropic sector. Historically, American philanthropy has been a powerful goad for government to improve its priorities and practices. The war on poverty, the civil rights movement, school funding, healthcare coverage, children's rights, women's rights, human rights—these are only some of the great advances that have been influenced by the philanthropic community. For example, we have seen private donations pay for social experiments that have led to a huge increase in the housing available to the poor of this country. Obviously, what's been accomplished is not enough, but the Ford Foundation almost single-handedly inspired the development of the nonprofit housing and community development system in this country. Banks and other foundations—and government—have added to those initiatives, but the seeds were planted by Ford. More recently, the Diamond Foundation provided the funding that led to the development of the AIDS "cocktail" that keeps thousands of HIV positive people alive. Most everyone reading this book can point to example after example of social benefits that have resulted from "good grants," be they either old-fashioned "charitable" grants or newfangled "strategic" ones.

Government expenditures as a percentage of the U.S. gross national product are at 31 percent.[i] This pays for a huge range of public goods, from roads and bridges built and maintained, to schools and head-start centers operated, to police, firefighting , and social services, up on the scale to national defense—and a bit of international aid. Thirty-one percent verses .5 percent. The ratio between government and philanthropic monies is barely a ratio. Corporations give about $9 billion or $10 billion a year to all their grantees, including colleges, universities, and hospitals, plus the other social causes they assist. But with all due respect, one federal program can cost that much each year.

With these realities in mind, I suggest that we keep our expectations for the harvest from the wondrous garden of philanthropy to a proper scale. Philanthropy matters, certainly. We can touch millions of people, but we can not cure all the ills of the world—social or physical. We can help the nation's nonprofits do their work, but we cannot help as many as we would like to help, nor as many as need our help.

Some years ago, I asked a hundred and fifty New York fundraisers if they'd ever tried to raise money from Chase Manhattan Bank. Almost all of them raised their hands. I then asked (with some nervousness) how many had gotten a grant. A delightful number, well more than half, raised their hands. The audience shared my relief. I then asked how many had gotten enough. I got a good laugh.

---

i.   Carl E. Van Horn, et al., *Politics and Public Policy*, 3rd edition (CQ Press, 2001), p. 48.

STEVEN A. SCHROEDER, M. D.

When Execution Trumps Strategy:

Looking Back on Twelve Years
at the Robert Wood Johnson Foundation

THE PRIVILEGE of serving as the president of the Robert Wood Johnson Foundation—RWJF—between 1990 and 2002 was the highlight of my professional life and a rich source of lessons, insights, and reflections about conducting successful philanthropy. The particular history of this foundation, as well as my earlier career, are germane to the story, so let me begin with a glimpse of each.

A Brief History

Robert Wood Johnson, the son and nephew of the founders of Johnson and Johnson, lost his father in 1910, when he was only seventeen. Rather then attending college, he went to work in the company, and he quickly rose to become its highly successful CEO. A visionary businessman and entrepreneur, in 1936 Johnson established a local founda-

Steven A. Schroeder is the Distinguished Professor of Health and Health Care in the Department of Medicine at the University of California, San Francisco. A graduate of Stanford University and Harvard Medical School, he founded the division of general internal medicine at UCSF and is currently chairman of the American Legacy Foundation. He has published extensively in the fields of clinical medicine, healthcare financing and organization, prevention, public health, and the workforce. Schroeder was president and CEO of the Robert Wood Johnson Foundation from 1990 to 2002.

tion for charitable causes in central New Jersey, and when he died, in 1968, he bequeathed to it the bulk of his fortune—1.2 billion dollars, a sum that transformed a small regional foundation into the nation's third-largest one. Johnson left no instructions concerning directions for the foundation to take, leaving that decision to the board of trustees, which soon established its new mission: "To improve the health and health care of all Americans."[i]

The initial focus of RWJF, under its founding president David Rogers, was on preparing the nation for the surge of demand that was sure to follow what he and his staff believed would be the imminent enactment of national health insurance. A decade later, as access to primary care and emergency services had improved but universal health coverage in America remained a mirage, the foundation shifted its priorities. It retained a focus on healthcare access but added two themes: increasing the cost-effectiveness of all kinds of care, and keeping healthy people healthy while improving the quality of care for those who are ill.

In 1988, the foundation's second president, Lee Cluff, articulated a set of ten specific interest areas for RWJF: 1) infants, children, and teens; 2) the chronically ill or disabled; 3) HIV/AIDS; 4) destructive behavior, including illicit drug and alcohol abuse; 5) mental illness; 6) the organization and financing of health care; 7) quality of care; 8) ethical issues; 9) the health workforce; and 10) medical technology impact. Programs in these areas, building on earlier foundation work, were supported for several years.

In conversations with the RWJF board as a candidate to be its third president, I argued that the foundation had undervalued the part of its mission that dealt with "improving the health" of all Americans, and that maximizing the health of the population would require more than just increased medical services. The best place to start in this arena, I argued, would be to foster healthier personal behavior, specifically reducing harm from substance abuse, including that related to tobacco, alcohol, and illegal drugs.

I joined RWJF in 1990 with a background as a general internist and additional training in epidemiology at the Centers for Disease Control in Atlanta. I had also served in three academic health centers—at Harvard and George Washington universities, and the University of California at San Francisco (UCSF). I had maintained an active practice of general internal medicine (both outpatient and hospital-based), taught medical students and residents, done research on health policy issues, served as founding medical director for two university-sponsored health maintenance organizations, and founded the Division of General Internal Medicine at UCSF. Because I was one of a relatively few physicians whose research interests fused clinical medicine and health economics, I had been invited to participate in many national organizations and activities. At that moment in its history, RWJF had been through a consolidation phase and was searching for a new president who would be a physician about fifty years old, steeped in foundation's fields of interest, energetic, and with managerial experience.

Timing was on my side. Our board was ready for change, and I benefited from a bull market that took our assets from $2.6 billion in January of 1990, when I was named president, to over $8 billion by the end of 2002. This increase in assets allowed me to promote the side of our mission that focused on preventive initiatives without diminishing our grantmaking in more traditional areas of health care. We developed many new programs aimed at combating the harm from substance abuse, especially tobacco—which kills 440,000 Americans annually. We were the first foundation to become involved in anti-tobacco work, and helped inspire others to join that important cause. We also developed programs to support compassionate care at the end of life, volunteer care-giving for home-bound disabled people, the expansion of health insurance coverage for poor children, the promotion of increased physical activity for people of all ages (an important wellness-enhancing factor), and the entry of more persons of minority backgrounds into the health professions. At the same time, we continued foundation programs that addressed issues affecting the healthcare workforce, access to care, and improved care for persons with chronic illnesses, including care at the end of life, in more traditional ways.

During my tenure, the Robert Wood Johnson Foundation awarded $4 billion in grants, 80 percent of its total grantmaking since 1972. My work was fascinating and stimulating, and yet often frustrating as well. Looking back now on that time, I can offer three kinds of reflections: on lessons learned, on regrets, and about institution building.[ii]

Lessons Learned

LESSON ONE: MISSION MATTERS. The mission statement created by the founding trustees of the Robert Wood Johnson Foundation—to improve the health and health care of all Americans—flowed naturally from the original source of the endowment, a fortune derived from a large medical supply and pharmaceutical company, and yet it was simple enough to allow for a wide choice of philanthropic activity. Over time, the breadth of that mission has proven to be both a powerful motivator and a recruiting magnet for staff and trustees. I have also found that its clarity often directed us to the decision that was right for our institution.

In 1999, for example, RWJF embarked on a significant programming redirection, one that reflected our concern that the health promotion part of our mission needed to be made permanent because it was in danger of being overshadowed by national obsessions about the financing and organization of medical care. Our decade's worth of work on the societal impact of tobacco, alcohol, and illicit drugs had amply demonstrated that non-medical factors were responsible for much suffering, and that such factors burden the healthcare system with tremendous and unnecessary costs. Although it was a dramatic shift for us in comparison to the foundation's activities in earlier years, the change was easy to make because it fit so well with our mission.

The RWJF mission statement defines the organization in a flexible way, achieving just the right balance between providing focus and leaving room for creative interpretation. While I was there, that statement told us who we were, motivated our work, directed and informed our expansion efforts, and even influenced how we decorated our headquarters, where pictures of grantees and those they serve predominate. I have seen other foundations pursue first one, then another program and goal, failing to achieve what they intended because they have not clearly defined where they are headed. If your organization is fortunate enough to have a powerful and cogent mission, exploit it to the hilt, use it to energize your efforts, and keep coming back to it. If your organization lacks a powerful mission, I strongly recommend changing it to something you can truly use.

LESSON TWO: FOCUS IS CRITICAL. Grantmakers face an almost irresistible temptation to strike out beyond the boundaries of current priorities and explore new territory. In part, this temptation is a natural reaction to the frustration of working with intractable, chronic issues; in part, it reflects the allure of the new; and in part, it comes from the understandable impulses of program officers to carve out their own special niches. Yet most experts—and I agree with them—advise having a well-defined focus to achieve maximum impact from the precious resources we are responsible for allocating.

One way we stayed focused at RWJF was to think specifically about what we would *not* fund—the "roads not taken," to adapt Robert Frost's phrase. The foundation's general guidelines exclude some types of grants we do not make, among them funding ongoing general operating expenses, basic biomedical research, or international programs;

in addition, many important topics (women's health and occupational health for example) fall outside the work of our program teams. Whenever staff members were developing specific programs and strategies, we always took care to discuss the kinds of projects that would not be funded under a particular initiative, which helped clarify the logic that lay beneath our planning process.

The problems most foundations try to alleviate are so large that progress is seldom possible without concentrated efforts. Because of the specificity of the RWJF mission, its focus is probably narrower than that of most other large philanthropies. Nevertheless, our staff debated regularly whether we had become too diffuse. I believe such discussions are essential—here and elsewhere—if grantmakers are to resist the relentless centrifugal forces to which they are subject.

LESSON THREE: EXECUTION TRUMPS STRATEGY. Foundation staff spend a great deal of time pondering how to approach complex social problems. If they do their homework, at a minimum they will understand what has been tried before, what the evidence shows, what confluence of forces affects a given problem, and the current thinking of experts, as well as the attitudes of the general public or more targeted constituencies. In the best of all possible worlds, they will then develop a well-designed strategy that aligns with the foundation's mission, culture, and resources. But the next, critical step is planning that strategy's execution. In my experience, a preoccupation with strategy all too often causes us to gloss over the equally important decisions about the way that a goal—or an individual program—will be implemented.

When I first arrived at RWJF, I wanted to harness the foundation's reputation and moral and financial capital to promote specific change strategies. In the years since, I have come to appreciate that in philanthropy leadership and tactics are every bit as important as strategy.

Identifying and cultivating individual leaders can be frustrating, because the outcome is not, and cannot be, totally within our control. The very human qualities of creativity, personality, unpredictability, and variability in performance always come into play, sometimes for good, sometimes not. Developing effective tactics requires a solid sense of how the world actually works (a messy science at best!) as conditions on the ground change, as progress is made (or not), as midcourse corrections are needed. Sometimes totally extrinsic events—like the September 11 terrorist attacks and their aftermath—can destabilize efforts that were previously on course.

After observing many organizations, including RWJF, I think that foundations tend to overemphasize strategy at the expense of execution for several reasons: because of internal reward structures, because of relative isolation from the front lines, and because foundations typically recruit staff whose backgrounds are stronger in conceptualization than in operations. Common mistakes in planning for the implementation of a program include selecting the wrong leader, permitting lines of authority between foundation staff and the program director to become tangled, missing opportunities to communicate about the program, and having unrealistic expectations that set grantees up to fail.

Achieving a proper balance between strategic design and implementation requires addressing each of these factors, in particular by shifting internal reward structures, staying more in tune with what is happening in the broad environment, and looking for staff who are strong in both strategy and execution. All of these are easier said than done, but at the end of the day what matters is the strength and usefulness of what has been built, not the elegance of the blueprint.

LESSON FOUR: SOCIAL CHANGE COMES HARD. The kinds of social problems that RWJF and many other foundations tackle are the "big, hairy, audacious" ones.[iii] Typically, they are problems with significant consequences and multiple causes and contributors. If they were easy, they would have been solved already. The example that comes immediately to mind is poverty, a problem many foundations address with energy and creativity, even though it was recognized as intractable more than 2,000 years ago: "For the poor always ye have with you" (John 12:8).

Increasing health insurance coverage, reducing smoking rates, and improving end-of-life care are three areas in which RWJF has worked extensively over the past decade, and in which we believe we have contributed to notable progress. Nevertheless, in each of these fields the problems have deep roots and are far from being solved in any comprehensive or permanent way.

Recognizing that it will be difficult to achieve the scale of social change that would completely solve stubborn problems, foundations still want to know whether their efforts are relevant and successful in moving us at least part way. How do we know how much we have accomplished? Sometimes the choice seems to be between picking easy targets that lend themselves to measurement and finding proxy measures for wider social change, neither of which may give a satisfactory status report. And sometimes we must decide that an avenue is worth pursuing even though our progress measures are not sensitive enough to guide us.

Even without adequate guideposts, foundations addressing complex problems must be prepared to take the long view. They must ask whether they can give themselves both the nourishment of optimism and a dose of realism when facing agonizingly slow progress, and whether they can sustain themselves in the face of persistent obstacles.

For foundations that choose to tackle problems that require social change, it is absolutely vital that we recognize the extra burden such problems place on the staff and the institution. And yet I believe that in making such attempts foundations fulfill one of philanthropy's essential roles in society.

LESSON FIVE: KNOW WHEN TO HOLD 'EM, KNOW WHEN TO FOLD 'EM. Knowing how long to stay with a particular goal, strategy, grantee, or program leader is one of the great arts of philanthropy. My colleague Terrance Keenan advises that the willingness to stick with a set of issues over a prolonged period is a distinguishing quality of foundations that "really make a difference."

Foundations have a natural wariness about staying too long in a particular field, pouring good money after bad, becoming unduly enamored of a favored set of grantees, pushing lost causes, or creating undue grantee dependence. At the same time, good foundation leaders recognize the risks of getting out of an area too early, perhaps just short of the tipping point, as well as the symbolic import of exiting a field, particularly for a large foundation like ours. The trick is in the timing. During my tenure, I'm bound to say, we made both errors—staying too long in some arenas and getting out too early in others.

Here is an example, however, of an instance in which we avoided both these pitfalls. My colleagues and I believed that one of RWJF's strongest programs, was—and is—the Local Initiatives Funding Partners Program. This program works in partnership with local foundations to provide matching grants to innovative community-based projects for underserved and at-risk people. The program didn't start out as such a success—in fact, it had serious problems—but rather than abandoning it, we made some necessary changes. Now it has made 240 grants totaling $80 million and has helped establish good relationships with funders nationwide as well as numerous grassroots organizations. No one can make a single, generalized recommendation about when a foundation should fold its hand and get up from the table, one that will fit all contingencies. But I can offer two bits of wisdom gleaned from the past twelve years: 1) Leave the table carefully: foundations generally exit too soon rather than too late. 2) Keep questioning and debating, internally and externally. This is the only way to gain clarity about when it's time to move on.

LESSON SIX: ESTABLISH A STRONG INTERNAL CULTURE. When I arrived at RWJF in 1990, I told our staff that my aspirations were simple: "Best possible programs, best possible place to work." Implicit in that formulation was the hope that these two goals would reinforce each other.

In a small philanthropic foundation, it may be possible for a single leader to drive program development, leaving the back-end functions of execution and monitoring to staff. A foundation of the size of RWJF, however, relies on the creativity and passion of its staff in the design of programs as well as their oversight and implementation. We recruited and retained the best possible people for this complex job and tried to establish working conditions that allowed them to flourish. Because it is almost as hard to assess individual accomplishment as it is to measure foundation performance overall, subtle incentives and institutional rewards take on heightened importance.

The combination of ambitious goals and ambiguous performance measures can create a permanent undertow of anxiety among a foundation's staff, who worry that they are not "doing enough." Staff may also feel a bit guilty when they compare their own relative conomic security with the turbulence faced by friends and colleagues working in industry, government, and smaller nonprofit organizations.

The key is to build a culture that will reinforce mission, stimulate and reward performance, and help with recruitment and retention. It remains important, as well, to give staff opportunities to help make the foundation a better place to work. At RWJF, we instituted a multidirectional performance feedback system for managers, who are now assessed by people above, below, and alongside themselves on the organizational chart. We also encouraged formal and informal staff development through mentoring, leadership development, and individual coaching.

To accomplish all of this requires holding certain principles dear: treating staff with respect and dignity and making sure they know that they are expected to treat grantees and applicants the same way; maintaining integrity of purpose and conduct; avoiding ostentation; undertaking a relentless internal quality improvement program for staff and for organizational processes; and instituting regular feedback about organizational and individual performance and goals, involving both internal colleagues and external constituencies. I also recommend sprinkling in a little humor; philanthropy sometimes takes itself too seriously, and its ambassadors can appear self-important.

LESSON SEVEN: PURSUE ACCOUNTABILITY. Accountability requires letting the world know the results of our grantmaking in depth, in ways that can be acted upon. As with any other kind of enterprise, foundations need to know if they are making a difference. The question is rarely whether to measure success; it is more often what to measure and how. Foundations lack the usual yardsticks of success used in business, government, or academia. No financial bottom lines, periodic election returns, or *U.S. News & World Report* rankings exist against which to calibrate performance.

Collectively, foundations vary greatly in their missions, goals, and strategies; the scope, scale, and nature of the grants we make; the time frames of our grantmaking; and the degree to which our contributions are even identifiable. Though I have enjoyed reading the occasional reports on the large foundations that are written by professional foundation-watchers (and they were generally very positive about RWJF), such reports are highly subjective and their methods are not reproducible.

At RWJF, we spent a great deal of time and energy developing and pursuing three interrelated approaches to assessing how we were doing: evaluations, performance measurements, and public disclosure. Independent, external evaluations of RWJF national programs and some major grants, conducted by some of the healthcare field's leading researchers, have long been a hallmark of the RWJF organization. Toward the last several years of my tenure, we developed a variety of internal performance measures—including development and assessment of strategic objectives within our program interest areas and periodic formal and informal assessments of how we were doing as judged by important audiences—with the intent of integrating the results and feeding them back into future grantmaking. We also spent an increasingly large proportion of our quarterly board of trustees meetings wrestling with the question of how to measure the impact of our proposed and existing programs.

Some of our pioneering efforts, in my view, lie in the realm of public disclosure—for example, our reports on grant results and the essays in the annual RWJF anthology, *To Improve Health and Health Care.* Our growing library of grant results reports (available online at www.rwjf.org) looks carefully at what was accomplished by the scores of grants completed each year. The anthology—available online and in paperback—attempts to provide a critical, in-depth review of individual foundation programs, grantmaking approaches, and impacts on specific fields. In terms of traditional evaluation, RWJF commits millions of dollars each year.

Despite these efforts, our quest for performance measurement remained incomplete. In part this is because it is so difficult to establish causality when working on complex social issues, especially since one's own efforts are often made alongside those of many others. For example, during the 1990s RWJF invested heavily in programs to reduce the number of Americans who lack health insurance. Despite our efforts, the number of uninsured resumed its upward climb, though the number of uninsured children did drop. Should RWJF accept some blame for that lack of progress? Or did our efforts prevent worse outcomes? How can we know?

Foundations sometimes make a hard job harder by not specifying up front exactly what they hope to achieve with a particular grant, program, or grantmaking strategy. Sometimes we oversell what we hope to accomplish, because we believe in it and because we want the support of our colleagues. And sometimes we are tempted to tackle trivial problems where we know we can measure our results, but I like to think that's a temptation we usually resist.

The widely disparate strategies we employ in program design and evaluation defy ready comparison, for they must be tailored to different situations and time frames. For example, seeing the results of efforts in leadership development takes years, if not decades, as compared to the next-day results we can obtain from a poll on a topical issue. While the latter may help us or others shape a short-term action, design a program, or make a policy decision, the former contributes in sometimes unquantifiable ways to the development of people who may or may not assume important leadership positions some two decades hence.

Despite these difficulties, we in philanthropy owe it to ourselves, our constituencies, and the fields in which we work to try as hard as possible to judge the worth of what we do. We must not abandon attempts at assessment just because the tools currently available are crude. I have watched RWJF get better and better at evaluation over the past decade, and I know that this essential effort will continue.

Regrets, I Have a Few

Those who remember the Frank Sinatra song "My Way" know that the above line continues "but then again, too few to mention." Though my list of regrets at RWJF is short, there are a few that I *would* like to mention. I will skip over the generic disappointments of foundation work, such as how hard it is to catalyze social change, the nagging sense that our precious resources might have been used more wisely, and the pain of disappointing worthy applicants. Rather, I will dwell on six specific themes that represent arenas in which I wish we—I—had done things differently.

THE DIFFICULTY OF MAKING PROGRESS ON RACIAL ISSUES. Among all nations, the United States is by far the most successful "melting pot," and yet we still have a very long way to go before we fully atone for our country's most grievous sin, slavery. Many legacies of slavery are evident specifically in American health and health care today: poorer general health status, especially for African-American men; racial disparities in access to medical care; inadequate representation in the health professions; and the loss of trust in the health establishment that persists in the wake of segregation and particularly as a legacy of the vile Tuskegee experiment that withheld effective therapy for syphilis to infected black men. To be sure, RWJF has a lot to be proud of: continuing and even expanding our minority health professionals programs in the wake of a backlash against affirmative action; sponsoring much of the research that demonstrates racial disparities in access to health care; paying particular attention in most of our program goal areas to problems that disproportionately affect poorer Americans, especially those of color; and creating a more diversified staff and board.

But I had hoped for more. I kept looking for a way to use health and health care to accelerate the healing of the great racial divide that has so plagued our nation. Alas, I never found one. Maybe there were no other ways than those we tried, and maybe we did the best we could do. Or maybe there were opportunities that we failed to see, or that our staff might have discovered had I pushed harder. I hope that the latter is true, and that our next president can use the influence of the Robert Wood Johnson Foundation to make our nation stronger by helping to heal its racial wounds.

OUR INABILITY TO ALLEVIATE THE TROUBLES OF THE HEALTH PROFESSIONS. It is a strange paradox. Americans have never been healthier, health care never more valued or promising, yet morale among health professionals, especially nurses, is in decline, as is the allure of the field for young people. The reasons for this state of affairs are complex and beyond the scope of this essay. It might be possible, however, for a foundation such as RWJF to address some of the root causes of these troubles. We could continue our work on expanding health insurance coverage, explore debt relief for medical and nursing students, find ways to expand the pool of nursing school applicants, stimulate a national debate about the choices facing the profession of medicine, search for ways to improve clinical practice conditions, revive health professions leadership, and bolster the images of medicine and nursing.

Why didn't we take these steps at RWJF when I was there? In some cases we did—e.g., working to expand health insurance coverage and trying to improve clinical practice—though we were more active with the former than the latter. With regard to the others, either we did not figure out a way to accomplish them with the resources at our disposal or other priorities supervened, and in the end I doubt that we had sufficient leverage to do them all. The foundation is, however, currently designing programs to improve the state of nursing, understanding that this is no small task.

I wish we had done more to improve the outlook of the healthcare professions. Perhaps we will in the future. But maybe the root causes of the professional discontent that pervades the field lie beyond our ability to have influence upon them because they are embedded in fundamental economic and political dilemmas, and because the forces at work here are complex, the problems difficult to remedy. The issues at hand are huge, including how health care is organized and paid for, how health professionals are educated, how they are socialized, and what the public expects of them.

THE LACK OF VIGOROUS ADVOCACY GROUPS ON BEHALF OF THE PREVENTION OF SUBSTANCE ABUSE. Even casual observers of health policy cannot help but be impressed with the power of passionate citizen activists and advocacy groups, especially those led by women. Whatever the cause—breast cancer research, research on diabetes or cystic fibrosis, the need for services for people afflicted with HIV/AIDS or mental illness, coverage for mammography screening—an organized group of articulate and energetic citizen-activists assures that the issue will get the kind of attention that makes for at least some positive results. And of course it always helps when a celebrity such as Michael J. Fox is involved. But despite all the damage caused by tobacco, alcohol, and illicit drugs, no organized citizen advocates support work on these issues, with the important exceptions of Mothers and Students Against Drunk Driving (MADD and SADD).

What could such advocacy groups do? They could exert pressure on the National Institutes of Health so that its research agenda includes the consideration of important questions about prevention and treatment. They could help shift the ways in which society frames the use of tobacco and illicit drugs, and the abuse of alcohol—a concept referred to as denormalization. They could press for specific legislation, such as raising tobacco taxes, lowering the permissible blood alcohol level for driving (as MADD has done so successfully), and expanding insurance coverage for treatments that help people break harmful patterns of addiction and/or substance abuse.

It is not hard to understand why no such groups have been formed. Leading the list of reasons is the matter of stigma. An addiction is still too often seen as a personal failing, rather than as the medical problem it is. If you lose a child to leukemia, you bear no stigma when you appear on television or in front of Congress on behalf of leukemia research. But it's a lot harder to go public if your relative suffered or died from one form or another of substance abuse. Whether you are a parent or a spouse, you may somehow feel at fault or in some way implicated.

Another factor here may be that the leadership of many health advocacy movements emerges from educated women in the middle and upper classes, for whom issues such as breast cancer seem much more salient and acceptable than that of substance abuse. It seems to me a curious thing that although more women die from lung cancer than from breast cancer, there is no "Race for the Cure" for lung cancer or smoking cessation.

The creation of substance abuse advocacy groups will require energetic and impassioned leaders, readily understandable action targets, and resources. For example, the American Legacy Foundation's new campaign, Circle of Friends, which focuses on middle-aged women who are dying as a result of tobacco use, features print and television advertisements in the form of letters to family members that express regret at ever having started smoking and at leaving them too soon as a result. Perhaps campaigns like this one will catalyze a women's advocacy movement against tobacco.

OUR FAILURE TO DEVELOP INTELLECTUAL PARTNERSHIPS WITH PRINCETON UNIVERSITY. Though lacking either a medical school or a school of public health, Princeton has the distinguished Woodrow Wilson School of Public and International Affairs, and many faculty who are major figures in health policy. One of the world's great universities is literally right down the street from RWJF, and one would think that many natural alliances between the foundation and Princeton would have occurred over the years. Alas, they have not.

The reasons for the separation run deep. RWJF is more action-oriented, Princeton more theoretical. Furthermore, because Princeton is not involved in graduate health education per se, the Wilson School has a limited involvement in health, despite the importance of this field nationally and globally and the large proportion of Princeton undergraduates who subsequently become health professionals. Despite these barriers, I believe there are potential benefits to a closer relationship. These include the opportunity for RWJF's research staff to engage more frequently with bright graduate students, for collaborative projects and for conceiving and testing new ideas about health policy. Princeton's new president, Shirley Tilghman, supports such moves, and I hope that collaborations will be explored, even as I recognize that the very real cultural differences between the two institutions may limit how far they can go.

THE CONDUCT OF "CONVERSATIONS ON HEALTH." In 1993, RWJF sponsored a series of four town meetings that were intended to inform the newly created Clinton Task Force on Health Care Reform. These meetings, which I moderated, were held in Florida, Iowa, Michigan, and Washington, D.C. Our goal was to provide forums that would give Hillary Rodham Clinton and her task force more experience with the public's views and expectations for healthcare reform. Technically, the Conversations on Health meetings were a success: they were well organized; featured local experts, many of whom were RWJF grantees, commenting on real problems; they received much local as well as national media coverage; and their content was excellent—substantive and nonpartisan.

But in hindsight we realized we had not been sufficiently sensitive to potential political minefields. The main media drawing card—Hillary Clinton herself—was not balanced at the events by the presence of a prominent Republican, so despite our intentions, our efforts were viewed by some, including Republican leaders in Congress, as partisan. This perception was later asserted by conspiracy theorists on the right as evidence that RWJF was the driving force behind the healthcare plan that the Clinton task force put forth in 1994, an initiative that eventually failed.

The take-home message from how we conducted our Conversations on Health is one that I mentioned earlier: execution trumps strategy. Simply put, we should have insisted that the meetings feature politicians from both political parties. Because we did not, I jeopardized both RWJF's reputation and its effectiveness, but fortunately the foundation was sound enough to overcome this incident.

Our Unwillingness to Make Grants outside the United States. Although the policy that limits RWJF support to domestic grantees was established by the phrase "for all Americans" in the 1972 trustees' mission mandate, during my tenure as the foundation's leader we revisited this restriction periodically, including at a retreat in June of 2001. And at that time we did authorize a one-time, 5-million-dollar exception that allowed us to join a consortium of funders supporting efforts to interrupt maternal-to-child transmission of HIV in Africa.

From my current perspective, I would not propose that RWJF become an international foundation along the lines of Gates, Ford, or Rockefeller, with offices all over the globe. But of course it's impossible to ignore the global nature of health threats in the twenty-first century, and I think RWJF should be open to learning from other countries' experiences with such issues as tobacco control, infection control, drug treatment, physical activity and obesity. Because the U.S.

healthcare system is so idiosyncratic, the lessons from foreign experiences may be less applicable to the "health care" side of RWJF's mission than to its health improvement and maintenance mandate. What I would propose is that RWJF stick to its current mission, while experimenting with a few overseas grants to see whether those experiences could advance its mission and grantmaking focus.

Of these six regrets, one, the conduct of Conversations on Health, is not possible to redress, though that experience is an invaluable object lesson for future efforts. The others point to areas worthy of consideration in years to come.

Reflections on Institution Building

As I prepared to depart RWJF at the end of 2002, I was asked about my philosophy of leadership, and about what contributions I had made to the success of that foundation, as well as to another organization, which I had founded, the Division of General Internal Medicine (DGIM) at the University of California, San Francisco (UCSF). Reflecting on the experience of leading these two high-functioning and highly effective organizations, I hold up six principles that guided me at both places.

START WITH INSTITUTIONS THAT ARE FUNDAMENTALLY SOUND. Both UCSF and RWJF are great institutions. They have clear missions, outstanding reputations, sound governance, adequate resources, and distinguished histories. Institutions that are fundamentally sound provide a secure base—whether for recruiting or retaining outstanding talent, marketing ideas, or (for UCSF) attracting new resources. This is not to say that much good cannot be accomplished at less well established institutions, but merely to acknowledge that whatever success I had was partly due to the bases I was able to build upon.

My role was very different at UCSF than at RWJF. As a founding division chief at UCSF, I had the luxury of recruiting all the faculty. That they were outstanding is evident from the fact that six are now members of the Institute of Medicine of the National Academy of Sciences. Together we defined the division's mission, shaped its programs, and established a strong new identity. We accomplished this in an institution whose reputation had been built on excellence in biomedical research and high-technology medical care, and was, at best, indifferent to the more inclusive principles of generalism in medicine.

It was even easier to foster excellence at RWJF, because I was able to build on such a strong existing platform and because the foundation's values were already so in sync with my own.

PUSH THE MISSION. Here I revisit one of the most important lessons I have learned in philanthropy. The RWJF mission statement is a wonderful guiding star—succinct, graphic, and visionary. Without it I doubt that we could have moved as aggressively on key health issues. At UCSF our mission was the promotion of excellence in generalism— including practice, teaching, and research. Though these three activities define what all academic medical centers do, in 1980—when the DGIM was created—there was not much enthusiasm for generalism at UCSF. The sense that we were establishing a beachhead helped create a unity of purpose among our faculty and staff and sustained us when times got tough.

RECRUIT GOOD PEOPLE. An institution can be only as good as the people who work there will make it. At UCSF I was fortunate to be able to recruit excellent young faculty who took a chance on our new venture. The earliest recruits were the most crucial, because they established the tone and made it easier to attract other excellent people. They were willing to come because they respected UCSF, were attracted to our new mission, and had a sense of adventure. Together we created one of the best academic generalist units in the world. Once a standard of excellence is set, it tends to perpetuate itself, because excellent people serve as magnets for others.

At RWJF, my aspiration was for the foundation to resemble the 1927 New York Yankees. That team, which included such players as Babe Ruth, Tony Lazzeri, Lou Gehrig, and Bill Dickey, was as close to an all-star team as has ever been assembled. It is exhilarating to work in such a setting. That was my goal, and I believe we came close to fulfilling it.

SUPPORT AND EMPOWER THOSE GOOD PEOPLE. Early on I accepted that it was okay to surround myself with people who outperformed me. Sometimes this was a little painful, as when I watched my clinical standing at UCSF slip in comparison with master clinicians, or witnessed the prodigious research efforts of young colleagues. But since an institution can be no better than its members, I needed not only to recruit the best but also to foster their maximal productivity. This entailed creating the best possible working environment, which was easier at RWJF than at UCSF, and finding ways to foster individual expression, which was harder at RWJF.

"MANAGE UP" TO MAKE IT SAFE. It is easier to do productive work if you feel safe. At UCSF we worked in an environment that did not reward generalism, either financially or with prestige, when we began. I saw it as part of my job to try to safeguard our division's resources and protect us against hard times by establishing good relations with senior officials. I needed to buffer our faculty and staff from frequent institutional worries about money and space. I was not entirely successful, but we did reasonably well.

At RWJF, cultivating a safe environment was simpler. It meant keeping our trustees abreast of what was happening, soliciting their views on foundation direction, informing them of our aspirations, exposing them to our outstanding staff, and avoiding surprises. Before I joined the foundation, I was warned to expect turbulent relations with the trustees, but nothing could have been further from the truth. The RWJF trustees were exceedingly supportive as we moved into grantmaking in health, explored new approaches to expanding health insurance coverage or care at the end of life, divided into health promotion and healthcare groups, and built a new facility. Without such support from the trustees, we could not have attracted or retained our excellent staff.

CULTIVATE SELF-KNOWLEDGE AS A LEADER. Early on in my career I made peace with my strengths and limitations. Since then I have paid close attention to leaders, heeding lessons about what they did well and not so well, and trying to adopt behaviors that were both successful and personally compatible. The attributes I have found particularly compelling are reliability, integrity, honesty, generosity, and the twin abilities to listen and to develop excellence in others.

Conclusion

The work that is carried on at the Robert Wood Johnson Foundation is harder than many on the outside suspect, but the cause is glorious and the rewards are great. It was not easy for me to leave, and I departed with a mixed sense of loss—at leaving such a wonderful job—and pride that the institution was now stronger than it had been when I had arrived. (That pride is tempered by the realization that at the end of her tenure, my successor, Dr. Risa Lavizzo-Mourey, will undoubtedly make the same statement!)

Serving as president of RWJF was a rare privilege. The combination of abundant resources, a supportive board of trustees, a talented and dedicated staff, and creative, hardworking grantees made it a pleasure to come to work each morning. To be sure, the problems that we tackled—and that remain to be wrestled with in the future—are daunting. We often felt more like Sisyphus than Sir Edmund Hillary. Still, we remained enthusiastic and committed because of our mission, our focus, our realism, and our culture. Looking back on those years, I often find myself rephrasing Robert Browning: "Ah, but a foundation's reach should exceed its grasp, / Or what's a heaven for?"

---

i.   L. G. Foster, *Robert Wood Johnson: The Gentleman Rebel* (State College, Pennsylvania: Lillian Press, 1999).

ii. The text describing "Lessons Learned" is adapted from "The President's Message: Reflections—Looking Back on Lessons Learned," *Robert Wood Johnson Foundation Annual Report 2001*. See also R. A. Schapiro, "A Conversation with Steven A. Schroeder," chapter 1 in *To Improve Health and Health Care: The Robert Wood Johnson Foundation Anthology*, vol. 6, edited by S. I. Isaacs and J. R. Knickman (San Francisco: Jossey Bass, 2002); and J. K. Inglehart, "Addressing Both Health and Health Care: An Interview with Steven A. Schroeder, *Health Affairs 21*, no. 6 (November/December 2002): 244-49.

iii. The phrase comes from J. C. Collins and J. I. Porras, *Built to Last: Successful Habits of Visionary Companies* (New York: HarperBusiness, 1994).

ADELE SIMMONS

Global Giving

PHILANTHROPIC GIVING across national borders is not a new phenomenon. For centuries, Western churches have supported missionaries working in every continent. Churches and wealthy donors funded Thomas Clarkson's movement to end slavery in the eighteenth century, and export official and journalist-turned-reformer E. D. Morel depended on private donors to support his exposure of the crimes in King Leopold's Congo. The founders of the first large foundations in the United States, such as John D. Rockefeller and Andrew Carnegie, were explicit in their support of what we would today call "global issues." The work of the Carnegie Corporation in challenging apartheid in South Africa and that of the Carnegie Endowment for International Peace in exploring how best to prevent deadly conflict are but a portion of Andrew Carnegie's legacy. The Rockefeller Foundation is widely known for supporting the development of hybrid seeds

Adele Simmons is president of the Global Philanthropy Partnership, a senior advisor to the World Economic Forum, and vice chair of Chicago Metropolis 2020. She was president of Hampshire College in Amherst, Massachusetts, and held senior positions at Princeton and Tufts universities. Simmons served as president of the John D. and Catherine T. MacArthur Foundation between 1989 and 1999, overseeing $1.5 billion in grants. The foundation's international programs focus on population and reproductive health, the environment, and peace and international security, with offices in Brazil, India, Mexico, Nigeria, and Russia.

that launched the Green Revolution. The Ford Foundation, which opened its first overseas office in 1952 in New Delhi, today has eleven offices outside the United States and is known for its crucial support, launched in the 1960s, for centers for international study.

The Kellogg, Mott, Packard, Hewlett, and MacArthur foundations and the German Marshall Fund are all major international donors. International intermediaries, from the Global Fund for Women and Global Greengrants to the newly formed Global Fund for Children and Fund for Global Human Rights, suggest that U.S.-based donors are seeking vehicles to help them make effective but very local, community-based grants in other countries. *Giving USA* reports that in 2001 over $4 billion in grant dollars left the United States for overseas destinations. This represents an increase of $1.5 billion in the last decade, but is still a modest portion of the $30.3 billion total in international giving.[i] Moreover, much of this increase can be attributed to a single donor, Bill Gates.

In the last decade, a new generation of donors began establishing foundations on a large scale. Three of these donors, George Soros, Ted Turner, and Bill Gates, are expressing a vision for a future in which the lives of many of those living in poverty, and without access to basic rights would improve. George Soros has committed an astounding $3.7 billion internationally over the past ten years, including about $1 billion to help build institutions to strengthen democracy in Russia alone. Ted Turner's United Nations Foundation supports international organizations' effort to address issues of population, health, peace and security, and the environment. And Bill Gates's commitment of over $3.2 billion to date, to programs directed at research and prevention of diseases that disproportionately affect poor countries—AIDS, malaria, and tuberculosis in particular—has not only provided immediate and flexible resources to combat these festering problems, but also galvanized global giving, attracting more donors and more visibility to an international movement to support public health in the new century.

In 1989, when I became president of the John D. and Catherine T. MacArthur Foundation, the organization was already committed to international work in three areas: peace and international cooperation, the environment, and population. Board members Murray Gell-Mann, a Nobel prize–winning physicist; Jonas Salk, the creator of the Salk vaccine; Jerome Wiesner, former president of M.I.T.; and Elizabeth McCormack, chair of the board of the Population Council, helped to design programs in each of these areas. My job was to build on the strengths of the existing programs, ensure that the work stayed on the proverbial cutting edge, and ensure that the grants we made had maximum impact. The lessons from these years offer important insights for grantmakers today.

Many of the same principles and strategies that underlie effective domestic grantmaking also shape effective international grantmaking. But bringing private resources to bear on global problems adds some complexities. Some foundations have a specific set of tools, e.g., they fund conferences, make large grants or small grants, provide scholarships and support individuals and/or institutions. These foundations typically do well when they find international problems and angles that match the tools in their domestic toolbox.

Other foundations start with a problem, then figure out which tools are needed to address it. A large foundation, such as MacArthur, has the luxury of being able to use all the tools available, from very large grants, to a series of carefully designed complementary smaller grants, to convening a group of stakeholders to find common ground.

In this essay, I will review some of the approaches to global grantmaking that the MacArthur Foundation used during my ten years as president, which I hope will help other donors understand ways in which strategically focused international grantmaking can make a

difference. The MacArthur Foundation's approach to global grantmaking included starting new institutions, strengthening the local
civil society infrastructure, building international networks to influence the outcome of significant international debates, and supporting
the research of scholars in the United States and abroad. In doing this
work we drew lessons from our U.S.-based grantmaking and also
learned new ones.

Context Matters

Efforts on the part of foundations and governments to revive inner-
city neighborhoods in the United States have foundered for many reasons, but high on the list is an arrogance that leads donors who have
never lived in a poor neighborhood to decide what such neighborhoods
need. Grantmakers apparently have to learn over and over again that
context matters, and that one needs to listen to those who are "on the
ground" before developing a strategy for intervention. This lesson
applies equally in global grantmaking. It may be obvious that a program to promote reproductive health in Northern Nigeria, where
Islam's sharia law prevails, must be different from a reproductive
health program in Brazil, where rock stars appear on TV calling for
condom use. But between these two obvious examples lie cultural and
political differences that are subtle as well as obvious and sometimes
very difficult for "gringo" donors to understand.

Want to bring U.S.-style fundraising to a local university? This is
not so easy in a context where most of the institution's board is composed of government officials, where there is no culture of local funding for public universities, and where fears of corruption and misuse of
funds cause individuals to back away.

Want to fund a local leader to set up a community health project?
This approach can get you in deep trouble in a culture that has a long
history of collective leadership, and in which the person who stands

out too much is often soon discredited. Donors who take the time to understand the context can figure out how their outside intervention can be effective and reduce the risk that such intervention may unintentionally cause more harm than good.

Some foreign donors never seem to learn. International agricultural workers worked side-by-side with Afghan farmers in the spring of 2003 to assist with wheat planting. The rains were right, and a bumper crop was ready to be harvested when an international group came in and unloaded tons and tons of free wheat. The price for the local wheat collapsed, and the farmers in this region are turning again to growing opium poppies. The cost of such colossal mistakes can be high, but the opportunities for U.S. foundations to have a positive global impact are significant.

Building the Capacities of Civil Society

Both at home and abroad, strong civil society organizations promote human rights and transparency, advocate for policies that ensure sustainability and democracy, and at the grassroots level provide opportunities for local initiatives outside of government. Apart from humanitarian organizations, governments rarely fund these civil society organizations, nor should they, particularly when an important role of civil society is to challenge government and/or hold governments accountable.

Civil society exists wherever ordinary citizens form social groups. These may be formal, not-for-profit, charitable organizations; they may be ad hoc social movements; they may be informal networks of concerned citizens. Foundations are a major source of support for civil society, whether global, national, or local. The MacArthur Foundation initially focused its attention on mobilizing the resources of U.S-based civil society groups that were working internationally. It helped launch new institutions that were designed to address big, cross-border problems and strengthen the local capacity of affiliates abroad. The stories below are examples of how one foundation, in its effort to deal with global issues, thought about strengthening civil society.

THE ESTABLISHMENT OF THE WORLD RESOURCES INSTITUTE. Shortly after it was established in 1978, the MacArthur Foundation had identified the global environment as a central issue. But in the array of U.S. environmental organizations, few were paying attention to the complex global forces that lead to the destruction of the environment. Acid rain from coal-fired energy plants in the United States is destroying forests in Canada and the ecosystems that depend upon them. Tropical rain forests are being either clear-cut or stripped of mahogany and teak, and animal species are dying along with the trees. It is not only consumer demand and private-sector profits that drive unsustainable development. In some cases, multilateral financial institutions also seem to encourage developing countries to include similarly destructive and unsustainable choices in their economic planning.

When we began our work, there were no environmentally focused global organizations fully engaged in the public debate about these resources. Yet there were visionary scientists and policy-savvy analysts who were acutely aware of the need for such debate. Gus Speth and Jessica Matthews were among the scientists and policymakers who helped the MacArthur Foundation's board decide that a new institution was needed. In 1982, after considerable consultation with leading environmentalists, the MacArthur Foundation made a $15 million grant to create the World Resources Institute (WRI), an independent policy research center designed to bridge the gap between the scientific world and the policymakers charged with addressing complex global environmental issues.

MacArthur wanted to invest sufficient funds to ensure that WRI had the capacity to quickly demonstrate the value of an institution that would be an authoritative source on critical issues from acid rain to global warming before they had attracted public attention as components of actual disasters. To ensure the permanence of WRI, MacArthur later provided an additional $22.5 million for an endowment, in part through a matching fund mechanism. The total institution-building commitment from MacArthur was $37.5 million over ten years.

WRI's influence has grown to the point where its staff of nearly 130 can produce a thorough documentation of the environmental consequences of, say, illegal logging in the world's remaining intact forests quickly enough to prevent further catastrophe. Its insightful analyses of international decision making provide roadmaps for implementing responsible and sustainable multilateral agreements on the setting and monitoring of environmental standards. WRI's pilot assessment of global ecosystems, for example, spawned the Millennium Ecosystem Assessment, endorsed by UN Secretary General Kofi Annan as an outstanding example of the sort of international scientific and political cooperation needed to further the cause of sustainable development. Similarly, WRI has developed and tested indicators that civil society and governments can use to measure citizens' "environmental procedural rights," including access to information, participation, and justice in decisions that affect their own local environments. Building on this work, a global partnership was launched at the World Summit on Sustainable Development in Johannesburg to assist government in efforts to improve environmental governance.

The foundation subsequently began to provide direct support to local environmental groups in other countries as well, believing that the bio-diversity of our planet would only be protected through a combination of international activity and the local actions of people who live in those "hot spots" where that bio-diversity is most threatened.

By the early 1990s, WRI had attracted diversified funding sources, and today MacArthur supports only those specific projects that are consistent with the overall mission of the foundation. WRI's annual budget is $20 million, and it has a $25 million endowment.

THE NATIONAL SECURITY ARCHIVE. The impact of U.S. foreign policy on global issues is not in question. Foundations have consistently supported policy centers and think tanks where analysts evaluate, critique, and offer suggestions concerning U.S. policy. But, as the Vietnam-era Pentagon Papers demonstrated, transparency relating to the making of foreign policy is of crucial importance. Substantive goals often compete with political aims in the conduct of foreign policy and the accountability of government suffers as a consequence.

Although the Freedom of Information Act (FOIA) had been law since 1966, it was not until after the Watergate revelations of abuse of governmental power came to light that the act's provisions were expanded. The 1974 amendments permitted citizens more access to information directly related to how the federal government was setting policy and determining its actions in the realm of national security. FOIA requests were subsequently filed by increasing numbers of individual journalists, political scientists, historians, and others monitoring a range of U.S. policies, particularly in Central America and Cuba, regions which underwent ongoing crises throughout the 1970s and into the 1980s. The responses from the different government agencies were uniformly slow; the agencies themselves were not especially cooperative. Indications were that the Department of Justice was actually coordinating a strategy to stymie these requests (it created a "hotline" to track them).

It became increasingly clear that an institutional counterweight to the bureaucratic institutions of government would be required if the public was ever going to benefit from the "freedom of information" that was its due under law. Ray Bonner, affiliated with the *New York*

Times; Scott Armstrong, still at the *Washington Post;* and Jim Moody, an economist, Peace Corps veteran, and member of Congress, collected and shared information about Central America. The physical burden of copying reams of documents (handled by a congressional intern, who was later supported by Mort Halperin at the ACLU) and the revelation that a member of Congress had to rely on investigative reporters to dig up information that the administration then in power should have been sharing freely, convinced them of the need to institutionalize this function. They envisioned an organization that would handle FOIA requests efficiently, one that would collect and catalogue information and keep it available in a retrievable, accessible way. They took the idea to the program staff at the Ford and MacArthur foundations.

With the input of Gary Sick at Ford and Ruth Adams at MacArthur, the group developed the concept of an organization that would be part law firm (to file requests), part library (to archive the material), and part think tank (to analyze the content developed). After much debate in writing and presentation, each funder made a $25,000 planning grant to allow Scott Armstrong, who had left the *Washington Post,* and journalist Tom Blanton to develop the design for a proposed National Security Archive (NSA). The NSA was to serve both as an archive of declassified federal government policy documents obtained through persistent application of the Freedom of Information Act and a source of analysis of these documents.

Careful analysis of the need for an organization focused on government transparency, combined with the successful search for imaginative leadership helped Ford and MacArthur make the decision to risk investing in a start-up operation. It also helped that two additional funders, the J. Roderick MacArthur Foundation and the Carnegie Corporation, came on board, effectively spreading the risk.[ii]

The NSA operated under the fiscal sponsorship of an umbrella

organization that provided various administrative cost-sharing benefits, including access to a sizeable line of credit. Then, in 1999, it spun
off on its own. The NSA is currently publishing a series of sourcebooks
on CIA reports on Osama Bin Laden and bioterrorism intelligence
material. Its skill at extracting and cross-referencing documents from
multiple sources allows the NSA to collect and collate materials that
one branch or another of the U.S. government—or of the government
of other country—refuses to officially declassify but that have already
been made public elsewhere. NSA's work makes it clear that clandes-
tine activities do, more often than not, lead to problems later on—
witness NSA's latest revelations about meetings between Donald
Rumsfeld and Saddam Hussein in the early 1980s.

The long-term relationship between the NSA and MacArthur cul-
minated in a \$1 million general support grant in 2003. The Knight
Foundation has also awarded it \$1 million, and Ford and the
Soros/Open Society Institute continue to support the growth of this
citizens counterweight to government secrecy as NSA expands to aid
citizens in other countries in their efforts to hold their own governments accountable. Currently NSA collaborates with partners in Mexico, Iran, and a consortium of NATO and Warsaw Pact countries.

The NSA is a superb example of an organization that would not
have been created without foundation help. The importance of a civil
society organization that insists on transparency in government decision making is evident. But governments will never fund this work,
and it does not have the appeal that draws most individual donors. The
NSA will rely on foundation support for years to come, and our democracy will be stronger because of it.

WORKING AT THE LOCAL LEVEL. Strengthening civil society at the
local level, especially in the environment and human rights fields, is
critical if change is to last and new ideas are to take hold. Local actors

and local movements are the drivers of change. The Ford Foundation's history of setting up "safe harbor" think tanks throughout Latin America during the period of military dictatorships permitted the survival of a modest civil society infrastructure in several countries. In the transition from dictatorship to democracy, the thinkers and strategists these centers insulated from reprisal became the intellectual leaders—in the case of Brazil's Enrique Cardoso, the elected leader —of reform. These think tanks also integrated research and advocacy in ways that have become central to many civil society groups across the ideological spectrum.

Local groups have a legitimacy that international civil society organizations (CSOs) do not necessarily share. Moreover, the views of local groups may differ significantly from those of large international organizations. In the late 1980s and early 1990s, the MacArthur Foundation funded Mexican environmental organizations directly, as well as through international intermediaries. By the time NAFTA was being negotiated, Mexican groups were strong enough to express views that were independent from and capable of influencing those of international environmental organizations. The foundation sought out local leaders working on both population and environmental issues to ensure that the perspectives of people living in remote areas of Mexico were a part of shaping programs and strategies. Local leaders did not exactly come flocking to the foundation's Mexico City office, but the foundation used an extensive network of advisors to locate emerging leaders in rural areas. These local leaders developed skills that helped them take advantage of resources outside their villages, and the foundation learned from these leaders how women's empowerment, indigenous rights, conservation management, and economic development affected their communities.

The strategy was different in support of human rights. At a time when the Mexican government consistently denied its complicity in human rights violations, only outside funding partners could support the nascent human rights organizations that were finding ways to expose government and police practices that violated the human rights of Mexican citizens. Working together, these organizations facilitated links between local groups and international civil society groups and played a part in the subsequent flowering of democracy in Mexico.

Simultaneously, research and leadership development initiatives, such as MacArthur's support of the Social Science Research Council's Fellowship Program, gave local actors the opportunity to directly engage with the broader community of human rights scholars and practitioners. Donors in the U.S. enabled Amnesty International, the Lawyers Committee for Human Rights, Human Rights Watch, and the Washington Office on Latin America to partner with Pro Juarez, Centro de Investigaciones y Estudioes Superiores en Anthropologia Social, Academia Mexicana de Derechos Humanos, and regional institutions like the Inter-American Institute for Human Rights in Costa Rica to advance human rights issues. The latter local groups struggle still with the legitimacy of human rights promotion as a requisite function of government: witness the recent disbanding of the department of human rights that Mexican President Vicente Fox created in 2000. To this day it remains a treacherous pursuit to defend human rights in Mexico, where workers for that cause are still in danger of being beaten and killed.

As international groups develop a deeper appreciation of the obstacles with which their various local counterparts must deal, however, they can provide new tools for overcoming them. They can increase the visibility of local human rights groups and thus provide them a measure of protection in their own countries.

As Mexican civil society became more established, the MacArthur Foundation introduced a new and very American concept to Mexico: the community foundation. The Ford Foundation has been a leader in starting new community foundations in the United States (including Puerto Rico) and overseas, most notably in India. Community foundations are managed by local boards that make decisions about supporting local civil society organizations.

Americans from Ford and Kellogg, collaborating with Mexican partners to establish the Oaxaca Community Foundation, found that they were constantly trying to decide when the "American way of doing things" or the "Mexican way" better suited an organization operating in Mexico. The proposed Oaxaca Foundation's board initially included U.S. funders, civil society leaders, and Mexican philanthropists. From the outset, it insisted that the search for an executive director be conducted in an open way, bypassing the Mexican proposal to appoint a relative of a founding donor without a search. The resulting discussions, which led to the formation of the Oaxaca Community Foundation, took several years, but ultimately succeeded; in 2002 the foundation gave away approximately $300,000 in grants, and double that amount in 2003. Sometimes a quick turnaround is essential in international grantmaking. But when new institutions are being established, time and patience are essential.

Anyone embarking on an effort to strengthen civil society, but especially in the context of another culture, should keep several things in mind. Foundations are only an enabling force. The success of a civil society organization depends upon its leadership, and for an international donor, identifying an effective leader is not always easy. The challenge is to find the person who commands local respect, and this is not necessarily the person who speaks the most elegant English. An intermediary institution may serve to make this link; groups such as the Synergos Institute, for instance, can help people respected by a community become "bridging leaders" who have the skills needed to be effective beyond their own venues and with new constituencies.

Building institutions takes time, and it takes even more time in countries where there is little history of strong civil society groups. Moreover, in countries where there is little philanthropic history, funders should be prepared to support an organization over the long haul, and to assist in the development of its fundraising capacity. Continuity can count even more than the volume of dollars committed.

Many issues may require several civil society organizations to address the same problem at different levels simultaneously. A local human rights group is effective, in part, because governments know that it can call in its international partners when needed. International human rights groups, in turn, depend on local organizations for information and the day-to-day monitoring of the situation "on the ground." While one donor cannot always support work at both levels, donors need to understand a field well enough to know where the gaps are and where their funding will bring the greatest benefit.

Building International Coalitions

Funders seeking to intervene in issues of global significance are acutely aware of the enormity of the task at hand. They also understand that the return on their investment might take the form of a paradigm shift in the approach to a worldwide problem or even a new treaty among nations.

By their nature, global issues are complex and interrelated, with economic, environmental, social, and cultural dimensions. Collaboration among international organizations, governments, and civil society is usually necessary to produce new approaches to familiar problems. But collaborations can work, and they represent a source of what the Kennedy School's Joseph Nye calls "soft power"—an alternative to political and military might that forces governments to work constructively on mutual, cross-border problems. Building a "soft power" network or coalition takes time and skill.

Security and sustainability were priorities for several funders in the

1980s and 1990s. As the UN began to sponsor regular global summits on women's issues, the environment, economic development, human rights, and human habitats, the foundation saw an opportunity to help reframe these issues in ways that would significantly change how they were viewed, in the process altering government policies and/or the activities of other major actors. Two UN conferences stand out in particular—the Earth Summit (the UN Conference on Environment and Development) in Rio de Janeiro in 1992, and the International Conference on Population and Development (ICPD) in Cairo in 1994.

THE EARTH SUMMIT, RIO, 1992. Maurice Strong, the secretary general of the Earth Summit gathering, realized quickly that only a highly visible and organized civil society presence could force governments to address issues of sustainability in a serious and accountable way. While the civil society groups would not have access to the formal discussions, he understood they could hold their own NGO forum, engage the press, and express the expectation that governments would respond to the findings of the meeting and be held responsible for fulfilling their pledges.

Foundations responded to Strong's argument; MacArthur, for one, established a fund of $1.5 million to support the participation of NGOs at Rio. Environmental groups from all over the world flocked to the city, holding daily meetings and press conferences, making it clear that they represented a vocal and influential constituency that demanded action. The final agreement among nations, calling for sustainability as an economic principle, was something that few had imagined possible. The implementation of that agreement has not matched expectations, and the Johannesburg Summit a decade later was arguably undermined by the United States. But in 1992 the issues were defined, and an international understanding of what was required was articulated clearly.

Civil society groups quickly recognized their own impact in the international arena, and organized for subsequent UN conferences, including the Vienna Conference (on human rights) in 1993, the ICPD in 1994, and the Social Summit in Copenhagen and the Beijing Women's Conference, both held in 1995. Creating the means for civil society to participate in the parallel NGO forum at Rio put immense pressure on governments to be accountable to their citizens, and the organizers of the conferences that followed learned from the Rio experience.

THE INTERNATIONAL CONFERENCE ON POPULATION AND DEVELOPMENT, CAIRO, 1994. Coordinated to a large extent by the International Women's Health Coalition, led by Joan Dunlop, foundations and civil society groups began planning more than a year in advance for the International Conference on Population and Development, held in Cairo in 1994. The goal was not only to have the United Nations conference support family planning activities, but also to shift the focus from the mechanics of birth control to a broad strategy focusing on women's reproductive health. Supplying condoms and IUDs was not enough. Women needed a full range of health and counseling services and needed to participate in decisions about their own reproductive choices.

For eighteen months leading up to the conference, women's organizations, representatives from sympathetic governments and foundations, and, when appropriate, from the UN Fund for Population (UNFPA) met and developed a Cairo strategy. Ford and MacArthur, among others, set aside funds to support these planning activities, and to strategically support women's organizations in the United States and in other countries where it was likely that these organizations could influence the views of their countries' official delegations to Cairo.

Precisely because the 1992 Earth Summit in Rio de Janeiro had demonstrated the powerful influence of a parallel NGO forum, subsequent UN conference organizers were wary of the civil society presence. UNFPA, the lead agency organizing the ICPD, was concerned that the CSOs at Cairo would create even greater discord and make it impossible to achieve a consensus among governments.

A collaborative of some dozen or so U.S. funders working in women's health issues, population, development, and human rights met with the director of UNFPA and her deputy in the year preceding the conference. In what participants have called a groundbreaking move, the group considered how to view the civil society interest as politically advantageous to UNFPA. The meeting defined ways in which this broadly representative, well-informed global constituency could be allies in the effort to persuade governments to address population policies more openly and progressively. This fundamental shift in the way the conference organizers perceived the role of civil society organizations is seen as significant in the adoption of the twenty-year ICPD Programme of Action and the explicit consideration of HIV and AIDS, violence against women, and gender inequality as development crises afflicting all regions of the world.[iii]

Shortly after the funder/UNFPA meeting, a few of those same funders leveraged their convening power once again to host a meeting of population, health, women's issues, and environmental CSOs in Brazil. The groups themselves were frustrated by the differences among them that threatened to divide them en route to Cairo. This forum, mediated by the presence of philanthropic supporters, was devised to help them seek common ground. At the forum, alternative goals were proposed and competing strategies debated. A consensus emerged to transform the message and change the paradigm away from specific doctrines that might fuel the opposition coming from fundamentalist sources worldwide. With representatives from over eighty countries, this pivotal meeting allowed a diverse group of civil society actors with varied skills and capacities to prepare a joint declaration to bring with them to Cairo so they could act as one.

Donors agreed to fund coalitions and networks of CSOs working on themes that included universal education; reducing infant, child, and maternal mortality; and reproductive health care, including family planning, assisted childbirth, and prevention of sexually transmitted infections, including HIV/AIDS. They supported alternative news organizations pre-, during, and post-Cairo, and paid for grassroots leaders to join the leaders of large international organizations at the conference. This funding approach sustained the cooperative spirit and enabled groups to participate at Cairo in a more concerted fashion.

The result was a major shift in the way issues relating to women and population were framed. The traditional emphasis on demographic targets was redirected to a concentration on the role and living conditions of women. The talent and energy of local NGO leaders was showcased on a world stage for their home governments to see. Governments began adding civil society representatives to their delegations to international conferences. In the end, the impact of civil society depends upon the quality of its organizations, but these organizations, even those that are supported by their memberships, continue to count on foundations for additional and vital support.

International Agreements

Determined and committed civil society organizations can claim the credit for the outcomes that led to the Kyoto Climate Change Treaty, the Treaty to Ban Land Mines, and the creation of the International Criminal Court. The MacArthur Foundation supported a coalition of civil society groups that brought about two of these international treaties.

THE INTERNATIONAL LAND MINE TREATY. When Bobby Muller from the Vietnam Veterans of America Foundation (VVAF) first met with the staff of the Peace and International Cooperation Program at MacArthur, to ask for support for his organization, he did not have a clear policy project in mind. But, he impressed the staff favorably and once a discussion about forming a coalition to work to ban land mines took shape, it was clear that the VVAF could be a key player. Any successful movement usually has several key players and uses multiple strategies. Jody Williams (who would later receive the Nobel Peace Prize for her efforts with the International Campaign to Ban Landmines) was identified as another invaluable contributor and was hired by VVAF to act as their policy person. MacArthur initially funded four organizations that worked independently and in collaboration with up to eighty others to ban anti-personnel landmines.

At the same time, Lloyd Axworthy, the foreign minister of Canada, was assembling a coalition of governments noted for their commitment to international organizations and peace to draft the treaty. Axworthy worked tirelessly to bring the United States into the treaty but was prepared to bring it forward without U.S. support. When, at the last minute, the United States decided it could not support the treaty, Axworthy did just that. It is unlikely that governments alone could have secured the ratification of the treaty without the organizing support of civil society groups and their funders, and it is certain that without sympathetic government leaders—no doubt emboldened by such widespread popular support—the treaty would not exist.

THE INTERNATIONAL CRIMINAL COURT. Foundations love to claim that all their work emerges from a clear strategy. Many times, however, serendipity plays a role. In MacArthur's case, our review of a five-year initiative on human rights grantmaking—an initiative that funded predominantly U.S.-based international human rights groups—led us to complement the institution-building approach with a more project-based approach. Simultaneously, grant seekers to the foundation came forward with proposals for consolidating procedures and lessons from the ad hoc tribunals for Yugoslavia and Rwanda in order to shape a more efficient and permanent process for global justice.

These visionaries impressed the foundation as having a strategy to match their big ideas. If justice is beyond reach, they thought, then reposition justice. The UN had authorized preparatory meetings to consider the establishment of a permanent International Criminal Court (ICC). MacArthur's funding strategy was to support the half dozen or so U.S. NGOs (including the center run by DePaul University professor Cherif Bassouni, a well-known grantee of the foundation) that were providing detailed analysis to aid the drafting of a treaty to create the ICC. Subsequently, MacArthur funded human rights groups in developing countries to participate in the 1998 United Nations Conference of Plenipotentiaries on the Establishment of an International Criminal Court to adopt the Treaty of Rome, an approach that leveraged the NGOs' power to return home and guide the public debate to support their governments in seeking to ratify the treaty and adopting the necessary domestic legislation to enable its application.

Because a number of philanthropic institutions recognized the timeliness and significance of global treaties in enforcing international norms, more NGOs than governments were represented in Rome. Among the initial groups were several that had established relationships with North American and European donors. The three largest private funders of human rights in the United States—Ford, MacArthur, and the Open Society Institute—were key philanthropic contributors to building a formal coalition, along with the international aid agencies of several European countries and Canada. Smaller countries, other private funders, individuals, and NGOs all followed suit.

The International Criminal Court came into being in July 2002, after the sixty-ninth country ratified the treaty. (Parties to the treaty now number ninety, with another seventy states having signed but not yet ratified it.) For the first time in history, all citizens of nearly every country have access to an instrument of international justice with the power to enforce human rights laws. Since the treaty has come into force, the Coalition for the ICC (CICC), which now counts more than two thousand groups as members, continues to build public awareness, provide expertise on the rules of procedure for the permanent court, and monitor the processes for all court functions. (The provision to give immunity to members of the U.S. military that the United States insists upon remains another focus of the CICC.) The role that civil society organizations played persuading their governments to commit to the process of forming the ICC, informing every stage of the development of the treaty's language and the court's operating procedures, is one of the more powerful examples of the effectiveness of philanthropic support for coalitions that come together for a common purpose.

Foundations, and their civil society grantees, have changed international frameworks in a number of areas, only a few of which are described here. But donors should exercise caution. They can help with planning and strategies, but unless there are effective civil society groups to fund, change will not occur. Foundations alone cannot create a movement. At MacArthur, we sometimes found this frustrating, either because in our enthusiasm to see progress we funded less strong groups with weak leadership, or because no civil society organization came forward with the brilliant plan that we, on the eleventh floor of 140 South Dearborn Street in Chicago, hoped for.

Research

Without knowledge—information and the theoretical framework that enables one to use information—efforts to effect change will very often prove to be misguided.

What are the possible strategies for preventing conflict? What is the relationship between mainstream religious organizations and fundamentalists? What is the impact of globalization on poor countries? How has NAFTA affected Mexican farmers? Why do some countries or regions seem to have better healthcare and educational systems than others? How does one explain the geopolitical differences between China and Russia? What kinds of rural health systems are the most effective? What are the advantages and limits of micro-credit lending? Where are the most vulnerable natural resources? What are the most effective ways of saving them? What strategies for promoting women's reproductive health work best in Muslim and Catholic societies? What prompts men to be involved in implementing reproductive health programs? What is the impact of genetically modified organisms? The questions we face are endless. Some are practical and have answers. Some are larger questions that may never be answered fully, but still need to be asked.

It appears to me that foundation funding for research on global issues is declining, in part because the impact of research does not lend itself to the kind of measurement fashionable in the foundation community today. One exception is the research on an AIDS vaccine and malaria eradication programs that the Gates Foundation and others are funding—research projects whose impact *can* be measured by conventional "metrics."

TIMING AND PERSPECTIVE. It is clear that foundation giving policies and the nature of their research agendas are interrelated. Timing is critical in this regard; listening well to grant seekers helps identify emerging trends. When funders follow their lead, they can accelerate the development of a field, enrich the discussion, and be a catalyst for new solutions. But of course many research strategies are limited to the concerns of the time.

In the last decades of the Cold War, for instance, most researchers were focusing on the comparative military strength of the United States and the Soviet Union. Only a relative handful of scholars were less interested in missile "throw weights" and more interested in the political dimensions of the conflict. It was only in the 1980s that some researchers began to focus on the political aspects of the Cold War and what the implications of its end might be.

The Berkeley-Stanford program in Soviet studies led by Gail Lapidus in collaboration with Brookings Institution scholar Ed Hewett, for example, brought economists, anthropologists, sociologists, and ethnographers together. These social scientists, not missile experts, were needed to parse the schisms within the former Soviet Union. Similarly, it was the ethnographers who anticipated that old ethnic rivalries would be rekindled and become violent once the Cold War was over; few paid heed to them until it was too late.

Today we might ask ourselves if it would not have been better if proposals by leading economists in the early and mid-90s to examine the downside of globalization had been funded instead of rejected by foundation officials who were unable to foresee the impacts of globalization and the power of the movement against it.

Funding research on global or domestic issues is complicated. The first question to ask is, Who is going to define the agenda? When I was president of Hampshire College, which was known for a faculty always engaged with new and unconventional ideas, I was often exasperated by funders who had a preset notion of which research areas and ideas were important. Time and again, foundations told me that they would only support work on issues that they had chosen and predefined. They had, in effect, closed the door to new ideas not their own.

When I came to MacArthur, I soon realized that the situation was worse than I had imagined, for the very nature of my position meant that it was impossible to have a brainstorming conversation about ideas. Most grant seekers are so focused on divining the agenda of the foundation president that they will never tell a person holding that job that his or her ideas make no sense. Even my closest friend in graduate school, who had since become a major figure in the peace and security field, was affected by this phenomenon; when I left the foundation she said she was glad because we could once again have an honest conversation. The conclusion is not, of course, to avoid research, but to let it be known that one is open to new thoughts and approaches, and to work hard to provide opportunities for people with unconventional ideas.

Funding research can, in fact, provide the room for innovation to flourish. The challenge is in finding researchers whose proposals are promising and then letting them direct the content and methodology of their projects. It is imperative to look beyond the traditional disciplines, and even the academy itself, in pursuit of new ideas and approaches. Funding journalists and freelance investigators and writers to work on international issues, especially at a time when there is little funding for more traditional research, pushes the boundaries of the mainstream, whereas foundation-directed initiatives that artificially delimit intellectual and procedural boundaries are unlikely to be relevant or responsive to social needs.

COLLABORATIONS. The MacArthur Foundation has also sought ways to encourage cross-discipline and cross-boundary research and worked to fund collaborations among institutions in different parts of the United States and different parts of the world. Some of these efforts were at least partly successful; others were not.

Our attempts to foster more North/South collaboration provide an example of an arena where our grantmaking strategy proved to be not as well conceived as it might have been. It was too manufactured to fit actual needs and often the timing was off. Many of the joint grants we made resulted in a pattern of parallel rather than integrated collaborative work, with the management of the research assumed or even usurped by the Northern-based institutions. We cannot simply yoke together, say, university and think tank programs from different places and hope that they will become collaborations to bring interdisciplinary and multinational perspectives together to forge new intellectual and international alliances. Attempts to force such collaborations, we discovered, will do little to breech the Northern domination of North/South institutional collaborations.

More successful was a long-term partnership with the Social Science Research Council to fund young academics from around the world who are working on pressing international issues. The program convened these young scholars at annual conferences to learn about their respective work. These conferences served as a base for networking and building relationships that extended well beyond the life of any individual research project, and these young scholars represent the generation of leadership that will inherit the responsibility of continuing to look for solutions to the many problems in the new century.

Responding to Special Opportunities

While focus and guidelines are important to good grantmaking, it is also important to be opportunistic. If a foundation has an area of interest that lends itself to, say, a timely response to a world event, it does not require a whole shift of focus to make some strategic grants fairly quickly. At other times, a new opportunity might arise in the form of a joint venture with another funder prepared to share the risk.

RUSSIA. One of the MacArthur Foundation's early initiatives was aimed at strengthening relations between academics and scientists in the Soviet Union and the United States, building on preexisting personal and professional relationship ties that some MacArthur board members and staff had developed long before the foundation was created. Thus, when the Soviet Union collapsed, the foundation was well positioned to begin work in the Commonwealth of Independent States. Many of the new leaders were close friends of ours, and to the extent that anyone understood how to function in the new context, MacArthur did. The foundation began grantmaking, after two years of consultations with advisors. As soon as the legal issues were clarified, MacArthur opened an office in Russia in 1992. In effect, this was a new program that got a running start without the long, complex process typical of a new foundation initiative.

The goal of the program was to help to build civil society in Russia, to support the emerging free press, and to protect scholars in transition by permitting them a measure of job security as they began to explore more unrestricted intellectual inquiry. Equally important to this funding strategy was setting standards for merit-based research and strengthening civil society capacity to disseminate information responsibly and effectively. These were new concepts, and some long-established Russian researchers and academics were stunned when carefully developed proposals, often by younger scholars and occasionally by women, were funded while their perfunctory submissions were not.

Intellectual freedom and institutional sustainability are long-term objectives. Foundations need to be prepared to make the commitment over decades to ensure some measure of success. Determining when that success has been achieved is not an exact science, to say the least. The Soros Foundations/Open Society Institute in Russia has already determined that there is enough capacity on the ground and in incipient community foundations to maintain future innovation; as a consequence they have announced that they will be leaving Russia. But it may well take another cycle of peaceful, democratic transfer of power in Russia and evidence of university vitality before the MacArthur Foundation feels it has accomplished its goals there.

Progress can be noted particularly in the emergence of new private institutions of higher learning, a MacArthur priority. Early grants helped establish the Moscow Higher School of Social and Economic Sciences and New Economics School. These models of higher education have trained a new generation of economists and social scientists now active in policymaking in Russia. Other grants enabled ethnographers to understand the ethnic divisions within Russia and subsequently advise government on policy concerning national minorities.

An Informed Congress

Guidelines and exit strategies are good things for a foundation to have. But it is important to be open to engage in an innovative program—in the case in point here, one that educates members of the United States Congress about critical foreign policy issues—even if it does not fit our guidelines, or have a neat exit strategy.

Most members of Congress do not have passports when they are elected. Fewer have an understanding of such complex issues as those surrounding the breakup of the Soviet Union, the nature of Islam, what is at stake in the civil conflict in Colombia, or the myriad ways in which Mexico and the United States depend on each other. As the phenomenon of globalization has expanded and taken shape—in the form of multilateral trade agreements, complex lending and debt arrangements, and the growth of huge, multinational private corporations with financial resources in excess of those of many of the world's smaller nations—U.S. policymakers are forced to consider its impact beyond their constituencies and national boundaries. Members of Congress desperately need a bipartisan forum where they can discuss major issues of foreign policy intensely for several days at a time days away from the business of governing.

In 1983, David Hamburg, then president of the Carnegie Corporation, committed start-up funding for the Aspen Institute's Congressional Seminars, to be directed by former Iowa Senator Dick Clark. Carnegie remained the sole funder for four years, after which the MacArthur Foundation, and subsequently others (Christopher Reynolds, W. Alton Jones and later Ford, Pew, and Kellogg), joined Carnegie as supporters of the seminars. The logic for MacArthur was compelling: all of the global issues of importance to the foundation were affected by U.S. government policies. And without a more informed Congress, those policies were not going to improve in the ways we hoped they would.

Focusing upon members of Congress as the key policy-making audience presents singular underwriting challenges. Public money cannot be used without running afoul of political ideologies and provoking calls for "equal time." And private corporate support is unethical due to conflicts of interest inherent in the U.S. campaign financing system. This is another case where philanthropy has a special responsibility— and a great opportunity—to help ensure that members of Congress are well informed as they make foreign policy decisions of global significance. To date the MacArthur Foundation has contributed nearly $7.8 million to the Aspen Institute Congressional Seminars. If these invaluable seminars are to continue, however, it and other foundations must continue to offer their support.

Conclusion

These stories from one foundation and its former leader illuminate some of the principles and considerations anyone interested in global grantmaking would, I think, be well-advised to take into account:

> ˒ Careful and strategic global grantmaking can make a difference.
> ˒ It is important to search out the perspectives of local leaders, not just in the capital city of a given country, but also in rural

areas, in order to understand and shape foundation efforts to the context.

’ Change, and particularly institution building, takes time, but local leadership can increase its long-term effectiveness.

’ A strong civil society is important to ensuring citizen participation in decisions. Support civil society groups at all levels— local, national, and international—that are transparent and have effective leadership. Be prepared to sponsor leadership training and to help ensure that these groups work to complement each other.

’ Look for unintended consequences; don't walk away when the original plan isn't working perfectly.

’ Be prepared to be the first in, and to stay the course even after other funders have left.

’ Support research and find ways to link research with practice.

’ Make research opportunities available to younger scholars and non-traditional investigators from journalism and other practitioner perspectives.

’ Be willing to take on big problems and admit you don't know what the answers are, or even exactly where they might come from.

Afterword

In the new century, individuals and foundations have increased their global giving, a phenomenon for which the leadership provided by Soros, Turner, and Gates is at least in part responsible. And events with worldwide implications, from the spread of AIDS in Africa to the terrorist attacks of 9/11, have contributed to a growing awareness of the interconnectedness of all people on the planet. In response, there is a growing infrastructure of organizations and institutions to support global donors.

The Global Equity Initiative at Harvard, directed by Lincoln Chen, former vice president of the Rockefeller Foundation, is engaged in research on new trends in global philanthropy, looking at substantive areas such as health and education, and new patterns of philanthropy within developing countries and among diaspora communities. The World Affairs Council in San Francisco now sponsors an annual conference primarily for West Coast global donors through the Global Philanthropy Forum, and the Chicago Council on Foreign Relations is beginning a similar group in Chicago.

The World Economic Forum has established an Advisory Group of Foundation Leaders, and cosponsors, with Synergos, a bimonthly newsletter, *Global Giving Matters.* The Synergos Institute's Global Philanthropist Circle has over fifty members who are invited to participate in field trips and participate in monthly events held on every continent. Boston-based Grantmakers Without Borders is a funders' network of 275 members that promotes international philanthropy through peer-to-peer support to current and new international funders, ranging from public and private charitable organizations to individual donors.

Above all, what I find most noticeable is the growth of what American grantmakers call "strategic philanthropy" or "high-impact philanthropy" in the countries of Europe and the global South (most advanced in Brazil, South Africa, the Philippines, and Mexico). Much of this has come from new philanthropic players who have brought us important new ideas and different approaches. In turn, they may learn from the lessons learned, successes, and mistakes of those who have been giving globally for many decades. I hope this essay will, in a modest way, help them do so.

i. AAFRAC Trust for Philanthropy, *Giving USA 2002: The Annual Report on Philanthropy for the Year 2001*; "Foundation Giving Trends," (The Foundation Center, 2003); "International Grantmaking II: An Update on US Foundation Trends, 2000" (The Foundation Center in cooperation with the Council on Foundations).

ii. Initially, the framers hoped that topical publications on critical foreign policy issues such as the Iran–Contra deceit, the Cuban missile crisis, and Watergate would earn income for the NSA. The ambition for this self-generating revenue was scaled back to the more realistic 10 to 12 percent of its annual revenues that it earns today from sales.

iii. This paragraph and the three that follow it are taken from my article, "The Role of Philanthropy in Globalization," publication pending.

Epilogue

THE TRAIN has arrived at the station from which it first set out. We look around, gather our belongings, and disembark, watching uncertainly as the train moves away and out of sight. Something is missing.

What Is Missing?

Philanthropy by itself cannot move mountains or solve the world's problems, but as this book illustrates in so many ways, there are powerful and persuasive reasons to use philanthropy to work toward and be part of the solutions. We thank the authors of *Just Money* for their contributions, not only to this volume but to our field as well. They are all what might be called *restless souls* and that is one of the reasons why the metaphors of a train and travelers seemed so apt to me.

Philanthropy's collective capacity, its talent, is in discovering those small differences, those tipping points, those gaps that can be filled to make positive change possible. In order to do so, gift-givers are challenged to recognize what new ways of understanding—of listening, communicating, and measuring—are needed to intelligently navigate the new world of the twenty-first century. One of the major themes that runs through the essays in *Just Money* is the inadequacy of conventional strategy and assessment tools and techniques. Something hard to describe is missing from the equation. This leads us to another major theme articulated by our contributors—the strong desire to accomplish more with our philanthropic efforts, come closer to fulfilling critical needs in a time of great uncertainty.

What may be missing is that we do not have a complete, integrated, picture of the realities of philanthropy, either from the perspective of our own motivation as donors or from a sound understanding of the variables of social behavior and social change. If that is true, it may help explain the feeling of restlessness that is so apparent in the essays in this book, and in the quote that follows:

> We do not see the full process of coming into being of social action; we do not see its descending movement from thought and conscious-ness to language, interpretations, and relationships. We see what we do. We also form theories about how we do things. But [we] are usu-ally unaware of the place from which we operate when we act. (Huai-Chin Nan)[i]

What we do and *how* we do it are more easily observable through the application of external methods like metrics and the collection of hard data. Those that are intangible, "the soft variables such as intentions, experience that is more personal, more subjective,"[ii] are more difficult to see and to articulate. In the philanthropic process, those intangible variables, those that constitute "the *place* from which we operate," include the values and passions that motivate us, the quality of choice in what we do and do not do, and the development of relationships that in turn motivate others. In the absence of a clear understanding of these "soft variables," the determination of areas of strategic focus and specific programmatic goals, and their measurement and evaluation, is incomplete. It simply doesn't tell the whole story, and this is what con-tributes to our complaint, increases our sense of restlessness, and, I believe, holds philanthropists back from more ambitious action. In these terms, what is needed is an integration, a synthesis of the intan-gible and tangible, the hard variables with the soft.

Huai-Chin Nan's concept of the place where our actions originate has other names, like wisdom or primary knowing or deep sourcing, and, in our own field, what one writer has called masterful philanthropy.[iii] It is that which appears in these lines from the poet Wallace Stevens:

> Light the first light of evening, as in a room
> In which we rest and, for small reason, think
> The world imagined is the ultimate good.
>
> This is, therefore, the intensest rendezvous.
> It is in that thought that we collect ourselves,
> Out of all the indifferences, into one thing. [iv]

Within the culture and system of philanthropy, that one "thing," perhaps, is the organic ebb and flow between the passions and needs of the gift-giver—individual, family, corporation, or foundation—and those of the recipients and other communities of interest, an interchange and union of purpose that provides the context for both. For the degrees of separation between these domains are more artificial than true.

Perhaps the integration I referred to earlier is about collecting ourselves, as Stevens put it, to move in better harmony into that ebb and flow, as individuals and networks and foundations interacting in ways that will in fact move mountains—thinking, imagining, and interacting to become what might be referred to as *gifted givers.*

The Gifted Giver

In addition to providing money, ideas, technical assistance, advice, and counsel, the *gifted giver* possesses a vision that transcends these particulars and becomes a catalyst for transformation. Here are some of the transcendent gifts that he or she may bring to philanthropy.

THE GIFT OF ENERGY. An act of generosity is a kind of transaction. Someone once said there are two types of people at any meeting, those who bring energy into the room and those who take it out. The *gifted giver* is one who brings a positive charge into the transaction of making a gift as opposed to draining the energy out of it.

THE GIFT OF TRUTH TELLING. When the parties pander to or "handle" one another, when they are secretive and lack the candor and the confidence to push back, to tolerate ambiguity, to tell the truth—then philanthropic giving can look like a dance or a charade. The *gifted giver* understands that philanthropy is a little bit like exercise: if it isn't sometimes uncomfortable, it isn't doing the job.

THE GIFT OF RESPECT. Charity can sometimes be a disguise for seeking personal power or social control, and all too often the kindly donor can become, to one degree or another, an oppressor. There is no greater sign of disrespect than to abuse a position of power, and in the field of philanthropy the giver has virtually all the power. Respect is the antidote, and one of the most important ways of putting respect into action is to listen. The *gifted giver* is first and foremost a listener.

THE GIFT OF LOVE. Love, so difficult to define, is the greatest motivator. It can transform and inspire any effort, and, by building confidence and feelings of self-worth, make all things, even the very difficult, seem possible. A gift in the spirit of love is the most powerful way of saying "I believe in you," but love from a *gifted giver* is not soft, but diamond hard.

THE GIFT OF JUSTICE. One view of justice is that it is nothing less than love distributed across a community or a society. Justice, whether it is defined in relation to the rule of law or as a doctrine of fairness, speaks to the larger issues of the human condition, those of access to economic and social opportunity. This view of justice is non-ideological, and the *gifted giver* is passionate about justice.

THE GIFT OF OPPORTUNITY. There are socially motivated street-smart leaders everywhere—with powerful ideas, energy, political savvy, and huge potential—champing at the bit, hoping against hope that through some miracle they can get a shot at realizing their vision. The *gifted giver* has antennae fully deployed to identify such people and opportunities, and eyes open to the potential of excellence wherever it lies.

THE GIFT OF HIGH EXPECTATIONS. Like metal to a magnet, we rise to high expectations. They push us to be the best that we can be. They encourage us to dream bigger dreams, and they make us more disciplined, more thoughtful, more focused on results. The *gifted giver* provides the challenge and the resources to encourage and nurture high expectations.

THE GIFT OF COURAGE. We are all afraid of acts of terrorism and other disasters looming in a world in turmoil. We are afraid for our selves and for our children. We are afraid of the "dark side," of the "Orks," of "the beast." A *gifted giver* stands with those who stand up for what they believe is right, those with their backs against the wall, those who refuse to give in to fear.

It is the hope of all the contributors to this book that whether you have only a small amount of money to give or are in a position to make a major philanthropic investment, these essays will help you answer one final question: How can I be a gifted giver? —H. PETER KAROFF

---

i.   From "Illuminating the Blind Spot: Leadership in the Context of Emerging Worlds," by W. Brian Arthur, Jonathan Day, Joseph Jaworski, Michael Jung, Ikujiro Nonaka, C. Otto Scharmer, and Peter M. Senge. Available at www.dialogonleadership.org.

ii. Ibid.

iii. The phrase "masterful philanthropy" comes from Theodore J. Mallon, author of *The Journey Toward Masterful Philanthropy*.

iv. Wallace Stevens, "Final Soliloquy of the Interior Paramour."

Stillness

Kykuit at Pocantico

Sequestered high, a great corner room,
Leaded glass windows, the river
Distant and still. Lights on the far shore
Soften in the rose colored mist of dawn.

The castle keep of a storied house.
Something here wants to suspend time,
To pronounce the word tableau, pastoral,
Rolling hills, headland, river like a sea.

I sit at a writing desk on a raised dais,
A woman's portrait in a silver frame –
Gowned in brocade, a brilliant evening
Begun and ended long ago.

Something wants to call the question.
Could that possibly be snow? No,
Only the last silent fall of leaves
Blanketing the garden paths below.

Something here wants to call my name
As though I am ordained to answer—
Meaning, still beauty, hallowed ground.
Go forth—take the river to its source.

I am now the only air in the room.
What force of will made this house
Dispersed now where, what remnant
Of huge ambition, what atonement.

If I take it all in, argue the devil
His due, spend the bearer bonds
Of legacy down to my last breath.
Would that do, and for whom.

It is too easy here, too safe.
Something wants the silence to end,
Come chaos, a cacophony of voices
Descend. I sit, a tightly coiled spring.

— H. Peter Karoff

Kykuit is the great house at Pocantico,
the Rockefeller Estate on the Hudson River in Tarrytown, N. Y.

Glossary of Terms

Community foundation. A public charity (a tax-exempt, non-profit, publicly supported philanthropic institution) dedicated to serving the long-term social needs of a community. Community foundations solicit donations from a broad base of private sources, and manage them under community control for charitable purposes. Typically, a community foundation focuses primarily on a community, region, or state. Community foundations provide an array of services to donors who often wish to establish an endowed fund without incurring the administrative and legal costs of starting an independent foundation. A community foundation's endowment usually consists of a general fund over which the foundation has full discretion in giving, numerous donor-advised funds, funding from support organizations, and other funds that are restricted for a specific charity or focus such education or youth programs. Community foundations, now numbering over 670 across the country, are the fastest growing segment of philanthropy in the United States today.

Community of interest. A group of individuals or organizations with a shared set of values or interests and, in the case of philanthropy, intellectual passions or concerns. A community of interest might consist of the stakeholders affected by an issue or organization, donors with an affinity with one another or a common focus, or people from a variety of sectors (e.g., academia, government, the nonprofit sector, business).

Corporate foundation. A private foundation that derives its grant-making funds primarily from the contributions of a profit-making business. Company-sponsored foundations often maintain close ties with their donor companies, but they are separate legal organizations, sometimes with their own endowments, and they are subject to the same rules and regulations that apply to other private foundations. There are more than 2,000 corporate foundations in the United States, holding some $15 billion in assets. Corporate foundations are typically only one vehicle through which a corporation makes charitable contributions.

Corporate social responsibility (CSR). Corporate social responsibility generally refers to the broader relationship of a corporation with society. CSR includes how corporate decisions and actions affect people, communities, and the environment, and it also involves operating a business in a manner that meets or exceeds the ethical, legal, commercial, and public expectations that society has of business. Corporate social responsibility can be defined as a comprehensive set of policies, practices, and programs that are integrated throughout the business operations of a company, that influence decision-making processes, and that are supported and rewarded by top management.

Council of Foundations. A U.S.-based membership organization of more than 2,000 grantmaking foundations and giving programs worldwide, the Council of Foundations provides leadership expertise, legal services, networking opportunities, and other services to its members and to the general public. The council also serves as the primary voice for what is commonly referred to as organized philanthropy, and acts as an advocate for foundations in Washington, D.C.

Donor-advised fund (DAF). A fund established by an individual or family at a public charity, such as a community foundation or a financial institution with a charitable gift fund. The public charity manages the money and handles administrative tasks when charitable gifts are made. The donor may recommend eligible charitable recipients for grants from the DAF. Under IRS rules, the community foundation or commercial charitable gift fund has the legal right to accept or reject the donor's funding recommendation. For many donors, DAFs have become a preferred means of organizing their philanthropy.

Due diligence. As applied to philanthropic gifts, the term due diligence refers to the research, inquiry, and discovery conducted by a donor to form a context in which to assess strengths, weaknesses, opportunities, and risks associated with a potential grant to an organization, project, or effort.

Giving and learning circles. Formal or informal alliances of donors with common interests who learn and/or give together. These groups enable members to get experience with grantmaking basics, learn about a particular issue, find other people with common interests, and leverage their combined impact through collective giving. They may be sponsored and staffed by a public or private foundation, or may operate outside any formal structure or sponsorship. Giving circles that wish to make joint gifts can do so through a variety of mechanisms.

Global social investing (GSI). While this term has no commonly accepted definition, it can refer to the strategic and systematic investment of private philanthropic resources to address complex, interconnected manifestations of chronic underdevelopment in the developing world.[i] Representative targets of global social investing include poverty, health, the environment, human security, and basic education. GSI is driven in part by the imperative to address vast inequities among rich and poor—the "haves" and "have-nots" of the world—and by the realization that many of the world's problems are global, threatening the health and security of people throughout the world regardless of their economic situation. Examples include drug-resistant infectious diseases, global warming, and escalating ethnic conflicts that threaten world peace.

Going to scale. The process of expanding, disseminating, replicating, or adapting a proven model, approach, or innovation in order to reach a much larger population or have a much broader impact than the original program or intervention.

Non-governmental organization (NGO). A term used in many parts of the world outside of the United States to refer to private organizations that are separate from government, non-profit-making, self-governing, voluntary, and of public benefit (see definition of nonprofit organization or NPO).

Nonprofit organization (NPO). A term used primarily in the United States to describe private organizations that are institutionally separate from government (i.e., neither part of government nor governed by a board dominated by government officials), non-profit-making (i.e., not dedicated to generating profits for owners, as distinguished from private businesses), self-governing (i.e., equipped to control their own activities, and with their own internal governance structures), voluntary (i.e., involving some degree of voluntary participation, often in the form of a voluntary board of directors), and of public benefit (i.e., serving some public purpose and contributing to the public good).[ii]

Operating foundation. A private foundation that uses the bulk of its income to provide charitable services or to run charitable programs of its own. Operating foundations make few, if any, grants to outside organizations. To qualify as an operating foundation, specific IRS rules must be followed. The Carnegie Endowment for International Peace and the Getty Trust are examples of operating foundations.

Place-based philanthropy. A term that typically refers to philanthropic efforts that target a particular neighborhood or community through a comprehensive array of strategies, which might include community and economic development, early childhood and youth development, efforts to improve public schools, community-building and family asset-building approaches. For example, the Annie E. Casey Foundation has worked for decades to advance strategies that produce improved results for disadvantaged children and their families by focusing on a specific place—a neighborhood or community—with an emphasis on strengthening families.

Regional association of grantmakers. A membership association of foundations in a particular state or region (e.g., Massachusetts, Northern California) that supports effective charitable giving through educational programs and other services. There are twenty-eight such grantmaker associations in the United States, which are members of a national network called the Forum of Regional Associations of Grantmakers.

Social entrepreneur. A leader in the nonprofit sector who applies the principals of entrepreneurship—finding new and better ways of doing things—to social issues. As articulated by the French economist Jean Baptiste Say around the turn of the nineteenth century, "The entrepreneur shifts resources out of an area of lower and into an area of higher productivity and greater yield." Social entrepreneurs may create value by creating a new organization or a more effective approach to a pressing social need. For example, members of the Ashoka Fellows, a network of 3,000 social activists around the world, are selected based on their characteristics as social entrepreneurs.

Social return on investment (SROI). A term referring to attempts to quantify the social benefits of a nonprofit organization. While the return on financial investments can be measured by the bottom line, the social return of philanthropic investments are more difficult to measure. Nonetheless, such investments do often have a real social impact, and with the right tools, this impact may be measurable to some extent. Various types of SROI scorecards and other schemes have been devised that attempt to bring greater discipline and metrics into the process.

Social venture capital. Philanthropy is often referred to as society's "risk capital" or "venture capital"—meaning the R&D money that supports social innovation and promotes social change. Many donors try to target their giving in ways that could produce long-term change — in some cases, by providing resources that enable social entrepreneurs and others in the nonprofit sector to experiment with new approaches to social issues.

Strategic philanthropy. For individual donors and private foundations, this term is often defined as high-impact philanthropy, where the donor develops a clear set of philanthropic goals along with strategies designed to accomplish those goals. For corporations, the term can also refer to philanthropic efforts that make strategic sense for the company while at the same time bringing social benefit to the community or communities where the company operates. TPI describes "strategic philanthropy" as philanthropy that is values- and passion-driven, focused, reality-based, proactive, diligent, goal-oriented and outcome-directed, with clearly defined roles and strategies that involve continuous learning, reflection, and refinement.

Venture philanthropy. While there are various definitions for this term, it is most often assumed to mean the process of adapting venture capital investment practices to the nonprofit sector to build organizations able to generate high rates of social return on their investments. Venture philanthropy rests on the premise that the best investments require talent, expertise, and strategic thinking as well as money. Like venture capitalists, venture philanthropists expect results and accountability from the organizations they support. In addition to financial support, venture philanthropists often share their managerial and technological expertise, leverage their network of contacts, and help organizations empower themselves to achieve their missions.

This glossary was compiled by Leslie Pine,
Senior Vice President for Program.

---

i.   Paula Johnson, *Global Social Investing* (Boston: The Philanthropic Initiative, Inc., 2003).

ii.   Lester Salamon, *America's Nonprofit Sector* (Foundation Center, 1999), pp. 10–11.